1971

University of St. Francis
GEN 822.33 Del
Elliott

S0-BRL-479

DRAMATIC PROVIDENCE
IN *MACBETH*

DRAMATIC PROVIDENCE IN *Macbeth*

A Study of Shakespeare's
Tragic Theme
of Humanity and Grace
with a Supplementary Essay
on *King Lear*

❖

BY G. R. ELLIOTT

GREENWOOD PRESS, PUBLISHERS
WESTPORT, CONNECTICUT

LIBRARY
College of St. Francis
JOLIET, ILL.

❖

G. R. Elliott, Litt.D. (Bowdoin), L.H.D. (Tufts),
was born in London, Ontario, and graduated from
the Collegiate Institute in that city and from University College of the University of Toronto. After
two years of journalism in Canada he studied lan-
guage, literature, philosophy, and history in Jena
University, Germany, and was awarded a Ph.D. for
a thesis on "Shakespeare's Significance for Browning,"
published in the German periodical *Anglia*. While
instructor in English in the University of Wisconsin
he became naturalized as an American citizen. Thereafter he taught English literature in Bowdoin and
Amherst Colleges. He is now Folger Professor of
English Emeritus in Amherst College, resident in
Brunswick, Maine. His chief books in order of pub-
lication are: *The Cycle of Modern Poetry; Human-
ism and Imagination; Church, College, and Nation;
Scourge and Minister* (on *Hamlet*) ; *Flaming Minister*
(on *Othello*) ; and *Dramatic Providence in Macbeth.*

❖

Copyright ©*1958, 1960 by Princeton University Press*

Reprinted with the permission
of Princeton University Press

First Greenwood Reprinting 1970

Library of Congress Catalogue Card Number 70-90501

SBN 8371-3091-3

Printed in the United States of America

822.33
Del.

To

my colleagues in the recently established

RENAISSANCE SOCIETY OF AMERICA

*whose researches are throwing fresh light upon
many great works of literature and art
including Shakespearean Tragedy*

56231

822.33
Del

 PREFACE

On Shakespeare and Grace

THE closing lines of *The Tragedy of Macbeth* allude to "the Grace of Grace."[1] Probably Shakespeare was as well aware as we are that this terse phrase is susceptible of various interpretations. One of them, perhaps the most substantive, is given by James Moffatt in his great book *Grace in the New Testament* (1932). He says (page 390f) that the phrase in question denotes the Grace of God or Christ or Providence, the second "Grace" being synonymous with those three in accordance with a medieval usage familiar to Shakespeare. Earlier in the same chapter (page 386) Moffatt calls attention to the fact that in Shakespeare's time the word "graceful" retained "the double sense of handsome and religious." Leontes could assure Prince Florizel that he has "a holy Father, / A gracefull Gentleman" (*Winter's Tale*, V.i.170f): the father, Polixenes, King of Bohemia, is both comely and replete with Grace. This idea is conveyed by the very movement and tone of the passage—the gracious *feel* of it—especially when read in the context of Leontes' speech as a whole. And a great many comparable passages are to be found in Shakespeare's works.

A good book could be written on the subject of Grace in Shakespeare. But its author would need to have the grace to remember that Shakespeare's intellect was such as to prevent his religious outlook from being identical with that 'of the average members of the audience in his theater. That fact is too often forgotten by recent investigators of religion in his plays. They are apt to regard him as not only responsive to but cabined and confined by the religious dogmas of his time.[2] This view is

---

[1] In modern editions "the grace of Grace." But the two capitals of the original edition (see *Note on the Text* below) may be truer to Shakespeare's intention.

[2] Among the happy exceptions is Kenneth Myrick's well-tempered essay

repugnant for those who believe in Shakespeare but not in Christianity; and it is, or should be, even more obnoxious to those who believe in both. For it traduces the freedom of spirit, at once religious and poetic, that is characteristic of both.

The Christian spirit at its best has always had a vitally ambiguous attitude towards the great dogmas of the Faith: accepting the essential truth of them but never fully satisfied, or not for long, with their forms; conscious that the Infinite Word cannot be adequately expressed in finite words, though these may wonderfully shadow it forth to a humble imagination. And surely that dual attitude was Shakespeare's. He lived in an age of religious questionings, disputes, and doubts; and no mind was more inquisitive and searching than his. Yet in his writings, though often very critical of Christians, he never slurs Christianity; his writings, together with the little we know of his life,[3] evince a deep and firm regard for the Christian doctrines. But his total work, when read impartially, testifies that the author, unlike the majority of his contemporaries, viewed the current forms of those doctrines with a marked detachment. Such is his attitude towards Original Sin, Damnation (more properly, Condemnation), Incarnation, and Atonement. His *explicit* references to them are few and casual; and these passages, couched in the contemporary terms which were natural for the dramatis personae who utter them, cannot be taken as precisely representing the dramatist's own opinions. The truths underlying those terms, however, are implicit in and basic for Shakespearean drama as a whole—a fact increasingly recognized by modern scholars. For instance, one of them speaks of the "essentially Christian spirit of the tragedies" and notes that the "sense

---

on "The Theme of Damnation in Shakespearean Tragedy," published in *Studies in Philology* (1941).

[3] See John de Groot's reliable book on *The Shakespeares and "The Old Faith"* (1947). It is certain that Shakespeare was very favorable to the religious (as distinguished from the contemporary political) tenets of the Roman Catholic Church. But it is also certain that his religious outlook was far more catholic, in the fullest sense of this term, than the *ordinary* views of either the Catholics or the Protestants *of his time.*

of reconciliation which remains to comfort us may well be called a sense of *atonement*" (italics mine).[4]

The doctrine of Grace had a very special fascination for Shakespeare. His allusions to it, explicit and implicit (continually, in accordance with Renaissance custom, he expresses Christian ideas in pagan terms), are innumerable. We may believe that for him as man it represented the essence of Christianity; we can be certain that for him as writer it pointed to a truth fundamental for human life and, hence, for vital poetry and drama. Grace in his view was less a Christian dogma than a human experience, an experience affording the greatest of all the contrasts that constitute the warp and woof of drama. A contrast is intensely dramatic in proportion as it comprises things radically different from each other yet closely related. And for Shakespeare the ultimate contrast was provided by Grace and Nature—by the spectacle of a divinely human will working in, through, and above our humanly defective wills. That dramatic spectacle gripped him more and more as his experience broadened and his art developed; and it was supremely displayed in the tragedies and semitragic comedies of the second half of his career.[5] The main theme of his work in that period may be summed up in words from the great poet who was his immediate predecessor, Edmund Spenser. It is inconceivable that Shakespeare, in his maturity at least, would write in the fashion of the lines quoted below.[6] But it is perfectly conceivable that in reading them—as

[4] From C. J. Sisson's "The Mythical Sorrows of Shakespeare" in *Proceedings of the British Academy* (1934).

[5] The passage on the Atonement in *Measure for Measure* (II.ii.72-79) is strikingly intense and forceful in comparison with earlier verses on the same topic, e.g. *Merchant of Venice*, IV.i.197-202. Of course it expresses the character of the speaker, Isabella. But also it intimates Shakespeare's preoccupation during his tragic period with the conflict of sin (particularly pride) and Grace.

[6] But compare his Sonnet 146:

Poore soule, the center of my sinfull earth,
[My sinfull earth] these rebell powers that thee array. . . .

The brackets are mine. Perhaps the senseless second line is a hasty jotting which Shakespeare, anxious to stress by repetition his "sinfull earth," intended to shape later into a proper verse. But if the printed text is corrupt, as generally assumed, the best substitute for the bracketed phrase is, I think, "Thrall to." Cf. Spenser's "thrall" at the end of the passage quoted above.

he doubtless did, some years before he wrote his chief tragedies[7] —he would do so with entire sympathy, finding there that "stedfast truth" in which he believed; though he would then proceed to peruse with keener interest the very dramatic canto which they introduce; wherein "heavenly grace" in *personal* form rescues a Christian knight from the sinful bands of "foolish pride."

> Ay me, how many perils doe enfold
> The righteous man, to make him daily fall?
> Were not that heavenly grace doth him uphold,
> And stedfast truth acquite him out of all.
> Her love is firme, her care continuall,
> So oft as he through his owne foolish pride,
> Or weaknesse, is to sinfull bands made thrall. . . .[8]
>
> *(The Faerie Queene*, I.viii.1)

Leontes, rescued very dramatically from that thralldom by "the Heavens" and the "blessed Gods" (*Winter's Tale*, III.ii. 147, V.i.168), is an outstanding instance of those persons in Shakespeare's later plays who yield to Grace. The outstanding instance of those who do not is the hero-villain of the *Tragedy of Macbeth*. But just for that reason the workings of Grace in this play are the more striking.[9] In the present book I have tried to bring out a *dramatic* phenomenon neglected by criticism: the constant striving of heaven, in various ways, to induce Macbeth to repent. In this matter the gracious spirit of King Duncan (who has generally been regarded as a very minor figure) is

[7] The first three books of *The Fairie Queene* were issued in 1589 when young Shakespeare was beginning his work as dramatist; the complete six books in 1596. Spenser's influence on Shakespeare has been demonstrated by a number of modern scholars. The most important consideration, however, is that both poets drew upon a common sixteenth-century fund of poetic and *dramatic* ideas.

[8] Obviously the phrase "heavenly grace" is here more or less synonymous with the divine "truth" and "love" of the next two lines; but its meaning is much wider. The "exceeding grace of highest God," as Spenser terms it elsewhere in the same poem (II.viii.1), is the full divine nature at work in human nature.

[9] Allusions to Grace (or equivalents) in *Macbeth* are numerous in various books and articles on Shakespeare, notably F. C. Kolbe's *Shakespeare's Way* (1930).

of great importance—for Macbeth and for all the other leading characters, above all for Macbeth's destined successor on the throne, Duncan's son Malcolm. The function of Duncan in the play is parallel to that of Polixenes in *Winter's Tale* though far more significant: a main feature of the plot is that Malcolm, like Florizel, had "a holy Father, a gracefull Gentleman."

But one must emphasize that for Shakespeare *as writer* the word "Grace" and all the other terms that he used as its equivalents (notably "heaven") had a poetic and dramatic more than (not instead of) a religious fascination. Of him must be said what has recently been finely said of Racine: "The only law which he always seeks to obey is the law of dramatic effect."[10] It was not a desire to embody the Elizabethan philosophy of Nature that caused Shakespeare to write *King Lear*: he was aiming, beyond his *Hamlet* and *Othello*, at a fresh and large simplicity of tragic impression. In *Macbeth*, reacting extremely from the loose comprehensiveness of *Lear*, he achieved a brilliant fusion of dramatic and theatrical effects (see my Introduction, below). In so doing he had recourse again to the Christian imagery so prominent in *Hamlet* and *Othello* but discarded in *Lear*. That imagery, however, is employed at once more sparingly and more effectually in *Macbeth* than in *Hamlet*. And *Macbeth* retains the large social meaning of *Lear* (a fact not sufficiently noticed by criticism) but in wonderfully succinct form. Indeed, as I have tried to demonstrate below, it is the most humanly representative of all Shakespeare's tragic plays. Macbeth himself is widely typical: nominally Christian, he is mainly pagan in spirit and liable, when strongly tempted, to become diabolic. But divine Grace, whether or not so termed, is at work in all men; and just because the atmosphere of this drama is for the most part murky and hellish, "the Heaven's breath," continually felt in the course of the action, "smells wooingly here" (I.vi.5f). And that human experience, whatever else it may be, is intensely dramatic.

[10] From Geoffrey Brereton's *Jean Racine, A Critical Biography* (1951), page 267.

Part B of my Introduction in preliminary form was given as one of the addresses at two conferences of Renaissance scholars, at Duke University, April 23, 1954, and at Tufts University, November 18, 1955. Acknowledgments to scholars will be found in my notes. Since completing this book I have read Professor Brents Stirling's remarkable *Unity in Shakespearian Tragedy* (New York, 1956). While differing from him in a number of points, especially in regard to the last Act of *Hamlet*, I am happy to find myself in main agreement with him. Professor Harold S. Wilson's very suggestive *On the Design of Shakespearian Tragedy* (Toronto, 1957) may profitably be compared with Stirling's book. My own view of *Macbeth* is closer to Stirling's view than to Wilson's. Franklin M. Dickey's penetrating *Not Wisely But Too Well* (San Marino, 1957) shows how fundamentally Shakespeare's Renaissance concept of love differs from the Romantic and modern view. In line with Dickey's thesis is the treatment of love and friendship in my books on *Hamlet* and *Othello* and in the present one on *Macbeth*. Irwin Smith's comprehensive and beautifully-composed *Shakespeare's Globe Playhouse* (New York, 1956) and Alfred Harbage's *Theatre for Shakespeare* (Toronto, 1955)—a keen critique of modern productions—have a bearing upon my Introduction, part A, below. An excellent background for the study of *Macbeth's* political and Christian aspects (notably in Act IV, Scene iii) is provided by Irving Ribner's *The English History Play in the Age of Shakespeare* (Princeton, 1957).

In this second edition the only main change is the inclusion of an essay, previously printed in the *Journal of English and Germanic Philology*, April 1959, on the initial phase of *Lear*. It is intended to be read in connection with my commentary on the corresponding phase of *Macbeth* (the first three scenes). Each of these two contemporary but vividly contrasting plays is contained embryonically in its initial phase. In *Lear* the Renaissance tragic motif of Pride, more or less subtle and covert in *Macbeth*, as in *Hamlet* and *Othello*, becomes violently overt.

Brunswick, Maine   G.R.E.
May 1960

NOTE ON THE TEXT

The prime authority for the text of Shakespeare's dramas (no manuscripts having survived) is the collected edition of 1623, the First Folio (F1), reissued with minor alterations in 1632 (F2), 1664 (F3), and 1685 (F4).[1] Before 1623, however, about half of the plays had appeared in small separate editions called quartos, differing much from the Folio texts of those plays, and generally less reliable, but in some passages closer apparently to Shakespeare's initial versions. We have quartos for *Hamlet*, *Othello*, and *Lear* but none unfortunately for *Macbeth*. And this drama in the Folio is not only at least as faultily printed as the rest of that great volume: it is also remarkably brief, especially in comparison with the three preceding tragedies. Hence several modern scholars think it represents a hasty abbreviation for stage purposes of Shakespeare's original version of the play —an opinion maintained vivaciously by John Dover Wilson in his New Shakespeare edition of *Macbeth* (1951). But most critics believe that the peculiarities of the text are mainly due to the author's deliberate and extraordinary concision in composing this fourth and last of his main tragedies.

Before emending *Macbeth*, except in the case of *indubitable* errors—which, if the adjective be heavily underlined, are found to be not too numerous—surely we should do, what I think has not yet been fully done: make the best of the play as we have it. In trying to do this I have had constantly before me a photostat of the text as given in Copy Seven of the First Folio in the Folger Shakespeare Library.[2] Significantly the editor of the revised edition of the play (1903) in the New Furness Variorum Shakespeare decided to reprint *Macbeth* letter by letter from the Folio (after collation of several copies), relegating all proposed alterations to the footnotes. Along with that book, and many oth-

---

[1] F2 has a number of more or less dubious corrections of F1.

[2] This text was tentatively recommended to me by Charlton Hinman, whose study of the variants in the different copies of the Folio was then (October 1953) far from complete. My quotations are made with the permission of the Director of the Folger Library.

ers, I have studied *The Tragedie of Macbeth, A Corrected Edition of the Text of the First Folio*, made about forty years ago by Henry Johnson, late Longfellow Professor of Modern Languages in Bowdoin College, embodying (without annotation) such changes as then seemed valid to that excellent scholar.[3] Especially helpful is Kenneth Muir's new Arden Edition of *Macbeth* (1953). While differing quite often from his opinions I have appreciated the exceptional breadth and fairness of his attitude.

In quotations from the play I have retained the F1 lineation of the verse—which seems to indicate generally, though not in every instance, the manner in which the speeches were intended to be spoken—and also the original capitalization: in the Elizabethan period capital letters were incessantly, though not consistently, employed for emphasis; and particularly in this play many words demand strong stress. Spelling and punctuation have been modernized only when likely to be misleading or distractive for the reader; but in repeating words already quoted I have often used modern spelling, for variety and clarity.

Arabic numerals (except when preceded by roman ones) in parentheses refer to lines in the scene under discussion. The line-numbering, as in my books on *Hamlet* and *Othello*, is the now commonly used numbering given in the Globe Edition of the *Works of Shakespeare*—except in the case of Act V, Scene vii (see Third Phase, footnote 103).

[3] Privately printed (1921); preserved in Bowdoin College Library. Professor Johnson used the Staunton and Preston Facsimile of F1 (London, 1866), advertised as "made from the best passages of the two best copies of the folio known, the one in the Bridgewater House, the other in the British Museum." After Professor Johnson's death in 1918 the proofreading was completed and a Preface provided by the late Professor Stanley P. Chase.

CONTENTS

CONTENTS

DRAMATIC PROVIDENCE

IN *MACBETH*

On *Macbeth* as Apex of Shakespearean Tragedy

A. *Its Dual Method*

THE popular notion that Shakespeare wrote his plays solely for
the stage, not for readers, makes him out to be less intelligent
than his readers are. For incessantly the reader finds in these
dramas subtle effects which stage-performance cannot well (if
at all) convey; and concerning which the reader, unless oddly
conceited, must believe that this very percipient author could
not have been entirely unaware. And those non-histrionic effects,
so to term them, have often been recognized by the actors themselves. Two of Shakespeare's fellow actors, who were also warm
friends of his, were certain that he wished his works to be read;
and they knew that incessant rereading was necessary for the full
enjoyment and understanding of them. So John Heminge and
Henry Condell asserted in the prefatory matter of the First
Folio (see my *Note on the Text*), the collected edition of Shakespeare's plays issued by them seven years after his premature
death at the age of fifty-two. They wished ardently that he
could have been his own "executor . . . that the Author himselfe had lived to have set forth and overseen his owne writings." And their lively, gently satiric address *"To the great
Variety of Readers"* concludes as follows: "Reade him, therefore; and againe, and againe. And if then you do not like him,
surely you are in some manifest danger not to understand him.
And so we leave you to other of his Friends, whom if you need,
can bee your guides: if you neede them not, you can leade yourselves, and others. And such Readers we wish him."

The allusion to "other of his Friends" is in its context very
suggestive. The implication is that they, like the two editors,
could not help an *intelligent* reader much. For Shakespeare was

not the sort of person who would discourse upon his writings to even his most intimate and admiring associates. No doubt when questioned by them in regard to his meanings he would give polite and candid replies; but these would be brief, casual, and noncommittal. Consummate as a writer, and also humble, he would feel that his written words conveyed his intentions as clearly as was possible *for him*, and that the readers would grasp those intentions as well as was possible *for them*. His attitude in this matter was caught and reproduced by his first editors. In the passage preceding their finale (quoted above) they declare: "His mind and hand went together; and what he thought he uttered with that easinesse that we have scarce received from him a blot in his papers. . . . And there [in his printed works] we hope, to your divers capacities, you will find enough both to draw and hold you." But thereupon they proceed, finally, to wish for him, as he himself must have wished, the very best sort of readers: those who, reading him "againe and againe" with liking, have the capacity to "leade yourselves and others" into an ever fuller understanding of him.

Such readers must have judiciousness (*Hamlet*, III.ii.31) together with love. In Sonnet 74 Shakespeare urges his Friend —an epitome, surely, of all his friends—to "review" his verses, after the death of his "body," and to find him living there: "My spirit is thine, the better part of me."[1] That presence was known to his two devoted friends and editors after his death; and always it becomes known to persistent and discerning readers (rather than spectators) of his works. They strive to "take" his "good meaning" (*Romeo and Juliet*, I.iv.46) more and more. He says to them ever: "If you do love me"—and look beneath *theatric* externals as judiciously as Bassanio did—"you will finde me out" (*Merchant of Venice*, III.ii.41).

In his everyday life as in his writings Shakespeare was extremely reticent regarding himself, in striking contrast with his friend Ben Jonson and with many other great writers. For this

[1] Macbeth just before his death speaks, with a difference, of "my better part of man" (V.vii.47).

reticence was an innate feature of his supreme dramatic genius.[2] His talk was genial and copious; but after listening to it with fascination for an hour or so, learning much about mankind, you would realize that you had learned nothing in particular about the man who was speaking. This reticence was not in the main due to secretiveness or even to his well-known modesty. It was due to the fact that he just naturally lived in two worlds: the everyday one, palpable, voluble, theatric; the other intensely dramatic, unseen except by his own "mind's eye" (*Hamlet,* I.ii.185), and, except to him, silent. It expressed itself to him vividly when he was meditating and writing in solitude. It demanded of him utter selflessness and, at his best, a highly concentrated energy of imagination and judgment, these two molten and fused together at white heat.

His great dramatic visions must have made his day-by-day existence seem comparatively (far from absolutely) trivial—a "poore Player" (*Macbeth,* V.v.24) upon the Stratford and London scene: he was not interested in expatiating upon it to others. And he simply could not speak to them, unless very casually, about the invisible and magnificent world wherein "the better part" of him lived most really. The words he wrote of it were exhaustive, and exhausting: they left nothing to be said; and they left him in extreme need of recreation. This was afforded by his external life. He put a great deal of energy into his extraordinarily busy career as a man among men; but it was different in kind from the effort required by his compositions, though it constantly yielded material for them. Thus his daily life gave him vital relief;[3] like that which appears in his best writings—for instance the "Martlet" and "Porter" episodes in *Macbeth* (I.vi.1ff, II.iii.1ff)—providing diversion for spectator, reader, and author while bearing significantly upon the main action. His strenuous outward life provided vital aid for, and vital

[2] Incidentally it is the basic reason for the meagerness of our knowledge of his life. The other reasons, usually more emphasized by biographers, are of secondary importance.

[3] Otherwise the immense total labor of his lifetime would have brought him still earlier to his grave.

diversion from, his strenuous inward life. Continually the theatrical world of every day played into and out of, out of and into, his invisible dramatic world. His "Genius" (in Macbeth's sense of the term, III.i.56) required that those two worlds should always be for him, unlike Macbeth, clearly distinct from each other but never separable: they were interpenetrative.

In visionary, and sometimes more or less satirical,[4] moments he saw all the world as a stage with "all the men and women merely Players" (*As You Like It*, II. vii.137ff), their "little life . . . rounded with a sleepe" (*The Tempest*, IV.i.157f). But in that "little," transient, theatric life he perceived a great reality at work very dramatically. This reality was "Nature" (*Macbeth*, IV.i.59) or Natural Law in the classic sense of the term, a sense not common today[5] but prevalent during the Renaissance: that is, the right and good constitution of human nature (and, only incidentally, physical nature) as designed by the Creator. But Shakespeare unlike the philosophers had small interest in Natural Law or Nature as abstractly conceived. In his writings the word "nature" is used, undefined, in all its manifold denotations, each clear enough in a particular concrete context, unclear if detached therefrom. He was not interested in Nature detached from nature. But he was intensely interested in the *dramatic* conflict, as it appeared in the lives of human beings, between the higher and the lower reaches of nature—between Nature and "nature's mischief" (*Macbeth*, I.v.51), between right volition and wrong desire. He discerned in "*all* the men and women" slight touches, at least, of the right Nature which appeared so wonderfully and beautifully in the few entirely noble ones. But the more he saw of that goodness, in his diurnal experience and in his omnivorous reading, the more he realized the great might of the evil that was continually undermining or striving to undermine it. This, however, made him envision afresh the rare, persistent, mysterious

---

[4] Normally he was *gently* satirical. In that respect his two editors seem to be imitating him in their "Address to the Great Variety of Readers," cited above.

[5] More prominent now, however, than it was a hundred years ago, and likely to become increasingly so.

strength of goodness—due, as he had to perceive ever more clearly, to the infusion of divine Grace in Nature.

Grace as a theological dogma did not engage Shakespeare any more than Nature or Natural Law or moral principles in the abstract. But he was captivated by the conduct of persons in whom human graces were mysteriously reinforced by Grace. Christianity appealed to him *as writer* on dramatic and poetic rather than religious grounds. It was not for him—what it was to become for many post-Renaissance authors—just one religion, though in some ways the greatest, among the many and various human creeds. For him it was universal religion in supremely dramatic form. Herein, and herein only, were time and eternity experienced, in vital paradox, as at once utterly different yet closely related—the ultimate dramatic contrast. He would have loved a bold verse upon Christ written by a younger contemporary: "Eternity, who yet was born and died."[6] Continually the spirit of Christ may be discerned by the reader in, through, and above the Shakespearean scene. But Christ as Person was excluded from that scene, not only by obvious secular-theatric necessity, but by the dramatic genius of Shakespeare himself. As writer he had to be intent always upon *imperfect* humanity: upon the dramatic, continually comic, but deeply tragic spectacle of men and women inadequately showing forth "the forms of things / Unknowne" (*Midsummer Night's Dream*, V.i.15); incarnating "eternal Love" in ever new and "fresh" (Sonnet 108) but piecemeal and transient fashion. His art is symbolic; but it is fundamentally different in quality from allegory and epic. Accordingly, unlike the majority of the leading Renaissance authors, notably Spenser, Dante, and Milton, he did not deliberately employ Christian doctrine as a mode of expression. But he was instinctively attracted by orthodox Christian theology in its main essentials. To him it was veritably orthodox, right, sound, and catholic in idea and image; it was approved by his judgment as much as it satisfied his imagination. Subconsciously, for the most part, it shaped his understanding of mankind and

[6] From Phineas Fletcher's *The Locusts* (1627), Canto I, line 97.

structured his compositions. The Shakespearean drama is "a uniquely true and powerful *mundane* vision of human life from the Christian standpoint."[7]

That vision is beyond the theater; the most accomplished actors cannot convey it; but if they will they can give suggestions of it. Certainly the actors in Shakespeare's own company gave incessant hints of it, and towards it, to him. They, performing on a stage that was complexly and admirably adapted to his needs (as modern scholarship has made increasingly clear), helped his mind's eye to see more graphically: the Elizabethan playhouse was a cardinal factor in the development of this poet's dramatic abilities; and it emblematized for him, in a small but very real way, the wide and universal theater of life. Of course as his vision deepened he increasingly felt the inadequacy of the playhouse. He had to wince when a performer in a serious role made "damnable Faces" or "strutted and bellowed"—strutting and fretting his hour upon the stage.[8] The excellent Globe Theater could seem merely a "Woodden O" and the actors tiny o's within it—"Cyphers." But "these flat unraised Spirits" could cause sympathetic souls in the audience to soar and range far beyond the theater. More importantly, they aided Shakespeare's own "thoughts" and "imaginary Forces"[9] to invent terms expressing his vision concretely *for readers.*

The "best" actors like the "worst" were merely "shadowes."[10] But so were the most "gorgeous" aspects of earthly life itself: the course of this "little life" was a "Pageant" as "insubstantial" as a play on the stage (*Tempest*, IV.i.148ff). Nevertheless that

[7] Quoted from an article of mine, "Shakespeare's Christian-Dramatic Charity," published in *The Church Review* (Washington), November 1952, and in *Theology* (London), December 1953. Essays on Shakespeare and religion have recently become very numerous. One of the most striking is Robert Speaight's "Shakespeare and Politics" in *Transactions of the Royal Society of Literature,* vol. 24, 1948, dealing with the religious theme of the history plays.

[8] *Hamlet,* III.ii.38,263; *Macbeth,* V.v.25.

[9] See Prologue to *Henry Fifth,* passim.

[10] *Midsummer Night's Dream,* V.i.213f.

passing show attracted Shakespeare very greatly because, like the other chief writers and thinkers of the Renaissance, he knew that in essence it is very great. The feeling of the essential largeness of earthly life underlies the whole of Prospero's monologue from which I am quoting, and is strong in its central verse: "The solemne Temples, the great Globe itselfe." Constantly in Shakespeare's view the insubstantial pageant of mundane existence shadowed forth a substantial, lasting, highly personal kind of life whose aspects were not "gorgeous" but glorious; not mainly theatric but intensely dramatic; as in Prospero's climactic speech regarding his vanquished enemies (*Tempest*, V.i.20ff):

> Though with their high wrongs I am struck to the quick,
> Yet with my nobler reason 'gainst my fury
> Do I take part: the rarer Action is
> In virtue than in vengeance: they being penitent,
> The sole drift of my purpose doth extend
> Not a frowne further.—Go release them, Ariel.—
> My Charmes I'll breake, their senses I'll restore,
> And they shall be themselves.

Their better and more real selves are restored, as the rest of the Act shows, by a power greater than Prospero's very temporary magic: by the action, in, through, and above him, of Providence—of divine charity, reasonable, just, and merciful. Contrastingly his magic held the foreground of the stage during the four preceding Acts. And in Act IV, which centers in his "insubstantial pageant" speech, Shakespeare stressed the theatric transience of mundane things, good and evil—the good, in the lovely "Iris" masque; the evil, in the bizarre, masque-like denouement of Caliban's conspiracy. Thus that Act is a telling preparation for the final Act's revelation of the workings of "immortal Providence" (V.i.189) in human affairs. Act V adumbrates, wonderfully, eternity *acting* in and throughout time: it shows the pageant of human life incarnating something of

> Beautie, Truth, and Raritie,
> Grace in all simplicitie. . . .[11]
> (*The Phoenix and the Turtle*, line 53f)

The fifth and last Act, while effectively theatric, is supernally dramatic.[12]

Certainly that fact may be apparent to actors and their audiences; but the full truth of it can be apprehended only by devoted readers. These, however, need to imitate Shakespeare's attitude towards the stage. One type of reader, more common formerly than now, cannot bear to see the master's great works mutilated in the theater. The opposite type, more common now than formerly, concentrates upon the playhouse aspects of those works and identifies "dramatic" with "theatric." Both types distort Shakespeare. He, though more practically and acutely aware than anyone else of the limitations of the playhouse, never despised it; he was grateful to it. Nor was he aware of the chasm that critics have discovered in his dramas between the poet and the playwright. For him, however, good drama and "good theater" (a term very current today) were far from being one and the same thing. The stage, dedicated mainly and necessarily to obviousness,[13] could at best provide only dim suggestions of those inmost conflicts in the human spirit which more and more fascinated him: the theatric must by its very nature be insufficiently dramatic. So while he wrote immediately for the stage he wrote ultimately for reflective readers—for those who (like himself) would be interested in and aided by, but never satisfied by, stage-performances of his plays; who, as his first editors urged, would read him repeatedly, endeavoring to discern his intentions completely.[14]

---

[11] When Caliban in the end resolves to "seeke for grace" (V.i.295) it would indeed be "Grace in all simplicity"!

[12] But in a New York production of *The Tempest* a few years ago Prospero's "insubstantial pageant" monologue was transferred to the end of Act V; it was played up to convey the modern sense of insecurity and unreality in life. That *theatric* trick negated Shakespeare's *dramatic* conception.

[13] He would not care for modernistic drama and verse dedicated to the unobvious and cryptic.

[14] Here I wish to record my gratitude for long and friendly association

The above considerations are especially pertinent to *The Tragedy of Macbeth*. The quality of this play has been very diversely estimated. Different critics have discovered in it many different defects; and modern audiences have viewed it with a curious mixture of repulsion and fascination. But surely those readers are right who, pondering it objectively, have deemed it Shakespeare's supreme work of poetic-dramatic art.[15] Its extraordinary concision[16] is due to his concentration here upon the very essence of his tragic vision: upon the fact that the *infernal* evil working in man more instantly than his *natural* goodness (his obedience to Nature or Natural Law as defined above) can ruin his humanity—so glorious at its best—unless it is sustained by the *supernal* power of Grace; without this, man's "ending is despaire" (Epilogue of *The Tempest*).[17] Shakespeare's awareness of that situation is apparent in his writings antecedent to *Macbeth*. It provides an underlying unity of outlook in his cycle of history plays; and it is very marked in his first three main tragedies, *Hamlet*, *Othello*, and *Lear*. But in those dramas, even in the very succinct *Othello*, the tragic theme appears discursive in comparison with the exceptional concentration of *Macbeth*.

Evil in this play is uniquely concentrated, insidious, and powerful; but also it is uniquely fantastic. The more potent it

---

with two actor-managers who, appreciating Shakespeare both as poet and as playwright, have done much for him on the academic stage: the late Florence (Mrs. Arthur) Brown, coach of "The Masque and Gown" of Bowdoin College, and her successor, George H. Quinby, Professor of Dramatics there. In consulting me they gave me far more help than I gave them. Happily their work has now resulted in the construction of Bowdoin's new and superb Pickard Theater.

[15] Some recent critics have awarded the palm to *Antony and Cleopatra*, regarding it as "glorious"; but a better adjective for this great tragical Romance is "gorgeous." See my treatment of those two terms above.

[16] Probably abetted by his new patron James the First's dislike of long plays.

[17] Cf. *The Faerie Queene*, Book I, cantos ix and x, particularly the closing stanzas of the former and the opening ones of the latter. The idea of Grace and Nature, a main source of the greatness of Renaissance literature and art, may become more prominent in the twenty-first century than it was in the nineteenth. It could rejuvenate poetic drama.

is in action the more abnormal is it seen to be in essence, from the standpoint of Nature and Grace. Accordingly *Macbeth*, Shakespeare's ultimate tragedy, is the precursor of his romances, culminating in *The Tempest*.[18] This visionary, masque-like poem repeats the ethical theme of *Macbeth* but with shifted emphasis: the innate abnormality of evil is stressed while its actual strength in the world is viewed at a divine distance. Significant, then, is the fact that the preposterousness of evil, though elaborately displayed in the romances, is shown more mightily in *Macbeth*. Shakespeare is true to human history (notably to the history of the middle twentieth century) in his conviction that we can realize the strangeness of evil only in proportion as we realize its terrific might in the world: the very fact that a thing so essentially thin and misty as evil, so air-like (*Macbeth*, I.iii.79-82), can be so powerful is highly fantastical. Hence *Macbeth* is at once greatly dramatic and, because of its fantastic element, extremely theatrical.

Therefore this play is both very alluring and very elusive for actors. They are constantly tempted to make it more theatric and less deeply dramatic than it really is. For instance, Macbeth's first speech to King Duncan (I.iv.22-27), avowing great loyalty, is "good theater" if it is spoken by the actor with histrionic hypocrisy; but that rendering, as I have tried to demonstrate in my comment below, spoils the dramatic (as well as the poetic) intent of this passage in the light of its total context.[19] And in fact the stage history of this play up to date is a record of gross simplifications for theatric effect—of productions more thoroughly distortive than in the case of Shakespeare's other tragedies. Particularly unfortunate is the truncation on the stage of Act IV, Scene iii, titled in my text "*healing Benediction.*" It

---

[18] The supernatural atmosphere, absent from *Antony and Cleopatra* and *Coriolanus*, passes over from *Macbeth* into the romances, above all *The Tempest*.

[19] Some reviewers of my books on *Hamlet* and *Othello* dismissed my interpretation of various passages as impossible for the stage, i.e. for the stage as they knew it, on the assumption that such an interpretation must necessarily be non-dramatic.

has been generally regarded as too long and too dull; critics have joined with producers—the former far more blameworthy than the latter—in condemning it. Conceivably, however, it could be rendered as effective on the stage as its author designed it to be: its political theme, the right and wrong traits of national leaders, is surely not less timely at present than it was in Shakespeare's day. In any case the reader, if not the spectator, can discover that for the mind's eye this scene is intensely and subtly dramatic.

According to a general opinion Shakespeare's subtilty, so outstanding in *Hamlet* and *Othello*, is supplanted by passionate forcefulness in *Lear* and *Macbeth*. That is true of *Lear* but not of *Macbeth*. This drama, while violent like *Lear*, resumes the subtilty of the first two main tragedies, though with a radical difference. Here it is fused with classic simplicity of whole design and with extreme tensity of episode. In this respect *Macbeth* is at the opposite pole from *Hamlet*. The opening scene of *Macbeth* says as much in ten lines—conveys as much of the play's whole meaning—as the first scene of *Hamlet* does in a hundred and sixty. The method of *Macbeth*, as in that opening scene, is *dramatic abruption*. In *Hamlet* Shakespeare meditates extensively. In *Macbeth* the net result of all his tragic thinkings is supremely and imaginationally condensed. The play is a series of abruptly shifting but subtly related images; they emerge from, and merge mystically into, a single vision.

But that single vision has two aspects; and the movement of the drama is double. *Macbeth* is a spiritual moving-picture in which close-ups and vistas fade into one another with insensible swiftness. Indeed they do not so much alternate as occur together: their profiles mingle. Close up, the realm of evil, of satanic wickedness abetting "nature's mischief" (I.v.51), appears hideously strong; but at the same time clear adumbrations are given of the encompassing world of good, of true "Nature" inspired by "Heaven" (I.v.46,54), which, seemingly distant at the moment, is supreme in beauty and ever ready, when occasion serves (as in IV.iii), to move close up powerfully, dimming though never obliterating the lurid contours of hell.

That twofold vision—climactically and superbly expressed in the fourth Act studied as a whole—is, in its fullness, far beyond the scope of the stage and of the cinema. But fine hints of it are continually given in the theater, hints suggestively various, and often fresh and penetrating, in different productions of the play. They can much assist the reader if he is also an appreciative though critical spectator. The outside of *Macbeth* is spectacular; and one must try to see it vividly, on the stage and in the imagination, while trying to see through it. Ultimately, however, this tragedy is designed for readers of Shakespeare, for those who in the words of his first editors will "reade him . . . againe and againe" in order to "understand him." This very theatrical play is fundamentally (and even more than *Lear*) non-theatric: it is the author's most subtly and profoundly *dramatic* poem.[20]

B. *Its Representativeness*

And *Macbeth* is a dramatic epitome of the tragic thought and art of the Renaissance. It embodies the idea of tragedy held by the chief authors and artists of that great movement, from Dante to Milton. But subsequently that idea was more and more modified or repudiated by philosophers and poets in favor of modern theories that seemed progressive. Nowadays, however, the brief and changeful modern period—the past two hundred years or so—is being viewed in critical perspective, and the validity of its cherished concepts is sharply questioned. Accordingly the Renaissance conception of tragedy is, in the opinion of a growing minority, truer than modern notions to the tragedy that really *is* in human life and history. And that view can illumine a significant paradox that emerges from the total modern criticism of *Macbeth*.

[20] Probably a perception of that fact, along with *Macbeth's* success on the stage, influenced the editors of the First Folio when they placed the last of Shakespeare's four main tragedies first, the order being *Macbeth, Hamlet, King Lear, Othello*. And his last play of all, *The Tempest*, is suggestively (in view of what is said of it above) placed first of all in the Folio.

This drama has been regarded by the critics, along with people in general, as the most gripping, whatever else it may be, of Shakespeare's plays. At the same time, however, the character of Macbeth himself as analyzed by the critics has increasingly come to seem very strange, far remote from ordinary humanity. A recent writer speaks for the majority when he says, "Macbeth is not a type but an individual."[21] But how can a play be so gripping for people in general if its central character, the one on whom the whole action turns far more than in the case of Shakespeare's other dramas, is not at all typical of people in general? Unless perchance the play is gripping in a merely melodramatic fashion; but that extreme view has not been maintained by the great majority of critics.

The interpreters of Macbeth may be divided roughly into two categories: the whiteners of his character and the blackeners of the same. The whitening tendency, though it still persists today, was at its height in the late eighteenth and the early nineteenth centuries. In those days a number of writers regarded Macbeth as unfortunate rather than sinful: they whitewashed him.[22] This, certainly, was not done by the chief Romantic critics, Coleridge and the others, nor by their distinguished successor in the early twentieth century, Professor A. C. Bradley. But these authors did not perceive in Macbeth the full depth of evil intended by Shakespeare with his Renaissance point of view; and so they may be regarded as honorary members, at least, of the guild of whiteners. As for the blackeners, their pioneer is George Fletcher who, reacting extremely from Romanticism, produced in 1847 a book wherein he claimed that Shakespeare designed Macbeth as an utter and detestable villain.[23] But especially since the black year 1914 the blackening cult has flour-

[21] G. F. Bradby in *Short Studies in Shakespeare* (1929), p. 104.

[22] Notably Thomas Whately in *Remarks on Some of the Characters of Shakespeare* (1785). His view was approved by John Kemble in *Macbeth Reconsidered* (1786).

[23] "It is no fault of his [Shakespeare's] if Macbeth's heartless whinings have ever extracted one emotion of pity from reader or auditor in lieu of that intensely aggravated abhorrence which they ought to inspire" (*Studies of Shakespeare*, p. 167).

ished; many critics have been impelled by modern evils to emphasize heavily Shakespeare's sense of evil. And a number of them, influenced by the comparatively recent discovery of Christianity in Shakespeare, have pronounced this drama a picture of a human soul on its way to hell.[24] That idea has been rejected, however, by other and more merciful Christian critics. In the upshot, the total mass of writings upon this character spells confusion worse confounded. And one must sympathize with those contemporary writers, notably Professor E. E. Stoll,[25] who urge that Macbeth's conduct was not rationally motivated by the dramatist.

Consider what happens in the final scene of the opening Act (I.vii). In the first half of this scene, beginning with the soliloquy "If it were done, when 'tis done," Macbeth adduces all his motives for *not* killing Duncan and decides not to do so. But in the second half, with the help of his wife, he determines to do so at once. Thus the dramatist attains what he is obviously aiming at, an extremely striking contrast between the opening and closing moods of this crucial scene; but in doing so has he not split his hero in two?[26] The initial movement of the scene culminates when the hero, accused by his wife of unmanly cowardice, replies:

> Prythee peace:
> I dare do all that may become a man;
> Who dares do more, is none.

[24] "Macbeth's spiritual experience is a representation on the stage of the traditional conception of a human soul on its way to the devil," says W. C. Curry in his *Shakespeare's Philosophical Patterns* (1937), p. 105. Roy Walker in *The Time is Free* (1949) says that Macbeth is "by nature predisposed to evil" (p. 6). Typical is Henri Fluchère's *Shakespeare* (1953). This author, who informs us that his work is based upon "English criticism of the last twenty-five years," declares that *"Macbeth* presents the complete triumph of evil, evil in its pure state, so to speak, evil without reason or issue" (p. 229). M. D. H. Parker in *The Slave of Life* (1955) terms *Macbeth* "Shakespeare's full length study of damnation" (p. 162).

[25] See his essay on "Slander in Drama" in the *Shakespeare Quarterly*, October 1953.

[26] Donald A. Stauffer in *Shakespeare's World of Images* (1949) says that Macbeth and also his Lady are "essentially unmotivated" in this scene (p. 213).

Certainly a manly principle. But is it humanly conceivable that the speaker should presently commit the most ignoble and unmanly of crimes: the secret stabbing of a helpless old person, his kinsman, guest, and king, who has heaped upon him honors, gratitude, and trust? Who, moreover, is loved and admired by all, including Macbeth himself! The dramatist deliberately intensified the situation by converting the Duncan of Holinshed's *Chronicles*, a very poor creature, into an excellent and even saintly monarch; thereby greatly aggravating the problem.

Bradley tries in modern fashion to save Shakespeare's face by arguing that in the passage under discussion Macbeth does not really mean what he says. But in quoting the passage Bradley omits the sharp opening sentence, "Prythee peace," which initiates a tone of complete assurance. And Shakespeare's point, I believe, is that Macbeth, so far from not meaning what he says, means it too much: in other words he is dangerously conscious of his own humanity. In this respect the speech is the acme of all those passages in Act I wherein the hero displays exuberantly his human-kindness; that is, his strong feeling for humankind, his humanness (rather than humaneness, though this is not excluded), his warm esprit de société. Accordingly Shakespeare's view of Lady Macbeth's characterization of her husband as "too full o' th' Milke of humane kindnesse" (I.v.18) is dramatically ironic. In reality Macbeth is "too full" of a lofty awareness of his own humanity. He relies too much upon it; he is proud of it, climactically in the first half of I.vii—and pride goes before a fall. Such, from the Renaissance standpoint, is the rational motivation of this scene; and I think it becomes very obvious and convincing when the scene is rightly performed on the stage.

In Act II, after the murder of Duncan, Macbeth, very humanly, tries to make himself feel better about it by giving vent to his human-kindness in speeches of piercing beauty. And he does likewise in the play's central crisis, the Feast scene (III.iv), after secretly disposing of his friend Banquo. To regard him as entirely hypocritical here when he proclaims his affection for his murdered friend is to miss the humanity of the scene. On the other hand if he were a mere emotionalist he would be too stupid to be interesting. Why, then, does he *twice* utter an ardent wish that Banquo could be present? The first appearance of the Ghost disturbs him greatly; the second appearance disconcerts him disastrously. But surely Macbeth is here doing, though in an extreme way, just what politician X does when he convinces himself of his own benevolence by publicly bemoaning the sudden demise of politician Y whom he has long desired to be rid of. And that phenomenon is not confined to politicians; it appears continually in the case of average persons, those who by nature are neither very good nor very bad. So that though Macbeth's conduct here is certainly extreme it is also extremely typical. Superficially it is melodramatic. Really it is a vivid dramatization of a common human trait; that is why this scene can arouse our sympathy, pity, and fear. Just because he has perpetrated two very wicked deeds, the second being the murder of his best friend, Macbeth strives ardently to assure himself, rather than the assembled thanes, that he is still very human. He illustrates a tragically deceptive achievement of the human soul: the cooperation of conscience and pride. The great remorse occasioned by his conscience, and richly felt by him, makes him greatly conscious of his human-kindness.[27]

In the Renaissance outlook wrong pride, as distinguished from right self-esteem—as indeed diametrically opposed to it—is not an *occasional* vice: it is an innate feature of human beings as such. This view, founded upon a realistic study of mankind, was of course due particularly to the Christian dogma of Original Sin together with the classic doctrine of hubris. Man is just naturally hubristic; he is, as Shakespeare terms him in *Measure for*

[27] Shakespeare's attitude in this matter harmonizes with the moral theology of his time. See Thomas Wood's *English Casuistical Divinity During the Seventeenth Century* (1952), especially pp. 132-136. Here Jeremy Taylor is shown to be characteristic of his predecessors, from the late sixteenth century on, in his critique of remorseful sentiment. Taylor urges that "tears are no duty, and the greatest sorrow is oftentimes the driest"; that "sensitive sorrow" is at best no more than a help to true repentance and, at its worst, a snare and a hindrance because of its self-centeredness.

Measure, "man, proud man." This belief persisted into the eighteenth century, though there it became more or less conventional, as in Pope's *Essay on Man*. But in the nineteenth century it was submerged: it mainly disappeared from the cultural realm and was rarely expressed in belles-lettres. Pride was regarded, not as being inherent in mankind, but as one vice among others which people might or might not have. For in that century, a time of extraordinary material progress, the danger of innate human pride was concealed. In 1913 western man was still certain that human-kindness (aided by modern science) could triumph over the worst human ills. This pride foreran the fall that was terribly revealed, though it did not begin, in 1914—the Fall of Man. That situation, recurrent in history and in individual lives, is the underlying theme of the *Tragedy of Macbeth*.

In 1904, a decade before the catastrophe of 1914, Bradley's great and influential book *Shakespearean Tragedy* was first published. Therein tragedy is defined as the waste of human values —a true definition so far as it goes, but too vague and naive from the Elizabethan standpoint. The modern period, supreme in natural science, has been comparatively superficial in its insights into human nature. The Renaissance, so naive (though seminal) in the field of science, was supreme in its grasp of human nature. Bradley interpreted Shakespeare in the light of the late nineteenth century in which he grew up rather than in the light of the late sixteenth century in which Shakespeare grew up. For this poet, as for the other great authors of his era, the waste of human values was fundamentally tragic only when it was due to human pride.[28] Comedy, in the Renaissance view, is the dif-

---

[28] Bradley remarks once and passingly that Macbeth's "disposition" is "proud" (p. 350); he fails, as already intimated above, to find any touch of this disposition in I.vii. G. Wilson Knight notes it here in connection with Macbeth's aspiring imagery, citing very appositely the passage in *Richard Second* (I.iii.129) upon "eagle-winged pride" (*The Imperial Theme*, 1931, p. 143). Cleanth Brooks in *The Well Wrought Urn* (1947) remarks that Macbeth becomes "the typical tragic protagonist when he yields to pride and *hybris*" (p. 41) but does not develop the point. It is a point of first importance for the right understanding of, particularly, English literature and drama from the time of Sir Thomas More to the time of Milton. J. H. Hexter's study of

ference between what a person is and what he thinks he is; tragedy, the difference between what he is and what he ought to be. Accordingly the motif of comedy is conceit; and the motif of tragedy is the pride that insulates a person and shackles him to what he is. Until that idea is plainly and fully recognized—in other words, until Shakespeare's outlook on life is seen to be essentially the same as that of the other leading poets of his era —the meaning of his tragedies will continue to be more or less modernized and distorted by criticism.

In modern criticism pride has of course been noted in Shakespeare's plays when it is very conspicuous, as in the main personages of *Lear*. But it has not been perceived, or at least not given its full due, when it is considerably disguised, as in Brutus, Hamlet, and Othello. This is the main reason (as I have tried to show elsewhere) for the extraordinary confusion in the interpretation of those three characters. And the same is the case with Macbeth. But here the confusion is especially disastrous because in him the pride is more humanly and tragically typical than it is in any other of Shakespeare's protagonists. The leading characters in his early tragical plays, *Titus Andronicus*, the *Henry Sixth* trilogy, above all *Richard Third*, are too brazenly arrogant to seem normally human. On the other hand, in the historical and tragic dramas from *Richard Second* to *Othello*, especially in *Hamlet*, the pride is extremely subtle; it is intertwined with other motives and, while basic, is not outstanding. It comes to the foreground again in the late tragedies from *Lear* to *Coriolanus* though not blatantly as in the early plays. But in *Macbeth* (contemporary with *Lear* though probably completed a little later) the pride is what it is in the average person: subtle without being supersubtle; constantly active while not too obtrusive; very tragic—but at the same time, and very humanly, *fantastical*. A famous passage in *Measure for Measure* (II.ii.110ff), which sounds the keynote of Renaissance tragedy as a whole, applies

---

More's *Utopia* (1952) demonstrates that this work "in its fundamental structure is a great social instrument for the subjugation of pride" as distinguished from right self-respect (pp. 80-91).

particularly to Macbeth; every phrase seems to point directly at him:

> .... man, proud man,
> Drest in a little briefe authoritie,
> Most ignorant of what he's most assured,
> His glassie Essence, like an angry Ape
> Plaies such phantastique tricks before high heaven,
> As makes the Angels weepe: who with our spleenes,
> Would all themselves laugh mortal.

In plain terms human pride, before high heaven, is always so unnatural and bizarre that it would be highly laughable if it were not so deeply tragic. That view, prominent in the Renaissance, is perennially true to human nature.

But the atmosphere of fantasticality so notable in the *Tragedy of Macbeth* centers in the hero's amazing imagination; and certainly in this respect he is *not* typical of average persons. He *is* typical in being from first to last a politician. Man is a political animal; and therefore when Shakespeare came to create the fourth and last of his main tragic heroes he made him, not a graduate of Wittenberg, not a Moorish soldier of fortune, not (like Lear) an imprudent old man, but an ambitious politician in the prime of life. But certainly not even the most eloquent politician, let alone the ordinary person who devours the political news in the daily papers, is possessed of the Macbethian imagination. Here Shakespeare employs poetic license, as he does in the case of all his leading dramatis personae, endowing them with a gift beyond common capacity; though Macbeth is especially outstanding because he is more worldly than the others: in real life this type of person does not speak so poetically. But be it noted that all ambitious persons use their modicum of imagination in exactly the same way as he uses his great gift. Everyone of us has one or another ambition which, like Macbeth, we manage to conceal at the first from other persons, excepting our spouses. We strongly desire something we have not, and we may desire it evilly if we let our imagination enhance its value inordinately. Bradley, under the influence of Romanticism, declares that Macbeth's imagination is, in itself, entirely good.[29] But the Renaissance view is more truly human: imagination is a great but neutral power, apt to be employed either for good or for evil ends. For instance, at the beginning of Act II "high heaven" (to adduce the *Measure for Measure* passage) enables Macbeth to have a "phantastique" but crucial vision of a bloody dagger which could forestall his slaughter of Duncan; but his evil will, swaying his evenly balancing imagination, makes that dagger usher him the way he was going. Of course his better imagination—that is, his imagination swayed by his better will—which has antecedently caused him to postpone the crime, brings terrible remorse upon him afterwards. But the remorse is mainly (not utterly) self-centered; and it comforts him falsely by renewing continually his sense of his innate human-kindness. In this respect he evinces strikingly a trait which, recurrent in Shakespeare's characters, is evidently regarded by him as a fateful human proclivity; namely one's ability to distract one's attention from the evil in oneself—thus preparing the way for further evildoing—by occupying his fantasy with the proud assurance that he is, after all, very human.

Along with pride Shakespeare makes use in this drama of three cognate ideas which, though they have not appealed to the modern mind, are deeply rooted in human consciousness and were prominent throughout the Renaissance. First, the supernatural origin of evil, in particular the belief that pride at its worst is devilish. Second, the supernatural origin of goodness, especially of the basic virtue, humility. Third, the possibility that even the most wicked person may at any time be converted if he allows his pride to be overcome by divine Grace. This idea enabled the dramatist, in a manner overlooked by criticism, to intensify greatly the element of suspense in Macbeth's career.

His blackeners claim that his resolve to murder Duncan was made completely and irrevocably before the opening of the play. On the other hand the whiteners, in their most extreme phase,

---

[29] *Shakespearean Tragedy*, pp. 352ff.

claim that this resolve was due entirely to Macbeth's encounter with the Witches. But in either case the full suspense designed by Shakespeare is missed. In the first Act, studied as a whole, it is quite evident that Macbeth did declare emphatically to his wife before the opening of the play an intention to destroy the king (see I.vii.47ff) but that this resolve, made by a very moody and human-kindly man, was far from irrevocable. In the first half of Scene iv that resolve is silently revoked by the hero, so entirely is he overpowered for the time being by the presence and gracious goodness of his sovereign. But thereupon, with acute dramatic irony, Duncan, sure of his most powerful thane's loyalty to the regime, appoints his son Malcolm his successor to the throne; with the result that Macbeth's evil design is revived and strengthened far more than it was by the Witches in the preceding scene. Thus Scene iv, with its vivid contrast between the hero's opening and closing moods, prefigures the great Scene vii, dealt with above, wherein for the first time Macbeth's evil volition becomes firmly fixed. The dramatist's point here, as so often in his plays, is that a wicked intention must in the end produce wicked action unless it is, not merely revoked by the protagonist's better feelings, but entirely eradicated by his inmost will, aided by divine Grace; which in Act I is mediated to Macbeth through the honesty of Banquo and, supremely, through the gracious generosity and trustfulness of Duncan. Only that view of the matter, I think, brings out the full dramatic quality of the first Act, particularly its suspensefulness.

Shakespeare was very bold in having his hero commit regicide as early as the start of Act II; for thereupon the suspense, hitherto great, collapses abruptly. But it is revived in the ensuing scene (II.ii) for those who, like the Elizabethan spectators, perceive that Macbeth's remorse, here profound, keeps open the possibility of his repentance. He hears a supernatural voice saying he shall sleep no more; he tries to pray to God, confesses that his guilt is ocean-like, and at the end of the scene wishes that his deed could be undone. And in the ensuing ensemble (II.iii) he seems, at first, likely to collapse. But his pride sustains him, as it is apt to do in the presence of others because of his strong, misemployed social sense. And in the climax he utters a lengthy, magnificent speech asseverating his love for the dead Duncan (II.iii.114ff). This monologue, in which the dramatist with fine art shows that the speaker is mainly sincere though unveracious, has two effects. It makes Macbeth king of Scotland but also it demonstrates conclusively that his conscience will not let him be happy on Duncan's throne. In the third Act his restless ecstasy brings about, but at the same time is intensified by, his destruction of Banquo. And in the close of the Feast scene (III.iv), alone with his wife, he is confronted definitively with two alternatives: he may repent; or he may harden his will by an orgy of evildoing. He chooses the second course. But he does so in such a vague and general fashion, not yet deciding upon any particular deed, that we are still kept in suspense.

Only in the end of the Cauldron scene (IV.i) does he definitely undertake his third and worst crime. Under the influence of the powers of evil, obeying their final injunction to "Be Lyonmettled, proud" (line 90)—the reader may recall the Lion in the outset of Dante's *Inferno*—he determines, in revenge for Macduff's flight to England, to slaughter his innocent wife and children. Here, deliberately cruel, Macbeth for the first time in his life chooses evil as evil. His pride in his human-kindness gives way entirely to his pride in the might of his evil will. But even here our suspense is not ended; for we cannot believe that he will succeed in extinguishing completely the remorsefulness displayed in the first three Acts. To be sure his present gracelessness stands out in vivid contrast with the conduct of Macduff, Malcolm, and Ross at the court of the saintly King Edward the Confessor of England (IV.iii). Here the theme of Grace, hitherto in the background, is brought to the fore. But in the Elizabethan outlook—formally, at least, Christian and certainly very dramatic (unlike modern lyric fatalism)—the fate of Macbeth's soul is still undecided. For the very Grace that can so remarkably animate his foes (who are far from unworldly by nature) may yet manage to lay hold of him too.

And in Act V he is certainly lifted above the subhuman, hellish level to which he sank in the preceding Act. Before he reappears on the stage his final state of mind is carefully foreshadowed by the dramatist in the first two scenes. In the Sleepwalking scene (V.i) the *extent* of Lady Macbeth's remorse is somewhat surprising. We easily imagine that if her husband with his larger conscience were the protagonist here his words would have been still more piercing. Thus Shakespeare, with the dramatic economy so characteristic of this play, disposes of the guilty queen while suggesting her royal husband's greater sense of guilt. Her vain attempt to cleanse her hands recalls inevitably his bloody hand incarnadining the ocean after his first murder (II.ii.59-63). And in the ensuing scene (V.ii) the dramatist, speaking through minor personages, tells us that Macbeth, now more than ever, feels his secret murders sticking on his hands, and that all that is within him condemns itself for being there. So that when he reappears in V.iii we know that his accumulated wicked deeds— not now mentioned by him explicitly but luridly recounted in V.i—are the essential cause of his great despair. And this despair, unlike that of Dante's and Milton's allegoric Satan, is entirely and grippingly human. It is touched, at least, with a humility he has not previously shown. Here at long last he knows that his career has been futile. He ceases to be ignorant of his glassy essence, of the glittering and brittle transiency of his earthly being. He sees he has been dressed in a little brief authority. His life is a "breefe Candle"; and, finally, he is "aweary of the Sunne" (V.v.23,49). But, continually alternating with that better attitude, is a very different one, a mood of defiant boastfulness, sustained by the lying predictions of the hellish spirits of the Cauldron scene. He brags: "The minde I sway by, and the heart I beare, / Shall never sagge with doubt, nor shake with feare" (V.iii.9f). And so we are kept in keen suspense, wondering what will be the outcome of the extremely ambivalent, though very human, state of his spirit.

56236

LIBRARY
College of St. Francis
JOLIET, ILL.

The last scene of all gives a supreme instance of Shakespeare's art of prepared surprise. Macbeth, surrounded by overwhelming forces but still fighting desperately, vaunting his determination to kill all he meets, is confronted suddenly with his greatest foe, Macduff, whom he is still certain of being able to defeat in single combat. Here he has the opportunity to cover himself, before his final exit, with the kind of glory he has always valued highly. He recoils from Macduff, however, and far more abjectly than he did in III.iv from the Ghost of Banquo; he cries out,

> Of all men else I have avoyded thee—
> But get thee backe, my soule is too much charged
> With blood of thine already.

This has been termed Macbeth's sole touch of real remorse; but that view overlooks the distinction, so sharp in the Renaissance mind, between remorse and penitence. Macbeth's remorse, though for the most part self-centered, has been real and great all along. But now he makes an impressive gesture, if nothing more, of penitence; that is, of willingness to sacrifice his lust of fame by way of compensating for the evil he has done. And the passage quoted above returns upon Lady Macbeth's fearful outcry at the heart and center of the Sleepwalking scene: "The Thane of Fife had a wife—where is she now?" There the speaker, who had absolutely nothing to do with the massacre of Macduff's family, expresses, as we are now clearly shown, that within Macbeth's "soule" which most condemns itself for being there. And presently, somewhat astonishingly, Macduff offers his great wronger the option of living out his natural life in a state of humiliating captivity—which is precisely the lot that Macbeth must endure if his penitence is to become real repentance. But this final and providential opportunity is rejected, only too naturally, by his resurgent pride; he fights Macduff and is slain. In contrast with the first Thane of Cawdor he does not at the end of his life "set forth a deepe Repentance" (I.iv.6f). He has shown, however, that he has some sense, however slight, of his need of purgatorial contrition. As for his eternal destiny, Shakespeare, unlike many of his modern critics, is characteristically willing to leave that matter to the Almighty.

Portia in *The Merchant of Venice* declares that earthly power doth then show likest God's when mercy seasons justice. And Shakespeare's earthly power, his power as a *secular* poetic dramatist, is singularly expressive of that divine charity in which justice and mercy season each other. His great art and his great charity are two aspects of one faculty; and this faculty appears supremely, I think, in the *Tragedy of Macbeth*.

The question as to the central meaning of this drama turns upon the difference, not commonly recognized by the modern secular mind, between the true charity, which is *justly and righteously kind*, and that inadequate sort of charity which is the *milk* of human-kindness. The word milk, here as elsewhere in Shakespeare's works, is ambiguous: it may denote either nourishment or weakness, chiefly the latter in the case of Macbeth. But he is very typical; his conduct evinces both the potential value and the tragic limitation of that fellow-feeling, that human-kindness, which most people have most of the time. Ordinarily it serves to cement human society; but this cement melts very quickly, and for most persons surprisingly, in the heat of selfish interests. In vivid contrast is the virtuous charity of King Duncan, so carefully shown by the dramatist in the first Act. Unlike Macbeth, Duncan is not proudly conscious of his own kindness; in him it is a subordinate and nourishing constituent of the true charity. This king bears his faculties meekly and is clear in his great office, gentle but firm, mercifully just. He has the manly meekness that inherits the earth in the sense that it alone can transform human society into a real human family. And Shakespeare, with beautiful art, makes the spirit of Duncan persist throughout the play after his death, to become victorious at the close.

While Duncan sleeps well in that eternal peace which appeared in his life on earth, his virtues do indeed plead trumpet-tongued against the deep damnation of his taking-off. Continually the recollection of "the gracious Duncan" (III.i.66), this "most-Sainted king" (IV.iii.109), is present to others for reproach or for inspiration. And his sort of charity appears in a number of other personages: in three minor characters, the Old Man in the end of Act II, Ross in Act IV, and the good Doctor in Act V; and in three important persons, Banquo, Macduff, and Malcolm. The character of Malcolm, developed in the last two Acts, reproduces that of his father: he reincarnates the humble benevolence and justness of Duncan. And in the play's final episode Malcolm, now king, is the head of a nation which has become again an organic society. The spirit of Duncan has triumphed, with the aid of "the Powers above" (IV.iii.238). In the closing lines of the play the new sovereign speaks of "the Grace of Grace," a striking phrase which seems to echo, at a reverent distance, the declaration in the first chapter of St. John's Gospel regarding the Word of God made flesh: "of his fullness have we all received, grace upon grace" (but see my Preface, above). Here the dramatist, speaking through Malcolm, alludes conclusively to a main theme of this play. In each and all of the six dramatis personae mentioned above, climactically in Malcolm, human-kindness is sublimated by divine Grace (as in Duncan) into true charity, humble, merciful, and righteous.

This drama in its whole pattern is the tragedy of human-kindness (or humanity) and ambitious evil—this rather than evil ambition. Macbeth's ambitiousness is not in itself evil. His very strong social sense, worldly but valuable, together with that gift of imaginative expression whereby he far outshines all the others, makes him naturally and rightly desirous of winning "Golden Opinions from all sorts of people" (I.vii.33) and of standing very high in the realm. But Shakespeare as a political thinker (an aspect of him well brought out by recent critics) shows that this hero, quite apart from his evil doings, is temperamentally unfitted for sovereignty at its best. He is designed by God and nature to be a very excellent second in command under the better balanced personalities of Duncan and Malcolm —the very position that devolves in the end upon the noble but temperamental Macduff, whose modesty and humility enable him to have a right self-esteem. But Macbeth slenderly knows himself, like Lear and Shakespeare's other tragic heroes, and like most persons in real life when blindly driven by one or another sort of ambition. So he yearns for a status higher than he is fitted to have. And as soon as his will is murderously tainted it becomes a vehicle for the ambitious evil of the powers of the air, who, unlike him, aim to reduce human society to chaos. They are symbolized, somewhat melodramatically, by the Witches; more humanly by their successor in the second half of the first Act, the demon-inspired Lady Macbeth; but most effectually by the murky or hellish imagery pervading the play, recurrent and most telling in the speeches of Macbeth himself. This diabolic atmosphere moves us deeply because all of us are aware at times of black desires arising in our consciousness suddenly and shockingly. These, we nowadays believe, derive from the subconscious fund of evil propensities accumulated in mankind during the past million years or so. That belief is comprised, really, in the outlook of Shakespeare though, for dramatic purposes at least, he also accepts the older belief that evil is fundamentally devilish, created by that which Macbeth terms "the common Enemie of Man" (III.i.69), Satan. For Shakespeare, as for Dante and most of the other great Renaissance writers, evil is both human and hellish. And the pressure of the hellish realm of evil upon Macbeth is so dreadfully heavy that he never completely loses our sympathy. But all of his wicked decisions, as the dramatist is careful to make clear, are ultimately his own: he has our human free will. His nightmare career is essentially very human. We ourselves could easily enter upon a similar "way of life," falling at last "into the Seare, the yellow Leafe" (V.iii.22f), if we should let our wills be swayed by the ambitious evil at work in the depths of human nature and, perhaps, of the universe.

In Macbeth Shakespeare has succeeded in creating a person who at his worst embodies the blackest evil but who, nevertheless, has a remarkable whiteness, a native candor. One of the meanest of human traits is our tendency to disparage—if only in the presence of our loyal spouses—some quite excellent person who happens to block our worldly advancement. Properly, however, we at least endeavor, carefully and sincerely, to give that person his just due; and in this regard Macbeth represents us at our best. He never, even when alone with his devoted wife, disparages those whom his ambition wishes to destroy—except on one occasion. In his conference with the prospective murderers of Banquo (III.i.74ff) Macbeth, descending to his very lowest level, utters a desperate falsehood defaming his friend. But this is the exception that proves the rule. Elsewhere, notably in the first part of that very scene, he appreciates the great qualities of Banquo, as he does those of Duncan, with fine human discernment, and without that effortful factitiousness that we may so easily evince when we are extolling those who stand in our way. He even goes the length of praising in Duncan, with tragical naïveté and pathos, that very humility the lack of which is to bring about his own ruin. And the really profound disturbance produced *in us* by the first two Acts of this drama is due mainly to the fact that here we are watching a hero who kills a person whom he does not hate while we (not heroic) are well aware of often hating a person whom we do not kill. Consciously or not we confront the truth, enunciated by religion and ethics at their best, that not the killing but the hating of a fellow man is the basal sin, a deadly spiritual sort of murder.

Macbeth's blackness and his whiteness are both accentuated through his relations with his wife. She, as the dramatist makes fully clear (certain critics to the contrary), has no regal yearnings of her own. She enters fully into her husband's ambition because of her intense and narrow love of him; and, despite her own considerable human-kindness, she manages with immense effort to assist him in his first crime because he has infected her deeply with the false notion that he can be entirely happy only if he attains the throne, even if he has to murder his way to it. His evil imagination begets the same in her; and so he is responsible for ruining the peace of this woman along with his own. On the other hand his love of her becomes not less but more intense as the action proceeds, a dramatic phenomenon which has been better perceived by actors than by academics. In this very condensed play the author has no room after the Feast scene (III.iv) for further dialogue between Macbeth and his wife; but during the last Act his remorseful love and grief for her are indicated clearly. When he learns of her death he is too much overcome—like Romeo on learning of Juliet's supposed demise (V.i.24ff)—to put his grief into words; it has to be expressed by the actor's mien and gestures. But his wife's fate is the *conclusive* cause of his great despair in Act V: he knows that, if she had lived on, the rest of her life like his, because of his evil past, would have been just tomorrow and tomorrow and tomorrow creeping in this petty pace from day to day. In short, his humanity, as well as his wickedness, is most strikingly shown in his bearing towards the one person other than himself whom he entirely and intensely loves.

The whitest feature of Macbeth, however, is that, like his wife and unlike a multitude of other sinners, he does not strive to cloak his wickedness with conventional religiosity. Many a tyrant in pagan and Christian times, including Henry Eighth, has succeeded in conceiving his evil doings as in the main condoned by the gods or God. But Macbeth, with all his imagination, never imagines that. In the close of the play, for the first time in his career, he has to hear himself utterly condemned to his face for his wickedness: two noble gentlemen, Young Siward and Macduff, representing a wide range of human society, tell him plainly and strongly that he has become a servant of hell and the devil. And he does not utter a single word in repudiation of that verdict. So that our sense of uplift at the end of this tragedy is due in no small measure to the fact that Macbeth has at least the grace not to claim for his doings any tinge of Grace. And in this respect he adumbrates a characteristic of Shakespeare himself, who continually in his works shows up the hollowness and black deceptiveness of a merely conventional, egoistic piety.

Of course Shakespeare is nothing of a preacher. With the possible exception of Homer he is the most sheerly artistic of the world's chief poets. His life-aim was merely to achieve the maximum of poetic and dramatic effects. We cannot know to what extent he had a *personal* belief in Renaissance doctrines; I have tried to show only that he used them for the purposes of his dramatic art. The question I have wished to raise is simply: what interpretation of *Macbeth* is truest to its author's aim of producing in this play the utmost of pity and fear, of dramatic suspense, irony, contrast, and surprise? In *Twelfth Night*, the last of his four main comedies, he achieved the utmost *comic* concentration and effect; in *Macbeth*, the last of his four main tragedies, he concentrated upon producing the utmost *tragic* effect. But in so doing he laid hold, consciously or not, of the most tragic feature of human life, man's overweening belief in the capability of his own nature, particularly his human-kindness —a belief all the more tragical just because human sympathy (or empathy) is so essential for us and at its best so lovely. Constantly in his writings Shakespeare shows an eager appreciation of any touch, no matter how slight and transient, of human-kindness. But also, and above all in *Macbeth*, he reveals his sharp awareness that *natural* benevolence cannot withstand the assault of supernatural (or preternatural) evil desire. This can be overcome only by supernatural (or preternatural) goodness; to the influence of which, however, man will not as a rule open his spirit simply and humbly. Instead he seeks a little brief authority for himself as man—proud man. Macbeth is a thoroughly representative human being. And the *Tragedy of Macbeth*, in its whole design, bodies forth the essence of the tragedy of mankind.

FIRST PHASE

THIS TERRIBLE FEAT

(ACT ONE)

ACT ONE

a. *with Macbeth* (I.i)

Red glares of lightning come and go in the rainy fog. The thunder is muffled and ominous, "not loud but deep," like the "curses" heard near the close of the play by a tortured imagination (V.iii.27). And the weird creatures approaching, three in number, now vague in the drifting masses of mist, now hellishly illumined by flaring lightning, might be things of the imagination, entirely "fantastical" (I.iii.53). But soon they are seen to be witches in form, footing the earth at present though "not like the inhabitants" of it; "wild in their attire," with indistinct faces bearded and "withered," and skinny gesturing fingers (I.iii.40-46) that rise towards their lips when they are about to utter a certain name. They typify a world of dire evil and disorder, of dubiety and incessant sudden questionings:

1. When shall we three meet againe?
   In Thunder, Lightning, or in Raine?
2. When the Hurley-burley's done,
   When the Battaile's lost, and wonne.
3. That will be ere the set of Sunne.   5
1. Where the place?   2. Upon the Heath.[1]
3. There to meet   with   *Macbeth*.

The liquid and soft sounds in the first five lines, distillations seemingly of rain and dim air,[2] are in contrast with the distant clashes of battle that mingle with the low pulsings of thunder. In lines 4 to 7 a sharp sibilance develops. Incidentally the sound, sense, and placing centralize the sad word "lost," though this is

---

[1] The spacings in the last two verses are of course mine; the sixth verse combines two lines of the Folio.

[2] The curious reader may count the l's, r's, m's, and n's, noting how they prepare for the "ain" and "un" rhymes.

gently contradicted by the "wonne." In the final line the swaying chant rises to a scream.

The name *Macbeth*, a very breathing of the whole murky scene—"Hell is murky" (V.i.40)—is the signal for an outburst of demonic laughter from beyond, superseding the shrill voices of the Witches. Presently come summoning catcalls, croaks, and shrieks from their familiar spirits in animal forms. The three mystic figures sway, retreat, and rise, and hover away, chanting in unison:

> Faire is foule, and foule is faire,
> Hover through the fogge and filthie ayre.   10

Certainly the "ayre" into which they have "vanished ... melted" (I.iii.80f) is foul and filthy with evil. But our world's air, generally, is very "faire," fair in sound and nature; and now it is enriched with the intense, visionary (though sinister) beauty of the great short poem that this scene is. And so our wonder is intense regarding the man "*Macbeth*." We feel that his air, his mien and nature, must be largely fair; but the emissaries of evil are to "meet with" him as with an accomplice. They are empowered, surely, by some foul trend in the very will of him; against which, however, he is struggling, confusedly: his inward "Battaile" (4) is swaying to and fro like the whole tone and movement of this mystic scene. He may dispel the evil, making it vanish into air; or he may incorporate it in his life and being. His final decision is hovering now between fair and foul, foul and fair; while the evil powers are yearning to transmute all the fairness of him into foggy, filthy wickedness.

b. *death ... Macbeth* (I.ii)

The fog thins; the thunder subsides while the noise of battle off stage heightens; the red lightning disappears: a blood-reddened man appears, staggering out of the mist, meeting King Duncan and his entourage. (In II.ii a bloody man will stagger forward out of midnight darkness after killing this king.)

B. DEATH . . . MACBETH *(I.ii)*

> King   What bloody man is that? he can report,
>   As seemeth by his plight, of the Revolt
>   The newest state.

Instantly our minds associate the misty evil in Macbeth with the word "Revolt." But soon the bleeding officer's speech, opening with the word "Doubtfull" (7), lets us know that the present rebel is the "mercilesse *Macdonwald*": he, with the "multiplying Villainies of Nature" swarming upon him and with masses of wild western troops swarming[3] after him, seems a momentary incarnation of the evil nature of the preceding scene. Momentary; for that rushing array of lawless, "damnèd" force,[4] fortunate at first, is quickly dissolved; "all's too weak":

> For brave *Macbeth* (well hee deserves that Name)
> Disdayning Fortune, with his brandisht Steele,
> Which smoaked with bloody execution
> (Like Valour's Minion) carved out his passage,
> Till hee faced the Slave: 20
> Which nev'r shooke hands, nor bade farewell to him,
> Till he unseamed him from the Nave to th' Chops,
> And fixed his Head upon our Battlements.

That flashing, smoking, crimson sword! We see it cutting its way through the crude mob, felling heavy-armed "gallowglasses" while "skipping kerns" take to their heels (13,30), till the hero faces the brutal Macdonwald—here a gasping pause; then the rude triumphant humor and slaughter of the three last lines. The rebel is suddenly confronted with a strange, bloody-armored apparition "which" is not here to shake hands with him, nor to bid farewell till[5] the sword rips him from jaws down to navel[6]—our imagination follows the ghastly unseaming in re-

---

[3] Compare the swarms of villains attacking the hero, Arthur, in Spenser's *Faerie Queene*, Book II, canto xi.

[4] The Folio has "damned Quarry." The second word has been variously interpreted.

[5] Note the effect of the repeated initial "Till" in the text (20, 22). Such repetition of words is characteristic of this play.

[6] Unless we conceive Macbeth as making here, with reversed sword, an upward stroke (22)! In either case the effect is grotesquely violent.

verse, from belly up to chin: thence the moving-picture skips up to the severed, fixed "Head." (A similar head will appear in the last phase of the play, IV.i.67ff, V.vii.82ff.) Here Macbeth's sword is the sword of "justice" (29), certainly, but bizarre and brutally violent.

And that atmosphere is heightened in the bleeding captain's preliminary account of a second battle, following swiftly upon the first but far more effortful and ominous. In the east, Sweno, king of Norway, taking advantage of the war in the west and newly supplied with men and arms, began a "fresh assault" (33), "direful" as a rising, wreckful storm (25f).[7] Macbeth, and Banquo with him now, met the terrible attack with the courage of eagles and lions, and with the violent force of overcharged cannon; but with doubtful result:

> So they doubly redoubled stroakes upon the Foe:
> Except they meant to bathe in reeking Wounds,
> Or memorize another *Golgotha*,   40
> I cannot tell—but I am faint,
> My Gashes cry for helpe.

The narrator sinks to the ground fainting, leaving us in keen suspense regarding the outcome of the battle.

The suspense heightens when Ross, entering with "haste" and "things strange" in his looks,[8] cries, "God save the King." Duncan, "great King," seems now to be in great peril. Ross has come from Fife

> Where the Norweyan Banners flowt the Skie,
> And fanne our people cold.[9]   50

But soon we learn that those banners, now brought to a standstill —some of them, apparently, captured by the Scots—are emblems

---

[7] Editors have supplied "break" after "thunders," which ends the line in the original. But "begins" (i.e. begin) is understood, being supplied from the preceding line.

[8] The iteration in "looks . . . look" (46) intensifies wonder. See note 5 above.

[9] This significant short line is filled out with the first two words of the next line in many modern editions.

of a hovering danger that has been overcome though with immense difficulty.[10] The difficulty and danger are rendered in rhetorical verses wherein Macbeth, whose name, however, is not mentioned by Ross, figures as the bridegroom of the goddess of war:

> *Norway* himselfe, with terrible numbers,
> Assisted by that most disloyall Traytor,
> The *Thane* of Cawdor, began a dismall Conflict,
> Till that *Bellona's* Bridegroome, lapt in proofe,[11]
> Confronted him with selfe-comparisons,   55
> Point against Point, rebellious Arme 'gainst Arme,
> Curbing his lavish spirit—and to conclude,
> The Victorie fell on us.

That word "Victorie" elicits a breathing of relief from the group on the stage and from the audience in the theater, expressed in Duncan's quiet exclamation "Great happinesse!" But a deep feeling remains in us of "things strange" and threatening.

For the nature of Macbeth's *outward* warfare, as the next scene will gradually make clear, results from and represents his "doubtful" (7), dreadful *inward* struggle. The "Strange Images of death" which he makes with his sword are nothing to him in comparison with the "horrid Image" in his mind of the potential murder of Duncan (I.iii.97,135). This image he tries to banish (as later he will try to banish the memory of the murder) by wading (III.iv.137) in "bloody execution" (18). His motives are mixed and confused. He fights with extraordinary bravery and desperate "Venture" of his life (I.iii.91) for King Duncan and, at the same time, for the kingship which he secretly yearns to have for himself. He has lost the simple, whole-hearted loyalty exemplified by the wounded officer so devoted to the king, to Malcolm, and to Macbeth himself (3ff). The secret disloy-

---

[10] Compare the Dragon in *The Faerie Queene*, I.xii, now dead but still menacing in appearance.

[11] Here, as not previously, Macbeth's *complete* armor is stressed: this time he needs it all.

alty of Cawdor, narrated in the climax of the scene, suggests the evil spirit that is trying to conquer Macbeth; but still the good in him may strenuously win the "Victory." Spiritual "death" hovers near the soul of "noble" Macbeth; but the gracious influence of his sovereign, whose every line in this scene breathes simple nobility, can serve to save him:

KING No more that *Thane* of Cawdor shall deceive
Our Bosome interest. Goe pronounce his present death,
And with his former Title greet *Macbeth*.   65
Ross I'll see it done.
KING What he hath lost, Noble *Macbeth* hath wonne.

c. *that suggestion* (I.iii)

The "done," "lost," and "won" of the last lines above echo, for us, the words of the Second Witch (I.i.3f). She, while awaiting the end of the hurlyburly with its bloody slaughter, has been "Killing Swine" (2). She whines that curt declaration balefully as the three appear again, this time to be seen more clearly. The fog, empty now of lurid lightning, is a deathlike grayness, hushed except for the low thunder muttering like a wicked charm. And though our sense of the presence of the great *invisible* powers of evil, a sense roused in the first scene and deepened in the second, remains very strong we are now made to feel the intimacy of the three "Sisters" (1,3,32)—not previously so termed—with each other and with earthly men, women, and events. To the pampered sailor-wife steadily munching chestnuts the First Witch is merely a despicable human hag (6); and the deeds that the three have been doing, recounted now to each other in vivid folk-verse, are those commonly attributed to witches.

But unconsciously, supernaturally, the three utter vague and distant hints of what will happen later. The solitary, bold wife of the adventurous "Master" of the ship called "*Tiger*" (7) is a prefiguration of the wife who, unwittingly, will help to bring ruin upon Macbeth, master of the state; the First Witch chants:

Sleepe shall neyther Night nor Day
Hang upon his Pent-house lid: 20
He shall live a man forbid. . . .
Though his Barke cannot be lost,
Yet it shall be Tempest-tost.

Again the piercing word "lost," this time in a context that recalls the tempestuous weather of I.i.2 and, more significantly,
the "Shipwracking Stormes" of the battle-story above (I.ii.26).

1. Here I have a Pilot's Thumbe,
    Wrackt, as homeward he did come.   *Drum within*
3. A Drumme,   a Drumme: 30
    Macbeth   doth come.·

The "Pilot" of the victorious army is returning. The throbs of
the drum, at first faint, come nearer and nearer, louder and
louder; while the three "weyward Sisters, hand in hand" move
in a circle, nod and sway, winding up their evil charm. They
retreat into fringes of the mist and stand rigid, silent, dim,[12]
while the tramping army off stage passes on quickly and the
drum-beat hushes.

Macbeth with bowed head, wrapped in thought, advances to
the front of the stage. Then, lifting his face, proud, handsome,
and haggard, he startles us by echoing the "fair" and "foul" of
the weird sisters in the close of the opening scene: "So foule and
faire a day I have not seene"—fair because it is "the day of suc-
cesse" (I.v.1); foul because of the stormy fog, and because his
success, the greatest in his life so far, has terribly quickened his
will to obtain the throne by killing his good king. Rapt, he pays
no heed to Banquo's matter-of-fact query, "How farre is't called
to Forres?" Macbeth's imagination, having sped thither, is
travelling very far beyond. But he rouses himself, slowly at first,
then quickly, when his companion, perceiving the misty figures,
questions them in a tone of rising though fearless wonder (39ff).

They, with nothing now of the familiar witchlike mien they

[12] John Dover Wilson imagines, mistakenly I think, that they are *completely*
hidden while Macbeth and Banquo enter.

evinced in the opening phase of this scene, are so unearthly and statuesque that they might be the three fates, in vaguely feminine form (45). Simultaneously they lay gaunt fingers on thin lips, speechless to Banquo, watching Macbeth's awed silence, ready to respond when he cries out suddenly, "Speake if you can: what are you?"

1. All haile, *Macbeth*, haile to thee *Thane* of Glamis.
2. All haile, *Macbeth*, haile to thee *Thane* of Cawdor.
3. All haile, *Macbeth*, that shalt be King hereafter.   50

That stanza, so beautiful in sound and rhythm, rising and falling, gradually ascending in tone, can seem the very "breath" and utterance of "the wind" (82). The iterated "aile" and "eth" sounds convey a strange wail, which, however, is belied by the full-toned "All" and the firm closing words of each line. And the wail is mainly dispelled, though still hovering, in the triumphant final verse, chanted by her who had announced the meeting (I.i.7) and the arrival (31) of Macbeth. She, terser than the other two in speech, and in figure more gaunt and tall, towers above them now in wild dignity, uttering the final dictum with Atropos-like assurance. She with her companions may be visionary instead of "outwardly" real; and whatever is foul in them is veiled by the mist and by the poetry of words that "sound so fair" (52-54).

But unlike Banquo his "Noble Partner," renowned for dauntless bravery, gives a violent start and recoils in terror; then stands fixed with bowed head again, deeply brooding, less, we perceive, upon outer than upon inner voices and images. Apparently he heeds not (though presently we learn that he hearkens to) what his fearless friend elicits from the weird speakers, the prophecy that Banquo will be lesser yet greater than Macbeth, not so happy yet happier, begetter of kings though himself not crowned: "So all haile *Macbeth*, and *Banquo* . . . *Banquo*, and *Macbeth*, all haile": foul and fair, fair and foul, mingle indifferently in that "Prophetique greeting" (78). Instantly, while Banquo maintains a skeptical calmness, not begging their "favors" nor fearing their "hate" (60f), the three begin to fade. But they stay momentarily when Macbeth, rousing from his long trance, adjures them excitedly:[18] "Stay you imperfect Speakers, tell me more" (70).

Multiplex irony[14] is in his declaration that "the *Thane* of Cawdor lives / A prosperous Gentleman": unconsciously he describes what he himself, by the pronouncement of Duncan, now outwardly is, while inwardly he is approximating "that most disloyal traitor," the preceding Cawdor (I.ii.52). Accordingly he betrays indifference to the prospect of becoming "King hereafter" (50) *by legitimate process.* At present it seems very likely, in the eyes of Banquo and doubtless many others, that upon the old king's decease "The Sovereignty will fall upon *Macbeth*" (II.iv.30), by decision of the peers, as "valiant Cousin" (I.ii.24) of Duncan and worthiest successor. But now the hero waives this "fair" (52) probability, asserting with specious modesty that it is unbelievable (74). Obviously he interprets the ambiguous prophecy to mean a soon and fateful achievement of which the three weird speakers have "strange Intelligence," imperfectly communicated to him "Upon this blasted Heath."

That sudden and dire word "blasted," prefixed by him to the "Heath" which they at the outset rhymed with *Macbeth* (I.i.6f) —the name conjoined with "death" in the second scene—indicates the imminent evil that can make his masterly spirit "dwindle, peake, and pine" (23).[15] His will, however, is entirely his own: it cannot be blasted from without. He "cannot be lost" (24) unless he loses his better self. So now when he charges the Witches to tell him more they vanish utterly; they have told him all they can: he must now speak crucially to his own soul. And the words he proceeds to say, along with the good Banquo, upon the unsubstantiality of the three fatelike visitants

---

[13] Hence no comma after the ensuing "Stay."

[14] Accordingly Shakespeare gives no clear explanation of Macbeth's ignorance of the first Cawdor's treachery: the unclearness is part of the irony and of the misty atmosphere.

[15] The word "blasted" in this context recalls a line from *Hamlet*: "Contagious blastments are most imminent" (I.iii.42).

(79-82) mean that the evil in his mind can become as immaterial as mists, bubbles, breaths of earth, water, and air, unless his will makes it "corporal," incorporates it in his own life and being. But his efforts to take as lightly as Banquo does the things they have seen and heard are very forced (82-88). And the effect upon him of the news brought now by Angus and Ross is shattering. In their speeches the greatness of his deeds and the greatness of the praise and gratitude of "our Royal Master" (101) are closely interwoven. Then suddenly Ross, like the weird sisters, proceeds to "haile" him as "Thane of Cawdor"! Macbeth starts more violently than before and utters a breathless question; then, during Angus's measured reply, stands at first dumb and staring like one whom a ghost has blasted, but gradually regains his self-control.

Banquo, affected sharply by the news but much more by his friend's reaction to it, drops his skeptical and neutral view of the Witches. He is sure now that they were emissaries of "the Devil" (107), speaking a truth with evil intent. And the prophecy that his own "Children shall be kings," mentioned somewhat lightly by Macbeth when the two were alone (86) but now repeated by him in a significant whisper (118), seems to Banquo a thing fraught with wicked possibilities. Worst of all is his friend's reference to "those that gave the Thane of Cawdor to me." The word "gave" is as ambiguous as the words of the devilish three themselves: it may mean either predict or decree. He replies, "That trusted home / Might yet enkindle you unto the Crowne"—might, in spite of long and newly demonstrated loyalty, inspire in you a fire[16] of impatient desire for the kingship:

> And oftentimes, to winne us to our harme,
> The Instruments of Darknesse tell us Truths,
> Winne us with honest Trifles, to betray us   125
> In deepest consequence.

[16] Here fire (implied by "enkindle"), the most aspiring and dangerous of the four elements, supersedes the other three, earth, water, and air, cited above (79-82).

Thus Providence gives Macbeth, through a close, tried, and admiring friend, the warning he needs at this moment. He nods his head, slowly and silently, as though in full agreement with Banquo; who, reassured, turns away to chat with Ross and Angus so as to afford the emotional hero a minute of solitude for accustoming himself to the "new Honors" with which he has been arrayed under such "strange" circumstances (122,144-146). And now we perceive that the ambitious spirit of Macbeth is rejecting his friend's providential warning as silently and absolutely as he had seemed to accept it. Resuming his broken soliloquy, "Glamis, and Thane of Cawdor! / The greatest is behinde" (116),[17] he repeats Banquo's word "Truths" with the "Instruments of Darknesse" (124) omitted:

> Two Truths are told,
> As happy Prologues to the swelling Act
> Of the Imperiall Theame.—I thanke you, Gentlemen.—
> This supernaturall solliciting   130
> Cannot be ill; cannot be good.
> If ill? why hath it given me earnest of successe,
> Commencing in a Truth? I am *Thane* of Cawdor.

Standing erect and firm, the chief peer of the realm, he feels himself protagonist in a grandly unfolding drama that will eventuate in imperial (royal is too weak a word for his swelling imagination) power for him. He is to be master of his own great destiny. For though this strange soliciting, now urgent *within him*— the three weird sisters have vanished for the present from his thoughts—is supernatural, it is also, he tries to feel, entirely neutral. Thus he intertwines truth and error: fair is foul, and foul is fair. Certainly his own will is to be the determinant factor; but this true perception of his is befouled by his denial of the hellish evil, the power of "Darknesse," in the supernatural soliciting.

---

[17] Compare the fascinating egoist, Meserve, in Robert Frost's "Snow," of whom it is stated that he talks straight on "from the last thing he said himself."

Yet if that soliciting is entirely neutral it cannot be good any more than ill. And "good" (131) sounds strange indeed in conjunction with his climactic word "Cawdor,"[18] now so direful. His new title, triumphantly declaimed by him, recalls at once the "hidden" (113), multiform, obscure[19] yet sure and certain treachery of Cawdor summed up tellingly by Angus a few moments ago. "*I am Thane of Cawdor,*" says Macbeth now—and pauses. Then his face, which with quick uneasy steps he brings close up to us, begins to fill with horror. He repeats his word "good," but now with fearful interrogation:[20]

> If good? why doe I yield to that suggestion,
> Whose horrid Image doth unfixe my Haire,   135
> And make my seated Heart knock at my Ribbes,
> Against the use of Nature? Present Feares
> Are lesse than horrible Imaginings:
> My Thought, whose Murther yet is but fantasticall,
> Shakes so my single state of Man,   140
> That Function is smothered in surmise,
> And nothing is, but what is not.

Oblivious of his three companions, he lets his mind work upon what he had hoped to regard as "things forgotten" (150),[21] namely the past occasions when he imagined himself as destroying Duncan. And just because he had entertained those "horrible Imaginings" (138) so often, without ever rejecting them definitively, they coalesce now into *one* "horrid Image" (134f), a "suggestion" (temptation) almost overwhelmingly powerful.

That immoral process is a common human experience: it brings Macbeth very close to us. Not often, of course, is human ambition so extremely imperious and the means of its fulfillment so

---

[18] Here spoken for the tenth and last time in this scene.

[19] The cryptic nature of Cawdor's doings, foreshadowing Macbeth's, has given needless concern to many critics. See note 14 above.

[20] But modern editions substitute a comma for the question-mark after "good" in line 134.

[21] For a different interpretation of these words see John Dover Wilson's edition, page 105, and Kenneth Muir's edition, page 22.

horribly wicked as in the case of this man. Yet along with his associates, notably his king and his comrade Banquo, we have come to admire him as normally a very worthy and noble gentleman. And now we have to be sympathetic as we watch him doing what we ourselves so often do when under great temptation: again he postpones decision, this time crucially, with "deepest consequence" (126). Pity and fear come upon us for this very human person who may become dreadfully inhuman. Shaken by his inner conflict he allows his "Function" (141),[22] his volitional action, to be smothered in a dreamy fog confusing the real and the unreal. The "day" so foul and fair of his opening line (38) becomes now merely "the roughest Day" (147)— and "Tempest-tost" (25), we know, his soul will soon be again. But now his face begins to clear when he determines to leave his future proceedings to "Chance" (143), to "Time, and the Houre" (147).

And perchance all may yet be well. When the good Banquo summons him, the "Worthy *Macbeth*" seems to resume, almost entirely, his better nature, dignified, grateful, courteous, full of fellow-feeling. He wishes his own heart to be as "free" (guiltless) as the heart of his comrade in arms when the two shall confer confidentially "upon what hath chanced" (153-155) in its bearing upon the dim future wherein "Chance" may crown Macbeth without his stir (143f).[23] To all three companions he says with full sincerity (149ff):

> Give me your favour . . .
> Kinde Gentlemen, your paines are registered
> [He lays his right hand on his heart]
> Where every day I turne the Leafe
> To reade them. [He takes their hands in his warmly]
> Let us toward the King. . . .
> Come, friends.

[22] Cf. "function" in *Hamlet*, II.ii.582.
[23] My interpretation, different from that in vogue, harmonizes with the tone of Macbeth's first speech in the next scene, and with Shakespeare's constant intention of achieving the strongest possible dramatic contrasts, here between the hero's better and worser selves.

That good "King" may become the medium of the effectual divine grace which he has so far waived and now needs desperately.

d. *loyalty ... black desires* (I.iv)

And as Macbeth leaves the stage the king reappears, with his devoted company, introduced this time by a happy *"Flourish"* of trumpets instead of the *"Alarum"* at the beginning of the second scene. And here his character is fully displayed. Duncan is *gracious* in the true and full sense of the term. Heavenly peace lives and moves in him—in, through, and above the admirable traits clearly recognized by Macbeth, his meekness, innocence, and manly virtue (I.vii.16-18). He was serene in the midst of the anxiety and turbulent haste of the Battle scene: constantly his words were calm, brief, and to the point, as in his final speech to the loyal wounded officer (I.ii.43f). And he evinced that high charity wherein mercy and justice season each other. Refraining from heaping opprobrium upon the Judas-like Cawdor whom he had taken to his bosom (I.ii.64) in love and trust, he pronounced his death-sentence with deep, quiet grief, a grief visibly tempering his great happiness (I.ii.58) in the victory of the second Cawdor, Macbeth.

That twofold state of mind reappears here. Duncan exhibits silent sorrow in listening to Malcolm's moving account of the former Cawdor's execution (2-11). And we feel the marked contrast between his own so open countenance and the "Face" he views again in retrospect:

> There's no Art, [he pauses in deep emotion]
> To find the Minde's construction in the Face:
> He was a Gentleman, on whom I built
> An absolute Trust.

But the sorrow expressed in those slow-brooding lines seems to him, presently, tainted with sinful ingratitude to heaven in view of the great victory and the great loyalty of his kinsman, the new Cawdor—on whom he is rebuilding his "Trust." "O worthyest Cousin," he exclaims to the entering Macbeth, "The sinne of my Ingratitude even now / Was heavie on me." So, banishing his mourning, he pours forth his thanks to the hero in "swiftest" (17), heartfelt, yet kingly terms, concluding: "More is thy due than more than all can pay."

There is ominous irony, for us, in that last line. But the omen is dispelled almost entirely when Macbeth, deeply moved, sinking to his knee in feudal and personal homage, replies tensely:

> The service, and the loyaltie I owe,
> In doing it, payes itself.[24]
> Your Highness' part, is to receive our Duties:
> And our Duties are to your Throne, and State,
> Children, and Servants; which doe but what they should,   25
> By doing everything safe toward your Love
> And Honor.

Verbally clear and simple, while effortful in movement and emotionally packed, that passage conveys to us the speaker's yearning to regain all the loyalty of soul he owes to his noble sovereign.[25] The former Cawdor, as we have just been informed, was overcome in the end by the thought of the goodness of Duncan, confessed his treasons, implored the absent king's forgiveness, and showed "a deepe Repentance" (5-7). And now Macbeth, in the living presence of the grateful, trusting, gracious Duncan, is similarly affected. He experiences an intense contrition which can lead to real repentance, to the "doing" of everything he ought to do (25f) by way of service to his king in a humble, "safe" (sane and healthy) spirit of loyal devotion.

And now a supreme opportunity for such repentance is offered to Macbeth providentially, and ironically. His noble

[24] This short line renders emphatic the speaker's allusion to Duncan's final word, "pay"; and the pause at the end of the line prepares the transition from the "I" of this sentence to the ensuing "our."

[25] To regard this passage as utterly hypocritical is to miss the dramatist's contrast between the initial and final moods of Macbeth in this scene. Moreover the passage is essential preparation for his divided state of mind in Scene v. See note 23 above.

speech, copestone apparently of all the loyalty won from all persons by the present regime, determines Duncan to take the crucial step of proclaiming his eldest son, Malcolm, Prince of Cumberland and successor to the throne. This decision, doubtless long weighed and now announced with utmost firmness, is eminently wise in the eyes of the Shakespearean audience.[26] The acute domestic and foreign dangers which have just been overcome may well recur in the future. And now, when sons, kinsmen, and thanes, particularly those "whose places are the nearest" (36) to the throne in power, namely Macbeth and Banquo, are loyal and harmonious—now is the time to drop the old custom whereby the peers, upon the king's decease, debate the question of his successor. Malcolm's bearing and his two excellent speeches (3ff, I.ii.3ff) indicate that he is (what he proves to be in the end) a worthy successor to his father. Above all, we perceive, and may infer the wise Duncan knows, that Macbeth is by temperament suited to be a great "Servant" of the throne and state (25), not the supreme ruler. "My worthy *Cawdor*" (46), as Duncan now terms him in contrast with the unworthy "*Cawdor*" (1) who brought about his own destruction, will do well to be content with the "growing" (29) rank and influence promised him by his king. Such is the fair way of repentance opened now to Macbeth.

But his proud self is cut to the quick by the elevation of Malcolm. Envious ambition battles in him against loyalty and contrition. Desperately restless[27] in spirit, and no longer able to face the serene king, he bows his head "humbly" when Duncan proposes, prudently, to "binde us further to you"—and, implicitly, to bind the chief thane further to the "Throne" and "State" (24)—by doing him the great honor of visiting him with full

---

[26] A modern American parallel would be the decision of a wise President, in a troubled time, to use all his influence in securing a worthy successor!

[27] This is hinted at, I think, by his ambiguous statement to Duncan, "The Rest is Labor, which is not used for you" (44). Macbeth can have no real peace of soul except in the service of his king. But now his soul is laboring restlessly under dire temptation. Hence the tremendous galloping speed of his homeward ride (I.v.35-38, I.vi.21-24). As the play proceeds, his vaulting ambition takes him further and further from "Rest."

court at his castle of Inverness; then as harbinger, apparently meek and "joyfull," Macbeth moves swiftly away with head still unraised (42-47). But, pausing and confronting us in soliloquy, he lifts to the gathering twilight a terribly contorted visage:

> The Prince of Cumberland!—that is a step,
> On which I must fall downe, or else o're-leape,
> For in my way it lyes. Starres, hide your fires,   50
> Let not Light see my black and deepe desires:
> The Eye winke at the Hand; yet let that bee,
> Which the Eye feares, when it is done, to see.

Above, the good king declared that the "signes of Noblenesse, like Starres, shall shine / On all deservers" (41f). But now Macbeth sees the emerging "Starres" of heaven as watchful eyes[28] above, pouring down a white fire of accusing "Light." Evil darkness is increasing in his soul: his black and deep desires, here first stated explicitly but in the past continually indulged—the source of his "horrible Imaginings" (I.iii.138)—have suddenly become very mighty. Previously they were checked by the very vision they caused, so hated and feared by him, the "horrid Image" of the "Murther" of the king, vivid in his mind, shaking his whole being (I.iii.135-142). But now that image diminishes to that "which the eye feares . . . to see," a deed which presently can be "done" (53) if he can keep it out of the magnifying and fearful eye of fantasy. His mind is preoccupied with the thing now blocking his way, on which he must fall down, like a horseman at a high barrier, if he does not overleap it. But he terms it a "step," not a barrier—mixing the metaphors in his confused mind—because he is thinking of the steps before a throne and his own "way" to the crown. Thus *our* thoughts are sent back to the "Throne" and "State" (24) so beautifully pictured by him, above, from the standpoint of a loyal subject—now silently but alluringly envisioned from the standpoint of a murderous traitor. His proud will is converting his imagination

---

[28] The repeated "see" (51, 53) together with the term "winke at" (cf. "hide") instantly connects the repeated "Eye" with "Starres."

—in itself a neutral power—from obstruction to furtherance of his wicked design.

But we know that his present mood, occasioned by a sudden and unforeseen crisis, need by no means be final. The fact that he recognizes so plainly the blackness of his desires is promising. And when the scene is closed by Duncan feeding happily upon Banquo's commendations of the "peerless kinsman" (54-58) who will "bid us welcome" at Inverness, we find it hard to conceive of Macbeth as murdering, in his own home, his royal and revered guest.

e. *This Night's great Business* (I.v)

"*Enter Macbeth's Wife alone with a Letter.*" She, the first personage in the play to appear alone, is indeed a solitary figure, and wordless at first, over against the background of the voluble and crowded previous scenes. She advances silently, slowly, her bent head moving from side to side as her eyes devour the missive gripped tensely in her hands. Soon she stands close before us, fixed and still, then reads aloud in a tone that gradually rises and quickens. "They met me . . . they have more in them than mortall knowledge . . . they made themselves Ayre, into which they vanished." Like her husband she is "rapt in the wonder of it." In imagination she is standing with him. She listens to the "Missives[29] from the King," listens avidly. She lowers the letter and looks off into far distance—while "these weyward[30] [weird] Sisters" salute him with "haile King that shalt be."

Glancing at the letter again she utters the rest of it hastily, dwelling however upon the phrase[31] "my dearest Partner of Greatnesse." She loves that title because, and only because, of her

[29] This curt allusion to the voluble Ross and Angus of Scene iii sharpens our awareness of the fact that none of the human beings involved are real to her except her husband. At present, having read the long letter from him over and over off stage, she is summarizing it, citing the passages that interest her most.

[30] This spelling, regularly used in the play, insists upon a dissyllabic and weighty pronunciation, particularly effective at the present moment.

[31] Parenthesized in the Folio text for emphasis, in accordance with Elizabethan custom.

intense love for him. Utterly and singularly void of self-love she, his "Partner," has the sole ambition of helping him to fulfill *his* ambition. She therefore smiles a little over his climactic adjuration to rejoice in "what Greatnesse is promised thee"; presses the letter to her "heart" (15); then, feeling his presence closer than ever, adjures him in words reversing his to her: "thou . . . shalt be / What thou art promised. . . ." Presently we gather that he, at some time in the past, confided to her an unholy (22) intention of destroying Duncan, as "the nearest way" (19) to the throne—a dramatic echo of his phrase "my way" above (I.iv.50). More than he, she shrinks from envisaging the dreadful deed; she cloaks it in continual and fearful periphrasis. And, beyond anyone else, she knows and appreciates his "Milke of humane kindness" (18), shown fitfully in the preceding scenes, shown fully now in his tender, strong, adoring, and confiding love of her. But the more she has come to admire his kindness, brooding in her solitude upon his nature and his public prospects, the more she has seen it as impeding his way to "the Golden Round" (29) he has set his heart on. She has a desperate "fear" (17) of his making himself wretchedly unhappy in fearing to do "that which" he wishes not to be left "undone" (25f); thus she echoes, mystically, the last words he said to himself above (I.iv. 52f).

And now in vision she sees him already crowned by the invisible world, by "Fate and Metaphysicall ayde" (30); and she nerves herself tremendously to pour her own "Spirits" into him when he comes home. He must "play false," for once, in order to "winne" (22f). Despite his human-kindness he must do the dreadful thing—she euphemizes it extremely in her final sentence (26-31)—which he told her must be done by him to the present king.[32] But instantly, now, an underling rushes in with news not given in Macbeth's letter.

[32] To read a fiendish attitude into Lady Macbeth in the opening thirty lines of the scene is to ruin the contrast between her mood here and her black mood that develops below. See note 25, above.

MESSENGER   The King comes here to Night.
LADY   Thou'rt mad to say it.[33]

That exclamation of hers is low and "hoarse" like the croaking "raven" heard presently in her fevered fancy (39f). A dead silence ensues for a moment while her slim figure totters, hand to head, as though she had suddenly gone "mad" herself. Then effortfully, rapidly, she questions the Messenger; he tells her of another fellow who exhausted himself in outspeeding Macbeth hither: she too is "almost dead for breath" as she ponders the "great news." Alone again, she decides with mad speed that Duncan's entrance under "my Battlements" ("my" instead of our) is fated (30) and "fatall" (40), and that she herself must assist in destroying him this very night. But how can her husband be brought to do to a royal guest in his home what he has long shrunk from doing anywhere?

And how can she bring her womanly self to take part in the horrible deed? Though not, like him, *too* full of the milk of human-kindness she has a normal degree of it, together with something far more potent in her case, the "Milke" in her "Woman's Breasts" (48f). But to let it weaken her now will mean ruination, she entirely believes, for the one person she loves entirely. And to help him suppress all kindness in himself she must suppress it in her own self. But now in striving to do so she realizes for the first time its strength: human and feminine kindness is active in her soul, in those very "Spirits" (27)[34] devoted to her husband's advancement—opposing strongly those other and remorseless "Spirits" experienced at times by every mortal mind. These she now addresses, urging them to transform her nature quickly, for once, for this night only. "Come, you Spirits," she exclaims with bent head and hands pressing her bosom,

[33] The very meaningful pause at the end of this line is eliminated in modern editions which, indenting the line, carry the end of it to the righthand margin.
[34] According to Elizabethan physiology the "spirits" were a fluid in the "blood" (44) connecting the soul with the body. But Shakespeare works the word for all it is worth.

That tend on mortall thoughts, unsex me here,
And fill me from the Crowne to the Toe, top-full
Of direst Crueltie: make thick my blood,
Stop up th' accesse and passage to Remorse,   45
That no compunctious visitings of Nature
Shake my fell purpose, nor keepe peace betweene
Th' effect and it. Come to my Woman's Breasts,
And take my Milke for Gall, you murth'ring Ministers,

[Here her head lifts, showing the fair face distorted ("fair is
foul") with horrorful determination, as she raises her hands
to those "Spirits," now felt as diabolical "Ministers" *above her*
in the darkening air]

Where-ever, in your sightlesse substances,   50
You wait on Nature's Mischiefe. Come, thick Night,
And pall thee in the dunnest smoake of Hell,
That my keene Knife see not the Wound it makes,
Nor Heaven peepe through the Blanket of the darke,
To cry, hold, hold.   55

The hellish fog that enveloped the ugly faces of the three
Witches is superseded here by the dunnest smoke of Hell, invisible, palling the spirit of this woman with the dreadfully
beautiful uplifted face. And that unholy "Wound" (never mentioned by Macbeth) which her imagination sees, and tries not to
see, concentrates for us the red lightning glares of the opening
scene and the "reeking Wounds" recalling "Golgotha" (I.ii.39f).
In one ecstatic moment she, inspired by love, and by Hell, conceives herself, instead of her husband, wielding the "keene
Knife." But "Nature" has, above the evil (51), "compunctious
visitings" (46) instilled by "Heaven" (54); and heaven itself
(like Macbeth's stars, I.iv.50) may peer down upon her through
the blanketing darkness—may even cry out to her suddenly,
"hold, hold!" Sinking her head she covers her eyes with her
hands convulsively. Then "*Enter Macbeth.*"
Swiftly clearing her face she addresses her approaching lord

in a tone of prophetic transport, repeating the final word he heard from his visitants on the blasted heath before they vanished, the First Witch's great concluding "all-haile" (56, I.iii. 69).[35] She seems a seductive reincarnation of that creature's spirit as she, Macbeth's "dearest Love" (59), embraces him with passionate devotion. Her every word, look, and gesture serve to make a foul project *bewitchingly* fair. The present ugly anxiety in their two hearts becomes merely "This ignorant present," negligible in view of the wonderful "future" pressing instantly upon them (58f). And the blackest possible sort of murder (49, I.iii.139) is transmuted into "This Night's great Businesse" . . .

> Which shall to all our Nights, and Dayes, to come,   70
> Give solely soveraigne sway, and Masterdome.

Thus she voices in masterly fashion the masterdom he yearns for —to be attained, if ever, this very night; else (she believes) no night, no day, in the future will be free from unhappiness for him, and hence also for her. And having upon his entrance cleared her countenance she keeps urging him now to clear his own.

But he does not do so. Unlike her he has not invoked the strong, secret aid of diabolic powers. Between this present moment and the great but abnormal future, he sees near and normal events occurring: "Duncan" coming "here" tonight as guest in their home, and going hence tomorrow "as he purposes" (59-61). Finally, however, his wife's desperate intimation of readiness to do the fearful deed herself (69, 74)—a thing he could nowise permit—draws from him a look of amazed and grateful admiration, unaware that her extreme courage is inspired by hell, momentarily, along with love. And so once more, this time very

---

[35]Contrast the context of "all-hailed" (8) in the letter as read aloud to us above. Lady Macbeth's phrase "the all-haile *hereafter*" (56) alludes to the Third Witch's royal greeting to Macbeth (I.iii.50), which, however, was not quoted in the letter. Thus an occult relation is suggested between the present mood of Lady Macbeth and the Witches, also between the evil spirits she has just been addressing and the evil spirits animating them (I.i.8ff).

fatefully, he postpones his decision: "We will speake further."
But he does not, he cannot, "looke up cleare." Still powerful in
him is a true and right "feare" of doing a great wrong (73,
I.iv.53, I.iii.51,137f).[36] And we know that this good fear may
be rendered decisive by the presence in his home of his gracious
king.

f. *our Graces towards him* (I.vi)

"*Hoboyes, and Torches. Enter King*," with full retinue. The
gracious mien of the king (ushered here, as not previously, by
hautboys) contends with the omen of the red torchlight, which
recalls the wavering lightning of the first scene; Duncan brings
hither, and finds here, a very different "ayre" (2, I.i.10). His
bearing is firm and serene like the exterior of the castle he views
in the fitful light, and gentle as the martins fluttering about their
nests on the multi-cornered walls. The scene with him at its
center has an air of love and trust, health and peace, indeed a
temple-haunting (4) holiness.

KING   This Castle hath a pleasant seat,
            The ayre nimbly and sweetly recommends itselfe
            Unto our gentle senses.

BANQUO   This Guest of Summer,
            The Temple-haunting Martlet, does approve,
            By his loved Mansionry, that the Heaven's breath 5
            Smells wooingly here. . . .
            Where they most breed, and haunt, I have observed
            The ayre is delicate.   *Enter Lady*

KING   See, see, our honored Hostesse—   10

Lady Macbeth, "Faire and Noble Hostesse" (24), seems entirely congruous with that air. But Duncan's courtly address to
her (11ff) conveys, by inspiration, a truth more deeply applica-
ble at present than he knows:

[36] The full force of this point is missed by those who share the modern de-
preciation of that sort of fear.

The Love that followes us, sometime is our trouble,
Which still we thanke as Love. Herein I teach you
How you shall bid God 'ild us for your paines,
And thanke us for your trouble.

This king, following Macbeth home and requiring of him and
his wife a full entertainment, symbolizes that pursuing, trou-
bling divine spirit for which we are grateful if we let it "teach"
us that it is "Love." But his hostess, visibly (to us) steeling herself against the urgings of "Heaven" (I.v.54), replies with a
loquacious gratitude, instead of the sincere intensity of Macbeth's
first speech to his sovereign, in Scene iv. Alluding neatly to Duncan's religious adjuration, her climactic hyperbole, "we rest your
Ermites" (19)—your hermits, ever praying gratefully to God
on your behalf, in our rural solitude—gives us a knifing sense
of her smooth and devilish hypocrisy here.

Immediately Duncan's thoughts, and ours, go to the new
"Thane of Cawdor" who, with indeed hermitlike strangeness,
still fails to appear; whose "great Love" for both his wife and
his king, so Duncan implies, spurred him homewards swiftly as
husband and as royal "Purveyor" (20-24).

Conduct me to mine Host, we love him highly,
And shall continue our Graces towards him.   30

g. *with fairest show* (I.vii)

Duncan's last words, above, make him central in our mental
picture of the offstage feast; while the hautboy music that pre-
luded the preceding scene rises again, sweet but eerie, mingled
with sounds of good cheer; and while many torch-led servitors
carrying dishes pass to and fro before our eyes. The best "banquet" for the good king, as we know, is "commendations" of his
leading thane (I.iv.54-58). And we imagine him evincing his
high "love" for "mine Host" in continual "Graces towards him"
at the festive ensemble; which typifies the new safety and harmony of the realm. But soon the stage empties; and all sounds
are softened as behind closed doors. "*Then enter Macbeth.*"

The "Host" has stolen away from the banquet, driven by the climactic battle now occurring in his breast.

His great soliloquy (quoted below) reveals that the Grace of "Heaven" (22) through the medium of the king is working upon him extremely, just when his lust for the kingship has become more extreme than ever. For while sitting at the feast with downcast eyes, secretly glorying in the honors he has won, showered with "Golden Opinions from all sorts of people" (33) —above all, from the fount of honor, the sovereign—he realized with overpowering vividness that the sovereign glory could be his own "quickly" (2), for just one "blow" (4). But now he reflects upon the dire consequences. At first he speaks in a low tone with rapid, syncopated style, avoiding mention of Duncan and employing (here only) the euphemistic term "assassination."

> If it were done, when 'tis done, then 'twere well
> It were done quickly: If th' Assassination
> Could trammell up the Consequence, and catch
> With his surcease, Successe: that but this blow
> Might be the be-all, and the end-all! Heere,   5
> But heere, upon this Banke and Shoale of time—[37]
> Wee'ld jumpe the life to come. But in these Cases,
> We still have judgement heere, that we but teach
> Bloody Instructions, which being taught, returne
> To plague th' Inventer. This even-handed Justice   10
> Commends th' Ingredience of our poyson'd Challice
> To our owne lips. . . .

The *temporal* danger, namely that a bloody deed teaches other persons to deal similarly with the doer, yields quickly in Mac-

---

[37] F1 has a period after "end-all" and a comma after "time." My dash represents the mental repetition of the condition stated in the five preceding lines. The customary modern reading of the fifth line, "Might be the be-all and the end-all here," is out of tune with the speaker's present emotion. Dover Wilson places four dots after "end-all" but retains the modern decapitalization of "Heere"; see his note. Joseph Quincy Adams in his edition of the play (1931) inserts two dashes, one after "end-all here," the other after "shoal of time."

beth's mind to the *spiritual* retribution imaged by the poisoned chalice.[38] This word, with its sacred and social implications, alludes to the royal feast within and deepens the meaning of the ensuing phrase "double trust" (12). He proceeds with rising tone and slow deliberation, viewing exactly, as never before—contrast the vagueness of I.iii.134-142—every poisonous feature of the murder; significantly the "heere" (12) echoes the threefold occurrence of the same word above (5-8); and the first person plural gives place to the singular "I":

> .... Hee's heere in double trust;
> First, as I am his Kinsman, and his Subject,
> Strong both against the Deed. Then, as his Host,
> Who should against his Murtherer shut the doore,   15
> Not beare the knife myselfe. Besides, this *Duncane*
> Hath borne his Faculties so meeke; hath bin
> So cleere in his great Office; that his Vertues
> Will pleade like Angels, Trumpet-tongued against
> The deepe damnation of his taking off—   20

Eternity, conceived at first as *beyond* "time" (6), a dim and silent ocean fleetingly sensed, is now felt as at work *within* time, through Duncan's supreme virtues; and it is imaged by awful angels pleading at the bar of *heavenly* "Justice" (10), in trumpet tones, against an utterly damnable crime.

Properly Macbeth (in the view of the Elizabethan audience and the seventeenth-century reader) would now entreat Heaven for a full measure of the Mercy and Grace he so desperately needs. Instead, he proceeds to invoke his own inadequate benevolence, attributing to it a strength and heavenly meaning which, apart from Grace, it cannot have. Accordingly his style, so powerfully simple hitherto, becomes grandiloquent and unveracious, albeit sincere enough and charming: it captivates us very much and the speaker himself completely:

[38] This object in relation to Claudius and Hamlet is dealt with in my book *Scourge and Minister*, page 202.

And Pitty, like a naked New-born-Babe,
Striding the blast, or Heaven's Cherubin, horsed
Upon the sightlesse Curriors of the Ayre,
Shall blow the horrid deed in every eye,
That teares shall drowne the winde. I have no Spurre   25
To pricke the sides of my intent, but onely
Vaulting Ambition, which ore-leapes itselfe,
And falles on th' other—   *Enter Lady*

That tiny, helpless infant fantastically bestriding a mighty wind, instead of nuzzling a mother's breast, is Macbeth's milky "humane kindnesse" (I.v.18) idealized by him prodigiously. The realistic vision of the judging angels, above, is instantly enfeebled by that babe and then superseded, elaborately, by the emotion-full cherubim riding swift and high on air—like the soul of Macbeth himself here. Ponder the hyperbolic picture of innumerable persons, including the speaker himself, pouring forth a rainstorm of tears immense and heavy enough to drown the very wind that has caused them! Contrast the simple, grateful "drops" shed by the king earlier (I.iv.35). Here Macbeth is doing what this Duncan who hath borne his faculties so meek would never do: he is proclaiming to his soul his own humaneness. And his proud self-satisfaction in so doing is a barrier to the Grace offered him through the king who is so clear and humble in his great office.

The character of Duncan is reminiscent of the good duke in an earlier play who had "with holy bell bin knowld to Church, / And sat at good men's feasts, and wiped our eyes / Of drops that sacred pity hath engendred" (*As You Like It*, II.vii.121ff). But Macbeth's "Pitty," instead of being simple and sacred, is supernally magniloquent. And very close beneath that stormy emotion, though overcast by it for the time being, gleams the sharp spur of his ambition. The last lines (25-28) allude with keen dramatic irony to the king's asseveration above: "But he rides well, / And his great Love (sharpe as his Spurre) hath holp him / To his home before us" (I.vi.22ff). We must feel that Macbeth's spurred and leaping man-and-horse—the beast and his rider consolidated by a startling image into a single strenuous creature, a terrific centaur—is really far more powerful than the foregoing cherubs horsed upon the tenuous winds.

A "young and rose-lipped" cherub, so Othello declares (IV.ii. 62ff), can turn his complexion in a crisis and "looke grim as hell." Rosily benevolent emotion, in actual life and continually in the Elizabethan drama, particularly in Shakespeare's works, may serve to conceal an evil will and may presently, swayed by that will, change its complexion to a hellish hue. Such is what happens to Macbeth in the course of this scene. Not that his present angelic feelings, though lacking the very real strength of his wicked ambition, are entirely unreal and weak: they are real and powerful enough to produce immense remorseful misery if he commits the vile deed. And right now those feelings may be converted into a good and effectual volition; as, again, often happens in life and the Elizabethan drama. Hence the acute suspense of the audience. Indeed it can be said, by way of anticipation, that we are never perfectly certain Macbeth will do the deed until he actually does it; so subtle and profound are Shakespeare's art and humanity. In the close of the next scene when he goes offstage to murder Duncan there is still a possibility—as when Othello comes on stage in V.ii to murder Desdemona—that the sight of the intended victim, reviving better thoughts and changing the will, may prevent the crime. That possibility is widely open at the close of Macbeth's present soliloquy: if he returns to the presence of his king at the love-feast (for so it may be termed) the crime may remain undone.

Obviously the lengthy reflections given above are not made by the spectator in the theater; but I believe they represent in extenso his actual state of mind. Surely he senses the fact that Macbeth in the last part of his great speech protests too much: that his highly emotional humaneness, though in a way propitious, is very vulnerable; and that the gliding-in of his Lady, just when he has declared he has no spur, has a spurlike sharpness of irony. Yet the sentence she interrupts denotes his definitive feeling that the more his ambition is spurred, by himself and by her, to leap wrongly and "quickly" (2)—the idea of heedless haste in the opening sentence of the soliloquy is repeated in the concluding one—the heavier shall be his fall into frustration and misery. And it is clear that when, as she says, he "left the chamber" (29) he wished to get away from the presence of his wife as well as of his king, renouncing her influence. Accordingly his first words to her here and now are repudiative and peremptory: "How now? What Newes? . . . Hath he ask'd for me?"

But when she replies that the king, as Macbeth must know, has certainly inquired for him there ensues a fateful moment of pause. Obviously he ought to return to his king at once—and, probably, be saved: the dramatic situation here is as simple as that. But he hesitates and is, perhaps, lost. Perhaps; for his next speech (31-35) is at first blush promising, though its secondary effect (to be dealt with later) is not so. He declares in a tone of utmost assurance and command: "We will proceed no further in this Businesse. . . ." The last two words puncture her ecstatic phrase in the close of their preceding conference, "This Night's great Businesse" (I.v.69), while the term "will" *may* intimate a real volition. And his urgent desire in the ensuing lines to rest content with his present great honors is a saving desire. When he declares that those honors "would be worne now in their newest glosse, / Not cast aside so soone," he does not mean merely that if he kills Duncan people will turn against him: he means that his own enjoyment of his honors will be poisoned (11): he himself shall have soiled and discarded them. This, precisely, is the valid motive that keeps most persons most of the time from letting their ambition overleap itself; Macbeth is representative. Here he cherishes the fair hope of learning to be entirely content and happy in his status of chief supporter of the throne and realm, a hope expressed with entire sincerity when in the presence and under the influence of his gracious king (I.iv.22ff). And now he motions as if to return to the nearly ended banquet and the royal presence.

But he hesitates for another and far more fateful moment.

Why? Because of the inward urge of wrong pride in contrast with the right pride, true self-esteem, which he has just expressed. All that we have seen of him hitherto has made clear (what the rest of the play will make still clearer) that this man was designed by God and nature to be the chief and very noble supporter of the king and the kingdom rather than to be king himself. The wise old Duncan, particularly in I.iv, has evinced full awareness of that fact. How successful a king, in Shakespeare's conception, this hero could have been if the high office had come to him legitimately is a matter for abstract speculation. The point pressed by the dramatist again and again is that Macbeth's special temperament and ability, though in a large measure "royal" (I.iii.56), fit him mainly to be second instead of first in the realm. This is what Macbeth himself has all along perceived in his lucid intervals of true self-estimation. But the very fact that he has just now made a climactic effort to be satisfied with his splendid but secondary station brings on a climactic urge of his devilish arrogance. He yearns more burningly than ever, as his wife easily discerns, for that which he esteems "*the* Ornament of Life" (42), "solely soveraigne sway, and Masterdome" (I.v.71).

The phrases just quoted are hers but the meaning is his own; and such is the case with all her utterances in the present scene. Though in the second half of the scene he is for the most part silent he is not at all a passive listener. His occasional words, his frequent gestures, and the workings of his face demonstrate that he is hearkening, more and more, to the tempter *within*. Every word she says not only appeals to but expresses his evil pride, expresses it exquisitely, making foul seem fair as her forerunners the Witches did and as he, vainly, wishes it to be.[39] She begins by catching up and distorting his new-garment metaphor. Can he be content with honors, however fine, in which others, not he himself, have dressed him? "Was the hope drunke, / Wherein you drest your selfe?" (35ff)—wherein he, not newly but of

[39] See Spenser's use of "fair" and "foul" in regard to Lucifera and her House of Pride (*Faerie Queene*, I.iv.5,10; I.v.48,53).

old, and constantly instead of intoxicatedly, arrayed himself by his own bold will. By implication she makes his fairer hope, that of being happy in his present status, look "greene, and pale"— exactly the complexion it has taken on in his own soul as soon as he has uttered it. His wife is his soul's echo.[40]

That fact is not really contradicted by his peremptory reply to her bitter imputation of cowardly unmanliness (39-44):

> MACBETH Prythee peace: 45
> I dare do all that may become a man,
> Who dares do more, is none.

Certainly a right sentiment. But the tone of the speech is absolutely wrong for a man crucially tempted and in desperate need of Grace. Here he has nothing at all of that awareness of the superintending "Heaven" (22) which came to him in the last part of his soliloquy. And his humaneness, there too conscious and airy, is here too solidly arrogant. His proud belief in the entireness of his manhood blinds him to the fact that in one respect, all along, he has been entirely beastly.

> LADY What Beast was't then
> That made you breake this enterprize to me?
> When you durst do it, then you were a man:
> And to be more than what you were, you would   50
> Be so much more the man. Nor time, nor place
> Did then adhere, and yet you would make both:
> They have made themselves, and that their fitnesse now
> Does unmake you. . . .

That word "Beast" was prepared for by the dramatist in his centaur-like image above (25ff). It reminds us tellingly of the constant conflict in mankind of the divine and the beastly, a conflict now at its height in Macbeth. But he is unwilling, here as ever, to see it in its true color: never, in his heaviest condemna-

---

[40] As Iago is of the soul of Othello in the Temptation scene (III.iii). But in the present scene, for several reasons, the situation is far more deeply human, convincing, and tragic.

tions of his evil "enterprize" (48), has he stigmatized it as beastly. And the reason is clear. Macbeth, like Everyman, can dissimulate his beastliness by means of the chief of the Seven Deadly Sins, Pride.

We know it is the beast in him, as in Everyman, that needs to be unmade (54). But he wills to believe that he, an entire man, greatly entire, is now being unmade by untimely yielding to humane sentiment. Hence his intense admiration for his wife's subjugation of that sentiment in herself. He veils, more than ever, the barbarism at work in himself by ignoring it in her when she utters her dreadful climactic lines:

> . . . I have given Sucke, and know
> How tender 'tis to love the Babe that milkes me—   55
> I would, while it was smyling in my Face,
> Have pluckt my Nipple from his Bonelesse Gummes,
> And dasht the Braines out, had I so sworne
> As you have done to this.

That slaughterous image (not the speaker herself, innately) is worse than subhuman: it is sub-animal, sub-brutal, beastly in the most savage sense of the word. Indeed it is so extreme as to be highly fantastic, like Macbeth's own imagery above (21ff). His wife's hapless "Babe" is the counterpart of his own naked newborn "Babe"—"Pity"—striding the blast grotesquely. Just now *he* is silently plucking it down, and dashing the brains out, while *she* speaks. His pride is telling him that such pity does not, in his present situation, when time and place have made themselves on his behalf (51-53), "become a man" (46): by dividing and softening him (39-41) it has well-nigh ruined his personal, manly integrity.

That integrity (he feels now) must be restored and maintained at all costs. Certainly its present price is dreadful. Horror is mingled with admiration in his face as he hearkens to his wife and, more, to the voice of Pride within, i.e. the devil, though he will not so term it; for, as a thoroughly natural man, unwilling to be plainly beastly, he is also unwilling to be plainly hellish. If he,

along with us, had heard the precursor of his wife's present
speech, her awful invocation to the powers of evil to "unsex" her,
exchanging her woman's "Milke for Gall," he would have been
completely repelled. But at present the devil is tempting him
with extreme seductiveness, from within and from without. His
wife, so far from being cruel, is by nature intensely loving. More
than half of what she said about the "Babe" is exquisitely tender
in phrase; and her tone is fierce only because of her fiercely
concentrated, purblind concern for her husband's happiness. Obviously he is far more really awed by the supernatural power
which he feels at work in her, but which he will not recognize as
hellish—compare his rejection of Banquo's warning against the
Witches as "Instruments of Darknesse" (I.iii.120-131)—than
he was by his visionary and all too airy (23) angels.[41] His wife
is here a dark angel of light: the devil allures him beautifully
through her intense love while seducing him inwardly, and effectually, through his own self-love. He is convinced that he can
regain his self-command only by doing the black deed that he
had "so sworn" (58) to do.

That word "sworn" is the superclimax of all she has been saying and of all Macbeth has been saying to himself. For us, certainly, it is news; but also it is a prime instance of proper dramatic surprise, a revelation reserved by the dramatist for the present great crisis while carefully prepared for all along. The fact
that before the opening of the play the hero determined to kill
Duncan when time and place (51f) should serve, and so informed
his wife with oathful vehemence, harmonizes with all we have
learned in Act I of him and of her. It illumines the Witches'
eagerness to "meet with *Macbeth*" (I.i.7) as with an accomplice;
it illumines his conduct during and after his encounter with
them; and it illumines Lady Macbeth's conviction that he will
never be content without the crown, however evilly attained.
That strong conviction of hers, stemming from her husband's

---

[41] Like many worldly persons Macbeth has a continual but vague flair for the
supernatural, conceived as a very atmospheric power, neutral or good or bad or
mixed according to one's emotional state at the moment.

vaulting ambition—from a "desire" that has long seemed to her as great and urgent and constant as his very "love" for her (39, 41, I.vi.23)—ensures our regarding her as human and womanly just now when her will-power seems most fiendish.

Above all, Shakespeare's present insistence upon his hero's evil pre-decision exemplifies a principle, at once moral and highly dramatic, that runs through his writings as a whole from first to last. Repeatedly he shows how a wrong volition, unless entirely eradicated, will grow strongly in the soul, for the most part subconsciously, until upon occasion it can stifle one's best reasonings, such as those of the hero in the first half of this scene, and bear sudden fruit of disastrous action. Macbeth's murderous pre-decision was a very real volition. But it was not obdurate, turning him into a permanent criminal at heart. He began to regret deeply his evil resolve soon after making it; but just as evidently he never really uprooted it, as shown in Scene iii. In the next scene his will to murder his king is suddenly accentuated by unexpected happenings. But resultant remorse appears in Scene v and, increasing off stage during the following scene, produces in Scene vii a desperate effort to rescind his initial wicked oath.

By now, however, extraordinary Grace is needed; and this is provided through the "Graces" (I.vi.30) of his great and loving king.[42] That fact is clearly apparent to the Shakespearean audience in the first thirty-five lines of Scene vii; and Macbeth himself is well aware of it in his inmost spirit, though ominously he does not state it so plainly as his words cause us to do.[43] But he has the grace (as the saying goes) to perceive more than ever

[42] A number of recent scholars have pointed out that in Shakespeare's frequent use of the word "grace," in its various denotations, the divine or spiritual sense is continually implied, sometimes punningly. See for instance the final episode of *Two Gentlemen of Verona* (V.iv.123,148,163-166). Note that earlier in the play Valentine had addressed the duke as "my lord" (II.iv.53,59) instead of "your Grace."

[43] Hence the deadly irony of his public exclamation after the murder, "Renowne and Grace is dead" (II.iii.99). Duncan is a special medium of spiritual grace because of his excellence both as man and as king. Both of those aspects of him are alluded to by Macbeth in the opening speech of the present scene (16ff).

the sheer horrorfulness of the deeply damnable deed (20) of murdering "this Duncan" (15f)—of doing that which "the Eye feares, when it is done, to see" (I.iv.53). That full horror is in his face and tone when he exclaims hoarsely to his wife, "If we should faile?" (59). He is not yet thinking of external difficulties (to fancy the contrary is to nullify the tragic force of those four words and to miss the point, as will be shown below, of her ensuing speech). He means: must not we, even if we combine our two will-powers in one fearful effort, recoil at the last minute from the dreadful deed? His supreme horror is evidenced by the fact that here—here only, and only for the moment—he conceives her as taking a physical part in the act which he so shrinks from performing alone, while at the same time he knows that her womanly nature must almost inevitably (as the sequel demonstrates, II.ii.13f)[44] prevent her from so doing. Here, despite the revival of Macbeth's evil resolution, we find it as difficult as he does to think of him as *not* failing, at the last moment, to destroy his very gracious king; especially if he now returns to the banquet (the renewed sounds of which should be heard off stage at this point).

But at once, with devilish inspiration, his wife draws a word-picture exactly calculated to reinforce his devilish volition. In the passage quoted below her initial adjuration to his "courage," so far from having a conclusive effect upon him, is merely a hasty introduction to that word-picture. Hence the rightness of the colon (changed to a period by modern editors) after "fayle" (61): note that thereafter the lines slacken in tempo while increasing in circumstantiality and effect.

LADY   We faile?
　　　　But screw your courage to the sticking place,　　60
　　　　And wee'll not fayle: when *Duncan* is asleepe,
　　　　(Whereto the rather shall his day's hard Journey
　　　　Soundly invite him) his two Chamberlaines

---

[44] "Had he not resembled / My Father as he slept, I had done't." A good actress will prepare for this by revealing to the audience Lady Macbeth's great difficulty in confronting Duncan with a face of innocent welcome in I.vi.

Will I with Wine, and Wassell, so convince,
That Memorie, the Warder of the Braine,   65
Shall be a Fume, and the Receipt of Reason
A Lymbeck onely: when in Swinish sleepe,
Their drenched Natures lyes as in a Death,
What cannot you and I performe upon
Th' unguarded *Duncan*? What not put upon   70
His spungie Officers? who shall beare the guilt
Of our great quell.

The word "Fume" recalls the speaker's "dunnest smoake of
Hell" (I.v.52) and the Witches' "fogge and filthie ayre" (I.i.
10). And the speech as a whole is a mounting deadly fume, representing, rather than causing, the process going on in the brain
(65) of Macbeth himself. As shown by his countenance—that
face which "is as a Booke where men / May reade strange matters" (I.v.63f)—he is allowing an evil vapor to drench his good
faculties and sentiments. His "Memorie" and "Reason" and
therewith his newborn pity (21) are drugged, with his consent,
into "Swinish sleepe." The end-word "sleepe" here (67), echoing the end-word "asleepe" above (61), serves to make one
tableau of the slumbering chamberlains and Duncan. The latter
is no longer a noble monarch living and moving and graciously
speaking, as at the banquet table: he is a mere physical form
along with two others so inert as to seem already defunct—"the
sleeping and the dead" have become "but as Pictures" (II.ii.
53f). Duncan, like his two grooms, lies "as in a Death" (68).
How easy to "performe" upon him the transformation of deathly sleep into sleep of death! A deadly, bewitching soul-fog, obliterating Macbeth's fearful vision of himself as "Murtherer"
(15), and making foul fair by metamorphosing the "horrid
deed" (24) into "our great quell" (72), stupefies the moral fear
that could make him in the moment of action shrink and fail.

But that bewitchment could not take place unless Macbeth
entirely so willed—just as he willed his preliminary bewitchment on the blasted heath (I.iii), in striking contrast with Ban-

quo, a contrast to be reemphasized by Shakespeare presently when
Banquo appeals to the "Mercifull Powers" to restrain in him the
"cursed thoughts" inspired by the Witches (II.i.7-9). Instead of
appealing to such Powers, Macbeth deliberately wills the be-
fogging of his moral sense. His full responsibility here is not
only in harmony with the Christian ethics of the Renaissance
and surely with the best ethical thought of today; it is essential
to the tragic effect aimed at by the dramatist. And it is made perfectly clear in the final dozen lines of Scene vii.

Consider the words "unguarded" and "guilt" (70f). Here for
the first time the hero confronts plainly, as he must now if he is
to do the deed, the atrocious act of slaughtering a completely
defenseless and helpless individual. From all we have learned
of Macbeth in the course of the first Act we know that this feature of the crime cannot in the least be softened for him by any
outside influence or sophistical consideration. "Th' unguarded
Duncan?" That phrase (the effect of which is weakened in modern editions by decapitalization of the ensuing "What") pierces
the audience to the core; and him it must pierce with an inevitable, shuddering sense of "guilt." For a moment he lowers and
hides his face convulsively. But with a definitive effort of evil
will he rouses himself and suppresses his saving sense of dastard-
liness. In this he is much aided by the vague intimation, so punc-
tuated in the Folio as to appear a hasty afterthought on his
wife's part, that the two drunken officers "shall beare the guilt"
—not only the external blame but, in Macbeth's distortive ap-
prehension, much of the actual criminality. (Afterwards in killing the grooms he tries blatantly to soothe his conscience with
that notion, II.iii.112ff.) In that respect, so far from being abnormally strange, he is highly characteristic of mankind. Like
him most men, just because they are normally not criminals, will
have recourse to strange devices for excusing themselves when
undertaking a criminal act: the more dastardly the act, the more
strange the dissimulation. Macbeth's case is certainly extreme but
also it is extremely typical, as in the following speech:

Bring forth Men-Children onely:
For thy undaunted Mettle should compose
Nothing but Males. Will it not be receiv'd,
When we have mark'd with blood those sleepie two   75
Of his own Chamber, and us'd their very Daggers,
That they have don't?

In the first of those two sentences he lauds in another, as many
a man does occasionally, a quality he is cherishing in himself.
For us there is momentous irony in the thought of childbearing
on the part of the woman who in spirit has unsexed herself
(I.v.42), in preparation for this very moment, with the aid of
the evil powers.[45] More deeply ironical, however, is the fact that
Macbeth's proud consciousness of his wife's and his own undaunted mettle covers up for him the hell working within him
—those hellish "Spirits" that "tend on mortal thoughts" (I.v.
41f) and are here mastering and also empowering him. Hence
the evil naturalness of his horrible second sentence above. With
devilish particularity he elaborates his wife's vague suggestion
of casting the blame on the grooms. Obviously he wishes thus
to prevent "Bloody" (9) reprisals. But this consideration is subordinate, as the whole context (including the first three scenes of
Act II) makes clear, to Macbeth's hypocritic effort to alleviate
an intolerable prospect which neither he nor his wife has ven-
tured so far to mention in this or in previous scenes: the sight of
the murdered king's "blood" (75). It is now alluded to by the
hero with subtle evasiveness, as if the "blood" were merely blood
in general, not that of the butchered "unguarded *Duncan*" (70).
By marking the sleepy two with it he hopes—in vain, as the
sequel shows (II.ii.28, 59ff)—to banish the thought of it dyeing
his own hands. And by using "their very Daggers" he can keep
his own unstained, submerging thus his conscience, which, how-

[45] Shakespeare lets us imagine, if we will, that she has had and lost at least
one child, a male (57); that she and her husband are hoping for another,
to be his heir; but that, in psychosomatic parlance, the state of her nerves has
now become such as to prevent conception: hence, ironically, Macbeth's "barren Scepter" (III.i.62).

ever, will presently stain for him a visionary "Dagger . . . in forme as palpable" as his own (II.i.33ff). With vivid self-deception he pictures the grooms as if already "they have don't" (77), nerving himself to get it "done quickly" (2). The abbreviation "don't" stresses the "done" and slurs the "it," the "it" redoubled so tellingly in the two opening lines of the scene, the dreadful anomalous thing that is to be done. The hero violently suppresses the mental image of it, so very much stranger than all the "Strange Images of death" he was "Nothing afeard" of making with his own hands (I.iii.96f) in the bloodily violent battling of Scene ii—the terrifically strange image of the bleeding king stabbed to death by Macbeth.

Intent upon holding that horrible vision at bay he pays scant heed to his wife's strident rejoinder, "Who dares receive it other, / As we shall make our Griefes and Clamor rore, / Upon his Death?"[46] She is preoccupied with the external effect of the deed afterwards; he, with its internal effect beforehand:

> I am settled, and bend up
> Each corporall Agent to this terrible Feat.   80
> Away, and mock the time with fairest show,
> False Face must hide what the false Heart doth know.

In that curt concluding speech the raptness and the hypocrisy evinced by him recurrently during Act I are fused and brought to their acme. The singular "I" is extremely striking over against the plural pronoun insistently used by his wife, above, and the "we" of his own preceding speech.[47] That "I," that ego, dominates all of the words that follow (as it will dominate all of his utterances in the next three scenes). Not looking at his wife

[46] In the four final lines of I.ii "death" and "Macbeth" are suggestively rhymed. He himself throughout Act I avoids (except in I.iii.71) the former word. His Lady uses it twice, capitalized, in their present colloquy (68, 79); and in the second case "Death" is immediately and significantly followed by the "I" of Macbeth.

[47] That "we" if taken literally would mean he intended his wife to take an actual part in stabbing Duncan with the grooms' daggers (75f). But surely he is thinking here of her spiritual, not physical, aid. This view harmonizes with his final speech in I.vii and his conduct in the next two scenes.

when he exclaims "Away" he addresses the two final lines main-ly, if not exclusively, to himself. The tone of the whole passage is that of rapt, intense, egotistic brooding. He takes upon his own self, his spiritual and "corporall" being, the full responsibility for the "Feat"—at the same time glozing the utter filthiness of the murder, particularly by means of the euphemistic adjec-tives "terrible" and "false." And now compare the closing couplets of the first and last scenes of Act I. The Witches' "fair" was "foul": Macbeth's "fairest" is merely "false." He hides from himself the extraordinary foulness[48] of his murderous proj-ect deep beneath its falsity.

The phrase "this terrible Feat" is exquisitely, tragically eu-phemistic. That "terrible" evades the far more accurate and repulsive terms haunting the mind of the audience: dastardly, foul, beastly, hellish. At the same time it allows the speaker to feel, as natural persons like to feel when about to do a great wrong, that his pronounced condemnation of the deed relieves his inmost self from utter condemnation, from deepest "damna-tion" (20). His intense awareness, displayed in the first half of the scene, that much of his soul is above the crime can veil the fact that the very essence of his soul, namely his will, has now become entirely evil. Such is the ultimate human hypocrisy, sus-tained by Pride. It centers here in a word not used by Macbeth hitherto—contrast his "deed" (24) and "Business" (31)—the climactic word "Feat," a term which, in context with "great quell" and "undaunted Mettle" (72f), suggests a great and bold achievement. The more "terrible" (here, and later) he adjudges that "Feat" to be, the more he can fancy himself as *in spirit* su-perior to it and, also, the more he can pride himself on the power of his will to achieve it.

[48]   Murther most foule, as in the best it is;
         But this most foule, strange, and unnatural.
   Those lines of the Ghost in *Hamlet* (I.v.27f) help us to realize vividly how *strangely and unnaturally* "foule"—far more than in the case of Claudius—the dramàtist succeeded in rendering Macbeth's crime, especially by means of the present scene, while at the same time making the motivation sufficiently natural.

The term "settled" (exactly prefiguring his state of mind in the following scene) has in it a "cold breath" (II.i.61) of devilish resolution. Thus it surpasses in evil overtone its predecessor, the warm word "sworne" above (58). Macbeth's ardent early determination to destroy his king was continually assailed and shaken by his better feelings. It became at the welcoming feast for the king unsettled in the extreme, but not uprooted: its taproot, wrong pride, remained deeply fixed. This pride dominates the present scene from first to last and unifies it deeply. That vice could have been overcome only if Macbeth, with right self-esteem, had humbled his spirit before the superior love, meekness, and constancy of "this *Duncan*" (16), opening his soul thus to the Grace he needs. Instead he tried to "drown" (25) his evil will by flooding it with his own humane emotions. In the upshot, with profound tragic irony—with pity and fear on our part—that indulgence in a fair show of lofty feeling gives place to, indeed assists him in undertaking, the "fairest show" (81) of loyalty with which he will now confront the king and the company again. Proud false trust in his own human-kindness foreruns the proud falseness of the four closing lines. The self-confidence of "We will proceed no further . . ." (31ff), a passage wherein he assumes that a good desire is a real volition, prepares the way for "I am settled . . ." where he finally and deliberately stabilizes his wicked will.

Here he utterly transcends Lady Macbeth in evil sublimity. Unlike her he is too strong and proud to feel the need of directly invoking demonic aid. Instead, he incorporates in himself, unconsciously, satanic wickedness and power. Later he will confess having given his soul to "the common Enemie of Man" (III.i.68f); still later he will pride himself on daring to face a sight that "might appall the Divell" (III.iv.60). But since it is of the essence of evil arrogance to be self-concealing he *never* calls the devil by his proper name, the one that denominates Macbeth himself in the present scene—the name of the Power that makes him here play "such phantastique tricks before high heaven" (*Measure for Measure* II.ii.121)—Pride.

YOUNG IN DEED

(ACT TWO—ACT THREE, SCENE FOUR)

a. *Nature seems dead* (II.i)

Enter Banquo and Fleance, with a Torch before him

BANQUO   How goes the Night, Boy?
FLEANCE   The Moone is down: I have not heard the Clock.
BANQUO   And she goes downe at Twelve.
FLEANCE   I take't, 'tis later, Sir.
BANQUO   Hold, take my Sword—
       There's Husbandry in Heaven,
       Their Candles are all out—take thee that too.
       A heavie Summons lyes like Lead upon me,
       And yet I would not sleepe:
       Mercifull Powers, restraine in me the cursed thoughts
       That Nature gives way to in repose—

Enter Macbeth, and a Servant with a Torch

       Give me my Sword—who's there?   10
MACBETH   A Friend.

Immediately upon Macbeth's settling himself, in the close of
Act I, to perform the murder the "Night" (1) settles down—as
though animated by the evil powers in response to the petitions
of the two principals (I.iv.50ff, I.v.51ff)—in deathly, unnatural quietude and blackness. The moon has gone down at
twelve; but the sound of the clock striking midnight (that very
human clock) has not been heard.[1] It seems to have been muffled by the preternatural air of drowsiness, the "heavie Summons" lying "like Lead" on Banquo, portending evil pressures

---

[1] This silence is more ominous than the sound of the castle clock striking
twelve in the beginning of *Hamlet* (I.i.7).

upon his soul in the night. His eye searching the murky sky can find no star: "there's Husbandry in Heaven, / Their Candles are all out." Yet those "Mercifull Powers" are present to his spirit. When he last appeared he said of this fatal castle, "the Heaven's breath / Smells wooingly here" (I.vi.5f). And now he breathes a simple, heartfelt prayer to heaven.

Such is, in preliminary form, the twofold atmosphere of this drama's second phase. In the pervading darkness there will be incessant intimations of supernal light. The black powers of evil will apparently be dominant. Heaven in its husbandry will not oppose them so directly as to stultify the freedom of human wills. But its strong working will be constant in the dark, and variously evident in persons and events, eminently in the awful increasing misery of Macbeth. He remains until the close of this phase "yet but young" in evil action (III.iv.144). And his child-ishness in this respect has in it a promise of true spiritual child-likeness. Time and again the Shakespearean audience—those (in all ages) who share the poet's sense of heavenly, and dramatic, mercy and suspense—will feel that Macbeth's passionate agony *may* overcome his cursed thoughts (8) and open his soul to repentance. In the present scene, however, he not only main-tains but manages to heighten his wicked composure, despite the providential dissuasion exerted upon him through Banquo, the visionary dagger, and the full horror of this night.

Preceded by his son with a torch Banquo entered the scene in a flickering circle of light. But soon (5ff) the light, still and steady, illumines his face as he strives to lift his spirit in prayer above his increasing premonitions—while Macbeth, followed by his torchbearing servant, enters at the rear with dark countenance. Banquo, starting and peering, grasps his sword, then relinquishes it slowly to his boy again when he recognizes his "Friend"—with a dramatic irony sharper than a sword.[2]

---

[2] All of the action here is packed with suggestion. Banquo's start recalls in ironic contrast that of Macbeth (I.iii.51), who this time is more composed than his friend. Fleance, appearing here for the first time and preceding his father as they enter, reminds us at once of the Witches' prophecy regarding the progeny of Banquo (I.iii.67); whose innocence, moreover, is accented for

Macbeth succeeds in making his tone and mien "mock the time with fairest show" (I.vii.81). To be sure he is visibly perturbed when Banquo describes, with simple beauty of speech, the "unusuall Pleasure" and "measurelesse content" of "the King," whom he has just seen to bed. "This Diamond" (15), which he suddenly produces from his pouch and offers to Macbeth for "your Wife"—conveying the king's final thanks to her "By the name of most kind Hostesse"—gleams in the night firm and clear like Duncan's character (I.vii.18) and also like Banquo's "clear" allegiance (28). Macbeth receives and contemplates it slowly, reluctantly. Then hastily stowing it away he avers in measured terms that, in spite of the king's generous satisfaction, his entertainment here has been very defective because of the unexpectedness of his visit; and that, "Being unprepared,"

> Our will became the servant to defect,
> Which else should free have wrought.

Under the surface that means, for Macbeth, a fatalistic palliation of his murderous design; for us, the present enslavement of his "free" will, through his own "defect," to the powers of evil. But Banquo, pleased with his friend's seeming modesty, reassures him by declaring that "All's well" and by reminding him of the highly deserved honors that have come to him: the weird Sisters have shown him "some truth."

And now Macbeth, speaking to that cue, tries with covert skill to make sure of the adherence of Banquo, next to himself the most powerful of the peers so far, in the imminent political crisis. He still wishes well to his friend; his tone, the other feels, is sincerely kind (24). And he intimates, truthfully, that he is not now relying on the Witches' foresight (21). His phrase "that Businesse" alludes with fine casual vagueness to the ques-

---

us by that of his "Boy." The "Sword," handed from one to the other, symbolizes the justice, suspended and uncertain in the second phase of the play, which in the end will descend upon Macbeth. Banquo's vague premonitions connect immediately in our minds with the entering Macbeth, before being partially explained by Banquo's dream of the Witches (20).

tion of the kingship in the uncertain future upon Duncan's decease. Silently present to the minds of both speakers is the possibility that the peers of the realm may eventually decide that the royal power should pass to Duncan's "valiant" and "worthiest Cousin" (I.ii.24, I.iv.14) rather than to his son Malcolm, the new "Prince of Cumberland" (I.iv.39). Banquo is ready to be counselled at leisure on that difficult point while taking care that his heart shall not be wrongly swayed by his natural appreciation of the higher status which, in that case, would come to himself (26-29). He sees nothing untoward in his friend's reminder that if he continues in the future to be Macbeth's supporter "it shall make Honor for you." But that declaration, conspicuously absent from their previous colloquy on this subject (I.iii.153-156), betrays to us the bold and fatal arrogance beneath the speaker's studied modesty: Macbeth's imagination has vaulted to the throne and is making "Honor" for his supporters. But, unlike Banquo, he has lost his soul's honor in seeking to "augment" (27) the honors he has deserved (I.vi.17ff, I.vii. 32ff).

The contrast between the two friends, between Banquo's "Bosome franchised" (28) and his companion's "false Heart" (I.vii. 82), is so powerfully rendered by the dramatist that we know Macbeth himself must be aware of it poignantly. With effortful calmness he wishes Banquo and his son "Good repose" (nevermore to be his own), dismisses his innocent servant, and watches the three torchlit figures disappear on their way "to bed." Then he sinks his head, waiting for his wife to "strike upon the Bell," summoning him to "strike"—with those "very Daggers" (I.vii. 76) so terribly vivid in his mind now, the daggers of the grooms, lying near the generous king asleep in his "measureless content" (17). He represses his conscience with an effort far more violent than ever before. Then, lifting his head strugglingly, he perceives a dim something shaped like a dagger (33) recumbent in the air: "Is this a Dagger . . . ?"

In the air! Earlier he watched the Witches making themselves air—assuming the nature of the air into which they vanished

(I.v.5), melting "as breath into the Winde" (I.iii.81f). And a short while ago he had an elaborate mental vision of condemning angels above him in the air, and cherubs riding the winds, the invisible "couriers of the Ayre" (I.vii.19ff). But the present airy form is simple, still, and close to him. And now it seems a veritable dagger with the "Handle toward my Hand." Stepping a pace forward and clutching at it in vain, he sees it still, at the same distance before him *though it has not moved.*[3] So he apprehends that it is a "Dagger of the Minde," proceeding from his "heat-oppressed Braine," oppressed by the double heat of ruthless ambition and remorseful horror molten together.

> I see thee yet, in forme as palpable   40
> As this which now I draw.—
> Thou marshall'st me the way that I was going,
> And such an Instrument I was to use.

Palpable now, certainly, is the warning of "Heaven" (I.vii.22), of all the "Mercifull Powers" (7). He can feel it, if he will, in each corporal agent (I.vii.80). He knows his wife is about to lay "ready" (31) the drugged grooms' daggers (II.ii.6,12). In imagination he grasps them as he grasps "this which now I draw." Staring down at it he feels his hand stabbing his king; and so, looking up again, he sees the airy instrument pointing now, like the wand of a "fatall" (36) invisible marshal (42), towards the door. Fearfully he covers his "Eyes" (44) with his other hand; uncovers them, and sees the thing still pointing— and suddenly, "on thy Blade, and Dudgeon, Gouts of Blood." He recoils in horror, bowing his head and shielding his eyes with his free arm. And now, finally and completely aware that the vision is an hallucination, he knows he can still turn back from the way he "*was* going," from that which he "*was*" to do (42f): the iterated past tense is significant. But the proud, bad integrity

[3] See Dover Wilson's text and notes for a different explication of the stage business and movements here. In my opinion, to conceive the dagger as first appearing on a table instead of in the air is to make the action more realistic in one way but less so in a more important way. See Kenneth Muir's convincing note.

he attained in the close of the preceding scene reasserts itself. Ashamed of his weakness he will not recognize the strong reality causing it, the heavenly power of conscience. He straightens himself more and more steadily; then, sheathing his dagger and peering defiantly into the air, he banishes the vision from his sight and from his soul. "There's no such thing":

> It is the bloody Businesse[4] which informs
> Thus to mine eyes.—Now o'er the one halfe World
> Nature seemes dead, and wicked Dreames abuse   50
> The Curtained sleepe. . . .

Deliberately deadening his better nature, he attunes his mood to the world of darkness and "stealthy" (54) evil, but at the same time mastering that realm, in his imagination, making it subservient to his own black ambition.

This soliloquy in midnight is the sequel to Lady Macbeth's in thickening twilight (I.v.41ff), but far more sinister. She entreated the help of the evil powers. He, tacitly receiving their aid, associates himself with them as a superior who comprehends and surpasses their activity. This is the hour when evil spirits are active in "wicked Dreames"[5] and in the orgies of "Witchcraft" (50-52); when, far more dreadfully, the spirit of "withered Murther . . . towards his designe / Moves like a Ghost"—like a very wraith of Macbeth himself. He is the reality, walking the "sure and firme-set Earth," fully aware that its homely naturalness is hostile to his design; glorying in the strength of his wicked will, his ability to face and consummate "the present horror" (59).

But that phrase, still more general and vague than its predecessor, "the bloody Businesse" (48), displays to us his vulnerability. Studiously, here as in the preceding scene, he avoids envisioning the great *particular* horror: the king's blood flowing from the

---

[4] The word business, here climactically used, is full of meaning derived from its previous occurrences (23, I.vii.31, I.vi.16, I.v.69).

[5] See the great passage upon spirits inspiring wicked dreams in *The Faerie Queene* (I.i.38ff).

king's stabbed body. Macbeth occupies his mind with the "World" of evil (49ff) to keep it from envisaging the actual details of the imminent murder. And very humanly he tries to mitigate his sin, even while priding himself on his evil strength, by regarding it as merely a small part of all the dark world's wickedness. He covers reality with night.

Hence the increasingly melodramatic air of his soliloquy, culminating in its fantastic close (60ff). He makes himself think of Duncan as an enemy who has to be destroyed: "Whiles I threat, he lives. . . ." Then *"A Bell rings."* A fearful shudder is instantly subdued by the great warrior, the "brave Macbeth" (I.ii.16). His lost battle seems to him won.

> I goe, and it is done: the Bell invites me.
> Heare it not, *Duncan*, for it is a Knell
> That summons thee to Heaven, or to Hell.[6]

That final word, so grotesque in relation to the saintly king, is Macbeth's unconscious proclamation of his own present state. Hell is worst when hidden. The hero is obeying the summons of inferno without acknowledging it: he has palled his soul in "the dunnest smoke of Hell" (I.v.52).

b. *this my Hand* (II.ii)

Lady Macbeth's dreadful suspense while "He is about it" heightens ours, as we hearken to her words of the opened "Doores," the "surfeited Groomes," "Death and Nature" contending (4-7). Her shudder when she hears the shriek of the owl (3), the "fatall Bell-man," following the fatal sound of the bell she has struck, prepares for the violent start she gives when Macbeth cries out within, "Who's there? what hoa?" (9). That wild, startled cry contradicts absolutely his bold mien on leaving the stage, above. And so we, along with her, but with opposite

[6] Cf. "down to Hell" exclaimed by Gloucester (Richard Third) to the saintly King Henry just before murdering him (3 *Henry Sixth*, V.vi.67). There as here the murderer relieves himself by proudly scorning the "Hell" which he is really obeying.

emotion, believe he may have recoiled from the deed at the last moment. To us it seems that he has felt the moving presence of someone suddenly intervening, some invisible "Who." She, however, fears "they have awaked" while he was groping for the "daggers" with great reluctance. She knows how awful "the deed" (11) was and is for him: she confesses to us, with strangely mixed remorse, that if "he," the unnamed victim, had "not resembled"

> My Father as he slept, I had done't.—
> My Husband! ?[7]

Those last two words are full of love and pity, horror, dismay, and questioning. Macbeth, soon after his outcry, has entered and advanced silently, staggeringly, with a dripping dagger in each red hand, held at stiff arm's length, down, back, away from him. He whispers hoarsely:

> I have done the deed: 15
> Didst *thou* not hear a noyse?[8]

Apparently he heard, as well as felt, the presence of the condemning "Who"; but this (unlike the airy dagger of the preceding scene) occurred after instead of before the murder, as he "descended" (17) the stairs from the bedroom story. To her astonishment he is unaware of his own outcry; to his great amazement she did not hear that by which it was caused, a dreadful sound, indeed an articulate voice (35), that he dare not speak of yet.

Instead his thoughts revert to the "second Chamber" (20), the lodging of the king's two sons, Malcolm and Donalbain. About to pass it, after his deed, he heard one of them "laugh" in his sleep and the other cry "Murther"—as though at once mocking and accusing him. He stood deadly still in the darkness

---

[7] Dash and exclamation-point inserted by me. For "done't" ("don't" in the Folio) see my comment on I.vii.77. A pause fills out the second line, while Macbeth advances. The suggestive alignment of "My Father" and "My Husband" is abandoned in modern editions.

[8] These two lines have become one in modern editions. Italics mine.

at their door while they, waking, said their "Prayers" before going "againe to sleepe." The closing words of those prayers pierced him and echoed and re-echoed in his brain: "God blesse us . . . Amen . . . Amen . . . God blesse us" (27-30). He himself struggled vainly to say "Amen." Now he utters the sacred word four times, yearningly but hollowly. Indirectly he confesses that by his deed he has rejected that of which he had "most need," the divine "Blessing" (32) and, therewith, the peace imaged by "the innocent Sleepe" (36). He is undergoing, more dreadfully than he foresaw, "deep damnation" and "judgement here" (I. vii.8,20).

And suddenly he pours forth what he has been suppressing: the awful experience he had while descending the stairs in the darkness with the unseen daggers in his bloody hands (21,28). The voice he heard (35) was personal—hence the repeated emphatic "Who" (9,44)—and yet superpersonal. It was the voice of God (27,30) speaking through nature, employing terms that were vivid in the guilty listener's mind. Macbeth, having murderously abused the beautiful "Curtained sleepe" (II.i.51), had just heard an innocent sleeping youth cry "Murther." And so—he begins in a whisper that quickly rises—

> Methought I heard a voyce cry, Sleep no more: 35
> *Macbeth* does murther Sleepe, the innocent Sleepe,
> Sleepe that knits up the ravelled Sleeve of Care,
> The death of each day's Life, sore Labor's Bath,
> Balme of hurt Mindes, great Nature's second Course,
> Chiefe nourisher in Life's Feast—   40
> Still it cryed, Sleepe no more, to all the House:
> *Glamis* hath murthered Sleepe, and therefore *Cawdor*
> Shall sleepe no more: *Macbeth* shall sleepe no more.[9]

At first the voice was quiet like thought (35), like the preceding "Dagger of the Mind" (II.i.38). But swiftly it loudened,

---

[9] Ruinous is the modern custom of placing parts of this speech (parts different with different editors) in quotation-marks to distinguish the voice's words from Macbeth's elaborations, a distinction not made by Macbeth and Shakespeare.

crying out like a trumpet-tongued "Angel" (I.vii.19) to "all the House." It mocks the screaming prophecy of the Witches (I.iii. 48ff): Glamis and Cawdor shall be "King hereafter"; but—in the close the tone sinks to its initial awful whisper—"*Macbeth shall sleepe no more!*" He shall indeed think at leisure upon that business (II.i.21-24).[10] He "*hath*" murdered, and therefore now and ever "*does*" murder, all his peace.

In the preceding scene his evil design made the nighttime seem entirely evil: nature seemed dead. But now, yearningly, he sees the nightly sleep as the natural and good "death" of each day's life for the sake of "Life" (38). Sleep, when innocent, as his own cannot again be, unravels our daily cares and restores ("knits up") our sense of vital pattern in human life, while refreshing labored bodies and soothing the hurts of minds. It is the chief nourisher in "Life's Feast"—recalling the genial festivity of last evening, crowned by Duncan's repose in measureless content (II.i.17). It is the revitalizing "second Course," alternating with the daytime course, of "great Nature," i.e. the Nature designed and blessed by God (27ff). Part of that "Nature" is Macbeth's "humane kindnesse" (I.v.18). His present beautiful speech is an expression of that and, at the same time, a piercing requiem for it.[11]

In pronouncing the final line of that speech he involuntarily lifts his right "Hand" (47) with its red-heavy burden. And his wife, pointing to it, manages unlike him to eye it fully and steadily. So far she has uttered merely low, brief adjurations, too unnerved to reflect until now that he has madly brought "these Daggers from the place" instead of letting them lie there after smearing the sleeping grooms, as he himself had proposed

[10] Thus, in the first two scenes of this Act, Shakespeare casually revives the thought of the Witches' fateful prophecy which, after being continually alluded to in I.iii and I.v, was dismissed from memory in the crucial I.vii so as to emphasize Macbeth's full responsibility for his evil decision. At the same time the dramatist stresses the fact that in the present scene Macbeth's great remorse annuls, for the time being, his great ambition: his allusion to the Witches' prediction omits, strikingly, the word "King" (42-43).

[11] Similar in that respect to Othello's lament for his gone occupation (III.iii.348ff).

(I.vii.75), "with blood" (50). But now that dreadful word "blood," hitherto unspoken in this scene, unmans him entirely. He dare not view his bleeding victim again: "I'll go no more. . . ." And she, breathing deeply, revives for his sake (and for the last time) all her evil "strength" (45) and firmness of "purpose" (52). She takes the daggers from his hands while he looks away. She nerves herself by speaking with artificial grimness. "If he doe bleed" (55)—that not to be named "he" (13)—she'll "guild" the very "Faces," as well as the hands, "of the Groomes withall." Immediately upon her exit her factitious realism is mocked by a sudden loud reality, a knocking at the outer door of the castle.

Macbeth, starting fearfully, peers into the lonely darkness in every direction. "Whence is that knocking?" For him it is not "a knocking at the South entry" (66): it is an appalling "noyse" (58) coming from every point of the compass, sequel of the noise (15) of the voice that cried out more and more loudly "to all the House": increasingly the "great Nature" he assailed is assailing him.[12] And now the empty crimson hands, which he unawares lifts high in awe at the noise, attack his sight. They are his and not his: "What Hands are here? hah! they pluck out mine Eyes" (59)—"mine Eyes" (II.i.44,49) that watched and dismissed the dripping dagger in the air. Now he scans with immense horror the right hand that did the deed. His wife had urged him to "get some Water" and "wash this filthie Witnesse from your Hand" (46f). Holding it off, waving it a little, slowly, he moans like the tides of the worldwide sea:

Will all great *Neptune's* Ocean wash this blood   60
Cleane from my Hand? no—this my Hand will rather
The multitudinous Seas incarnadine,
Making the Greene   one   Red.[13]

---

[12] As intimated above the word "noyse" occurs just twice in this scene and the homonymous "voyce" just once, in between. Contrariwise the word "done," which has recurred incessantly since I.iv.53, is frequent in this scene, up to line 51.

[13] The spacing in this line is of course mine. The Folio has a comma after "one," indicating that the actor should pause after as well as before that word:

Immediately Lady Macbeth reappears with red "Hands" and with a "Heart," she avers, not "white"! At once the knocking at the gate redoubles. "A little Water," she declares with vast unconscious irony, "cleares us of this deed" (67).

For him, however, ignoring her "us," "this deed" is entirely "my deed" (73), and he cannot be cleared of it. He stands brooding silently upon "this my Hand," oblivious to all external danger, while the knockings without grow ever louder and his wife's importunings more insistent.[14] She, strained almost to the breaking point, expects instant ruination for him. At last, with awful love, she clasps his red hand in both of her bloody ones, pulls it down out of sight, and says with calm firmness in his ear: "be not lost / So poorely in your thoughts" (71f). He has completely lost, for the present, the proud evil integrity and "Constancie" (68) he attained at the end of Act I and exhibited in II.i. His inward division has gone more "deepely" (30) down than ever. He is "afraid to," but has to, "thinke what I have done" (51). "To know my deed, / 'Twere best not know my selfe" (73): he cannot envisage the full wickedness of his deed without utterly detesting the self that did it. That repeated word "know" is new in his vocabulary: the elaborate imaginational "thought" (I.iii.138f) in which he had wrapped his crime beforehand seems now not to have been real knowing. Thus his final speech in this scene has a new confessional simplicity:

> To know my deed,
> 'Twere best not know my selfe—   73
> Wake *Duncan* with thy knocking:
> I would thou could'st.[15]

---

it is at once a pronoun qualified by "Greene" and an adjective qualifying "Red." Macbeth *feels*, as well as sees, the red flesh ("flesh" implied by the second syllable of "incarnadine") of his hand staining the multifarious waters comprised in the world's one green ocean. And the ocean of eternity is adumbrated, encompassing this bank and shoal of time (I.vii.6).

[14] Compare and contrast Othello's state of mind when he hears Emilia at the door just after his murder of Desdemona (V.ii.84ff). That dramatic situation is repeated here with tremendous intensification.

[15] Contrast those four short, irregular lines (printed as two in modern editions) with his closing verses in the two preceding scenes. The nameless per-

Will Macbeth's deepening remorse open the way for true humility and repentance? That major question overshadows the minor one: will his guilt be discovered by his peers? Our twofold suspense is relieved on the surface, but deepened underneath, by the humorous Porter who opens the next scene; and who unwittingly provides his master with plenty of time to take hold of himself again—for good or for ill.

c. *the great Hand of God* (II.iii)

In the beginning of the preceding scene Macbeth staggered onto the stage hearkening fearfully to a soundless voice. Here a tousled underling staggers forward, soggy with drink and sleep, giving ear drolly to the noisy knocking within, which is now impatiently quick and heavy. Repeatedly he waves in its direction a flaunting, gesturing hand (not redly burdened like his master's). He thinks of the uncommon labor "a man" (1) —not a devil!—would have if he were "Porter of Hell Gate." Unaware of the real "Hell" (II.i.64) created by his master in this "pleasant" castle (I.vi.1) he creates, in fancy, a ludicrous inferno here. The fantastical aspect of evil, developed more and more inwardly in the course of the drama hitherto, is here displayed in outward, frolicsome guise. The Porter, in a prose soliloquy that caricatures the poetic imagination of Macbeth's speeches, invents "strange" yet homely "images" (I.iii.97,135) of specters who have incurred "damnation" (I.vii.20) for crimes trivial in comparison with the one just perpetrated. We laugh at and with him. But his comical body-shaking shiver in the close of the speech makes us reflect that "this place" is not, as he avers, "too cold for Hell" (18). Hell indeed sweats (8) with heat; but also it shivers with cold.

And in the upshot his recurrent topic of "equivocation," alluding unawares to a theme recurrent in this tragedy as a whole, penetrates us shiveringly though he quilts it with absurdities.

sistently summoning "thou" who can *not* wake Duncan is sequel to the mystic voice proclaiming to all the house that Macbeth himself shall sleep no more.

The "Equivocator . . . who committed Treason . . . yet could not equivocate to Heaven" (10ff) figures in the middle of the soliloquy flanked by two ridiculous ghosts, the greedy suicidal farmer and the thieving tailor. Thus subordinated, the "Equivocator" may seem merely one casual figure in the parade of "all Professions that goe the Primrose way to th' everlasting Bonfire" (20-22). But he outlasts that parade in the Porter's imagination. When the fellow eventually admits Macduff and Lennox he extenuates his remissness by jocose moralizing upon "Drinke," particularly with regard to its ambiguous relation to "Lecherie." Consequently the "Equivocator" reappears (35), this time in the form of "Drinke" and, also, in that of the grossly equivocating joker himself. Here the talk is relievingly far from tragedy. But it keeps us in mind of the treasonable "Equivocator," to whom the "Porter of Hell Gate" exclaimed sharply, "oh, come in, Equivocator!" (14).[16] And presently, after the Porter and Macduff have joked equivocally upon lying (40ff), "*Enter Macbeth.*"

While the alcoholic Porter retreats to the rear in clumsy haste on shaky legs, the protagonist advances slowly, steadily, with expressionless face. His hands are clean, now, and welcoming. His first three replies to the newcomers are laconically polite, and his reserved manner causes Macduff to apologize for the "joyfull trouble" (53) of ushering him to "the King" (50). Joyful! Instantly Macbeth's utterance, hitherto extremely simple, becomes labored and artificial, while a dignified bow conceals his joylessness: "The labour we delight in Physicks paine." And instead of bringing (52) Macduff to the royal chamber he points, without looking, towards the entrance of the joyless, awful stairway which he lately descended and cannot, at the present moment, make himself re-ascend: "This is the Doore" (55).

That is the door through which Duncan, escorted by the loyal

[16] This word, continually repeated or alluded to in the first forty lines of the scene, is emphasized particularly here (14) by its position at the end of an exclamatory sentence. The Porter's welcome to the "Equivocator" is gravidly concise in contrast with the elaborate joking that follows the word "come" in the case of the farmer (6-8) and the tailor (15f).

and innocent Banquo, went to his bed in unusual pleasure and measureless contentment (II.i.12-17).[17] It is the door through which he would reappear if only he could be waked (II.ii.74), if only he could go "hence" today as he purposed (I.v.60f): "he did appoint so" (58). Macbeth, after Macduff's exit, hearkens with bent head and fearful tensity for sounds behind that door, at the same time giving ear to young Lennox's account of other fearsome sounds, the "unruly" and unholy noises of the past "Night" (59-68). Lennox heard violent, destructive blasts of wind and the "obscure Bird," hidden creature of darkness, clamoring "the live-long Night."[18] And he reports that others discerned, with and beyond those sounds, supernatural voices, "lamentings heard i' th' Ayre, / Strange Schreemes of Death, / And Prophesying, with Accents terrible, / Of dyre Combustion, and confused Events / New hatched to th' wofull time." The speech expresses for us the wild tumult in the heart of the silent Macbeth as well as the "feverous" (66) universal disorder signified by his hell-inspired crime. Above all it prepares for Macduff's ensuing outcry (quoted below) with its horrorful sense of "Confusion" (71).

The effect of that outcry is heightened by Macduff's words and bearing, above, before leaving the stage. Significantly he, not Banquo or Macbeth, was chosen by the king for service this morning. That appointment, emphasized by the dramatist (50-56), suggests that this great thane is, though new to us, a very intimate counsellor of the prudent Duncan. He equals Macbeth in strength of physique and dignity of mien. And while devoid of the other's rich poetic imagination he has a plain, patient, fellowly humor (24-47) lacked by Macbeth. Harmonious with that quality are his selfless devotion to Duncan and, especially,

---

[17] A certain type of critic might remark that Duncan, for all we know, may have used another door!

[18] Lady Macbeth in a fatal moment of that night heard "the Owle schreame, and the Crickets cry" (II.ii.16). In the present passage the bird is weirdly, effectively nameless. The winds suggestively precede and introduce the airy lamentings etc.; and "The obscure Bird" with its clamorings caps the climax of the "confused events."

a highly religious conception of kingship not hitherto expressed in the play.[19] No sooner has Macbeth managed to mutter to Lennox evasively, " 'Twas a rough Night"—recalling his earlier evasive "roughest Day" (I.iii.147)—than Macduff, so entirely composed above, rushes in with utmost perturbation and dismay:

O horror, horror, horror!—[20]
Tongue nor Heart cannot conceive nor name thee. . . . 70
Confusion now hath made his Master-piece:
Most sacrilegious Murther hath broke ope
The Lord's anoynted Temple, and stole thence
The Life of the Building!

The Christian conception of the human body as designed temple of the Lord's Spirit applies with full force to the gracious person and anointed king, Duncan. And now Macbeth cannot evade doing what in the preceding scene he dared not do: he must go and look again upon that anointed, now horrifically bloodied body whence he has stolen the "Life": he echoes that word (74f) fearfully. Must he not, then, break down? Shall he not betray himself when he returns to the courtyard where Macduff is now proclaiming, like the mystic voice previously, the evil deed "to all the House"?

During Macbeth's absence from the stage Macduff is the central figure. For this devout nobleman the present dim dawn, revealing secret "Murther and Treason" of the most sacrilegious sort, prefigures the Day of Judgment, when the dead shall rise and walk. He summons Banquo and the king's sons to rise from sleep like spirits from graves, each (he imagines) reflecting with ghastly "countenance," like the speaker's own, the "horror" of the time (79-85). It is not they, however, who arrive first. With

---

[19] But it was prepared for by the attitude of Banquo, of the minor personages, and of Macbeth himself, at his best, towards the king. In the beginning Ross exclaimed, expressing the general sentiment, "God save the King!" (I.ii.47).

[20] My exclamation point and dash replace the original comma. The speaker struggles for utterance. But the first two lines are modernly printed thus:

O horror, horror, horror! Tongue nor heart
Cannot conceive nor name thee!

ghostlike mien Lady Macbeth appears, in night attire, her face deadly pale with fatigue and anxiety. The castle's loud "Alarum Bell," rung at Macduff's command, is the antithetic sequel of the little "Bell" she herself struck a while ago (II.i.32,62). She compares the present menacing clang to "a hideous Trumpet" convoking the "sleepers of the House" (87f)—thus unconsciously alluding to the trumpet of Doomsday and countenancing Macduff's "image" (83). He, with fine gentility—resembling Duncan's (I.vi.10ff) and contrasting with the studied courtesy of Macbeth—tries to soften for her the terrible news:

> O gentle Lady,
> 'Tis not for you to heare what I can speake:
> The repetition in a Woman's eare   90
> Would murther as it fell.

But he has to sob out, as Banquo enters, "O *Banquo, Banquo,* our Royall Master's murthered." And she, near to collapse, exclaims unwarily, "Woe, alas: / What, in our House?" Here as ever her husband's safety and worldly honor, not her own, are in her thoughts, as when she thanked the king for "those Honors deep and broad" conferred by him upon "our House" (I.vi.17f).[21] "Too cruell any where," Banquo avers sharply, while Macduff regards her fixedly and silently. She shrinks away, then stands rigid, with hands half raised towards her re-entering husband.[22]

Macbeth, followed by Lennox and Ross, advances silently and blindly, as though his "sight" had indeed been destroyed by a "new Gorgon" (76f).[23] When he finds voice his requiem for the king is handsomer than any words anyone else could compass. Here is a supreme, ironic instance of the fact that an ambitious politician is usually at his best, his *emotionally sincere* best, when

[21] For Macbeth's ironically different "House" see the final sentence of my preceding paragraph.

[22] To give Macbeth the center of the stage the two men also step aside, in opposite directions, Macduff still facing towards Lady Macbeth; see line 124.

[23] The fact that the sight of Medusa's head turned men to stone is mainly irrelevant here; Macduff, and Shakespeare, omit it nicely.

commemorating a noble leader who no longer stands in his way. The first personal pronoun, conspicuously absent from Macduff's lamentation above, is prominent in the two opening lines; yet these have a piercing sadness:

> Had I but died an houre before this chance,
> I had lived a blessed time: for from this instant,
> There's nothing serious in Mortalitie:
> All is but Toyes—Renowne and Grace is dead,
> The Wine of Life is drawne, and the meere Lees   100
> Is left this Vault, to brag of.

In that speech the initial simplicity yields gradually to embellishment. But the whole passage is imbued with what is, and will increasingly be, the tragedy of Macbeth. This mortal human life, for which he has such an intense poetic feeling, will lose real meaning for him more and more, until it finally signifies "nothing" (V.v.28). In killing Duncan, his meek and clear sovereign (I.vii.17f), he has killed the embodiment of true renown, of human and divine grace (99); hence these, as he now feels despairingly, are utterly lost for himself. His "blessed time" is over and gone, the days when he might have died with heaven's blessing on him. A while ago, in "most need," he tried without avail to seek God's "blessing" and mercy (II.ii.31-33); now, seemingly, "Grace is dead," as "Nature" seemed "dead" beforehand (II.i.50). He lifts his hands a little towards the misty sky overarching a world of vacancy; then drops them inertly at his sides. His universe, "this Vault," is emptied of "The Wine of Life." Nothing is left but dregs, and trifles (toys), and vainglory (101).

In that passage, certainly, Macbeth seems to know his "deed" and his "self" (II.ii.73) more deeply than ever before. And the lines evince, covertly, an enlarging remorse. The red guilt of his hand staining all the world's seas (II.ii.60-63) means now a blank desolation pervading all the universe and every hour of time. So the final effect of the speech upon us is intense suspense.

How can this man endure the coming hours (96) and days and, particularly, the situation immediately confronting him? What can he say to the king's sons, now entering, whose prophetic fear and innocent prayers he listened to after one of the two—he does not know which—cried out "Murther" (II.ii. 23ff)? Glancing at them, then lowering his gaze, Macbeth says with effort: "The Spring, the Head, the Fountaine of your Blood / Is stopt, the very Source of it is stopt." Similitude of this stopped crimson wellspring was the red drawn wine of life in his preceding speech. He cannot forget that awful royal "Blood" shed by him in the darkness of night and, just now, plainly viewed in the dawn; he must speak of it; but he cannot do so except in euphemisms. And his tongue will not frame the word murder. When Macduff announces to the sons, "Your Royall Father's murthered," and Malcolm cries out "Oh, by whom?" Macbeth is speechless. He beckons Lennox, then listens stonily while the other describes a sight which certainly his "young remembrance" cannot "parallel" (67):

> Those of his Chamber, as it seemed, had done't:
> Their Hands and Faces were all badged with blood,
> So were their Daggers, which unwiped we found
> Upon their Pillowes: they stared and were distracted—   110
> No man's Life was to be trusted with them.   ,

The word "seemed" in the first line gives parenthetic intimation of the doubt that breaks forth in the packed, stumbling penultimate line.[24] We can see the roused, innocent grooms staring at those ghastly pillows with horrified and wild amazement—no one can believe that they did the deed, *if* they did it, on their own volition. But now the speaker, glancing at Macbeth with fear in his eyes, adds hastily his final and deprecatory line: it is, in the fullest sense, the other's cue. And the hero, in a voice more

[24] But the typical modern editor, putting a full stop after "pillows," begins a new verse with "They." Kenneth Muir and Henry Johnson (see my Note on the Text, above) retain the Folio lineation here. The dash, as usual, is mine.

"distracted" than the dumbness of the grooms, cries out: "O, yet I doe repent me of my furie, / That I did kill them."

That speech, a wild wave with its quick crest in the word "repent," sweeps away our feeling that Macbeth's immense remorse might presently occasion true repentance.[25] We know, now, that the agony of his soul when he viewed Duncan's corpse impelled him to a second murder: he tried to kill his conscience by killing the grooms. But he succeeded only in submersing it, thereby strengthening its torturing undertow, as evidenced by his "Wine of Life" elegy above. And now he does indeed sincerely and bitterly "repent," not of his sinfulness, but of the futile fury which, while deepening his misery of heart, has aroused deep suspicion in his present companions. He confesses to them,[26] in lieu of the true kind of confession, his emotional error in killing the grooms without questioning them.

But when Macduff demands with accusing sternness "Wherefore did you so?" Macbeth's vaulting ambition, thus spurred, resumes all its impetus. It enables him to exert the self-control achieved in the end of Act I, lost after the murder, and not completely regained during the present scene until now. His previous words to Macduff were uneasily brief and intermittent (49-74). Now he addresses him, and with him the other peers, in a passage (quoted below) of free-flowing eloquence and of such masterly political rhetoric as he has not hitherto displayed. Here Duncan's wouldbe successor claims for himself the kingly virtues of wisdom, temperance, and "Reason" (114-117); surpassed in his soul only, and properly, by the sublime virtue, "Love" (so signally shown by his questioner, Macduff); together with the basal virtue, "Courage" (124), for which the speaker is already famous. This climactic word, nicely reminding his hearers of the "valiant Cousin" (I.ii.24) approved by Duncan who saved the realm in battle, intimates that he has also *moral* courage.

---

[25] For real repentance succeeding great remorse note the case of Leontes in *The Winter's Tale*, III.ii and later. His voluntary and very heavy penance is stressed by Shakespeare.

[26] As indicated by his vocative "O" (112); contrast the "Oh" of Malcolm above (105), wrongly changed to "O" in modern texts.

Heedless of incurring dreadful suspicion (so he artfully suggests) he executed prematurely the bloody grooms, whom here for the first time he terms "the Murtherers," crowning his continual equivocation with a downright falsehood.[27] He was violently (116) moved, he says, by the sight of them and the slaughtered, gracious Duncan prostrate before his eyes: the terms used here, especially the "Golden Blood," indicate rhetorically the beauty and sacredness of the dead king's nature. He *had* to give way to his "heart," a "heart" pulsing with "love," a "love"[28] that must show itself immediately in action (122-124).

> Who can be wise, amazed, temperate, and furious,
> Loyall and Neutrall, in a moment? No man: 115
> Th' expedition of my violent Love
> Out-run the pauser, Reason. Here lay *Duncan*,
> His Silver skinne laced with his Golden Blood,
> And his gashed Stabs looked like a Breach in Nature,
> For Ruine's wastefull entrance—there the Murtherers,   120
> Steeped in the Colours of their Trade; their Daggers
> Unmannerly breeched with gore: who could refraine,
> That had a heart to love; and in that heart
> Courage, to make 's love knowne?

Could Macduff have refrained? Such is the implied query. Certainly a nobleman worthy to be Duncan's successor could not have refrained!

For us that oration is a fantastic yet very human mixture of truth and fiction, deception and sincerity; above all, pride and conscience.[29] With the despairing "Wine of Life" speech fresh in mind we must feel in every line of the "Golden Blood" speech (so to name them) a deep sense of "Ruin," not only in "Nature"

---

[27] Above he hastily qualified his untruthful assertion about the king's going "hence today" (57f), showing the uneasiness which he now succeeds in hiding entirely.

[28] The verbal repetitions characteristic of this play, and revealing Shakespeare's careless haste according to some critics, are here designed to express a simple, unreflective, full-hearted love.

[29] This theme is fundamental in Shakespearean tragedy. See "pride and conscience" in the indexes of my *Scourge and Minister* and *Flaming Minister*.

(119f) but in the speaker's own soul, due to his repressed but implacable conscience. That sense is surmounted, however, by ambition and arrogance—by his pride in mastering at once his own emotions and those of the assembled peers.[30] For them, as not for us, Macbeth's apologia must seem mainly, though far from completely, plausible. If they suspected him overwhelmingly of regicide they would now crowd upon him and place him under durance, led by Macduff. But this great thane, who (I think) grasped his sword-hilt, above (113), has gradually withdrawn his hand from it; and he makes no reply, here or during the rest of the scene, to Macbeth's irrefragable declaration. Macduff, though far more deeply suspicious than the others in regard to Macbeth, is too righteous to take action against him until he shall have sure and certain grounds.

And, no less kind than carefully just, Macduff is the first to heed the distress of the only "Woman" present, Macbeth's "gentle Lady" (88-91,124). Now she cries out desperately, "Helpe me hence, hoa!" tottering, one hand covering her eyes, the other groping for a way, any way, "hence." After her previous misfortunate outcry (93f)—so different from the clamorous grief she had planned to show upon the discovery of Duncan's death (I.vii.77-79)—she weakened more and more. She listened, rigid and deadly pale, while Lennox with terrible vividness described, unwittingly, what she herself had done. Those "Faces of the Groomes" which she in darkness hastily gilded (II.ii.56f), she had now to see clearly and fully through the horrified eyes of young Lennox: in the dawn he found their "Hands and Faces . . . all badged with blood," the king's blood. "*If* he doe bleed . . ." (II.ii.55) she had exclaimed beforehand, wondering if the old man who resembled her father as he slept (II.ii.13f) would still be bleeding when she returned to his chamber with the daggers. What she discovered there appalled her—and will horrify

[30] The commonalty in the background can be represented on the stage by the Porter, now quite sober, and as many other underlings as the troupe can afford. Their faces and gestures here should surely express convinced and awed admiration of the great-hearted hero!

her increasingly, as she broods upon it, until the end of her life: "who would have thought the olde man to have had so much blood in him!" (V.i.44f). That horror she masked from her husband, with great effort, for his sake (II.ii.64ff). And just now she has managed to stand upright while he orated of the "Golden Blood" with which she gilded the grooms, not only their hands but their very faces, though, swaying, she must cover her own face with her hand. But his speech is successful; he has made the "fairest show" (I.vii.81): her husband will be king! Immense relief added to dumb, shuddering horror sinks her to the pavement.[31] There for a moment she supports herself on her hands, struggling to keep her head up—watched by all except Malcolm and Donalbain, who are stage-whispering to each other and to us —then falls prone in a dead swoon. Banquo, who has been eying the two princes questioningly, repeats Macduff's "Looke to the Lady" (124, 131). She is carried out.

And now the thanes, shaken by "Feares and scruples" (135), stare at one another and at the king's sons, doubtfully, confusedly. Who was it that employed the grooms to kill the king, or smeared them with blood after murdering him with their daggers, or with another and now hidden dagger? Some suspicion must attach to Macbeth. The immediate beneficiary, however, is the designated successor to the crown, Malcolm, Prince of Cumberland (I.iv.39). His quick conference aside with his brother was dubious; so is their present, uneasy, tearless silence (125,129): probably enough, they may have an understanding with Macbeth. And he, the king-maker, would be the chief power behind the throne of Malcolm—supported by his companion in arms, Banquo. Therefore to this nobleman, so silent since his leader's entrance (95), all eyes now turn. His ensuing apologia (131-138) concludes in a manner extremely impressive for all. Appealing to heaven with lifted hands he declares:

[31] Compare Hermione's swoon from mixed emotions: grief for her son's death on top of joy for the oracle's proclamation of her own innocence (*Winter's Tale*, III.ii.125-150). The notion that Lady Macbeth's faint is merely simulated, to cover Macbeth's indiscretion, misses the depth of Shakespeare's humanity and art in the climax of this great scene.

In the Great Hand of God I stand, and thence,
Against the undivulged pretence, I fight,
Of Treasonous Malice.

That "Hand" is rendered emphatic by the rhythm of the lines, by the two internal rhymes, and by the warrior's gesture when he exclaims "I fight": he drops his hands upon the cross of his sword-hilt, pledging himself as a fighter, a spiritual one now, on behalf of the justice of that vast invisible grasp *within* which, as he says, "I stand." That tremendous "Hand" is the end-sequel of all the hands that have figured in the play hitherto: Macbeth's fierce "hands" in gory battle (I.ii.21); the skinny hands of the weird Sisters gesturing in the mist or clasping one another (I.iii.32); the fearful hands of Lady Macbeth invoking evil spirits (I.v.41ff); Macbeth's "Hand" trying to clutch the airy dagger (II.i.34); and, especially, the bloody hands exhibited in the preceding scene (II.ii) and those pictured in the present scene (108). Previously we have been made to feel often the presence and oversight of "Heaven" (I.v.54, I.vi.5, I.vii.22, II.i.4-9) and of God Himself (II.ii.27ff). Now we are called upon to recognize the "Great Hand of God"—symbol of the unseen world of good, working in, through, and above men and nature; working in this drama hitherto, now, and doubtless in the "undivulged" (137) events to come; promoting affection which is humble, just, and merciful; gradually conquering "Treasonous Malice," i.e. treacherous wickedness, and establishing that which is right.

"And so doe I," says Macduff, laconically approving Banquo's assertion. "So all," the others declare in quick loud chorus—including Macbeth, speaking far more ironically than he knows (providentially he will "fight" against himself and shall not long be able to "stand"). Unanimously, too, all chime with Macbeth when he urges, significantly, "manly readinesse"—a quality far from apparent in the present demeanor of Duncan's sons—and when he seconds Banquo's proposal to "meet" (132-135,139f) for a thorough judicial questioning of "this most bloody piece of worke." Thus all agree in postponing decision in regard to the crowning of Malcolm. And they cast upon him, as they move off stage, looks of doubtful sympathy: in their view he is very possibly not guiltless. Thus *evil good-fortune* has favored Macbeth in a manner he did not foresee.

"Let's not consort with them," says Malcolm decisively when alone with his brother. The two princes know that it is easy for nobles to feign more "Sorrow" (142) than they really feel for the death of a king; and that the "Smiles" accorded to an heir after the destruction of a royal father may have "Daggers" in them (146). Certainly Macbeth is the one most to be feared— "The neere in blood, the neerer bloody"—but the others are also to be suspected as active or, at least, passive accomplices.[32] And since the secret killer would for obvious reasons try to do away with both the heirs at once, if opportunity offered, the two brothers determine to seek refuge in different localities, the younger in Ireland, the older in England. Involuntarily they are clearing Macbeth's way to the throne; but also, supposing they can save their lives, they will render his future dubious.

Thus the ensemble, owing to Macbeth's impious crime, ends in an atmosphere of general suspicion, suspense, and disorder; as will be vividly emphasized in the ensuing scene.

d. *the good Macduff* (II.iv)

The Old Man, pondering all the "Houres" he has seen, could well be an embodiment of "Time" (2f) itself.[33] When he alludes so knowingly to the very dreadful and strange "things" of the past "sore Night" we may feel, for the moment, that he has some mystical awareness of Macbeth's wicked doings. But he is roused from his broodings by his younger companion, Ross,

[32] Another notion that flattens the climax (see the preceding note) is the popular belief that the two brothers really suspect only Macbeth; see my next paragraph. Incidentally that notion is untrue to the conditions frequently depicted in Shakespeare's history plays, notably in Act II of *Richard the Third*.

[33] Hence his symbolic significance is narrowed when he is represented on the stage as a priest.

who points out that the "Night" still continues: "Ha,[34] good Father,"

> Thou seest the Heavens, as troubled with man's Act,   5
> Threatens his bloody Stage: by th' Clock 'tis Day,
> And yet darke Night strangles the travailing[35] Lampe. . . .

That metaphor is violently unnatural like the time: the journeying sun is laboring in the strangling, murderous clutch of murky air; though by human time—by the "Clock," unheard, that introduced the present act (II.i.2)—it is called "Day." The deathly silence of nature here, in contrast with the night's "unruly" noises reported by Lennox above (II.iii.59-66), renders the dark sky tomblike: "Darknesse does the Face of Earth intombe, / When living Light should kisse it" (9f).[36] Primeval chaos seems come again. The Old Man exclaims: " 'Tis unnaturall, / Even like the deed that's done." And now the strange images from inanimate nature are followed by intimations of the unnatural conduct of living creatures, all the way up from the mean mousing owl to Duncan's beautiful and swift "Horses" (14), emblems of vital loyalty. They turned "wilde in nature . . . / Contending 'gainst Obedience, as they would / Make Warre with Mankinde." Also they preyed viciously and amazingly upon each other (18-20)—as human beings do when they revolt against the natural moral law ruling "Mankind."

In direct contrast to all of that is "the good Macduff" (20), now entering with firm and quiet mien. He is very different, too, from his questioner and "Cousin" (36), the conventional Ross, who was conspicuously speechless in the preceding scene. And unlike Macbeth, Macduff has in his soul that high "Love"

---

[34] This exclamation is more fitting than the milder "Ah" substituted by Rowe and accepted by later editors: Ross, as stated above, is rousing the Old Man.

[35] This word and "traveling" were closely associated in the Elizabethan mind because of the great difficulty and danger of travel in those days.

[36] No doubt Shakespeare has in mind *Genesis* 1:2-5. The present passage goes far beyond Macbeth's gloomy allusion to "this Vault" (II.iii.101): he did not perceive the dreadful disorder, like that of the primal chaos, brought about by his crime.

(II.iii.116) or Charity wherein justice and mercy season each other,[37] free from the sentimentality that negates true sentiment, strong in right detachment and patience. Inwardly certain, now, that the new king, Macbeth, was guilty of the murder of Duncan he will give him no countenance. But he will take no action against him, now legally his sovereign, without sure objective grounds. Nor does he condemn the other leading nobles (including Banquo, here unmentioned) for choosing Macbeth as king (30f); and he condones the multitude of minor personages, represented by Ross, who without much reluctance are concurring in that decision. Such is the way of "the world" (21). Macduff recounts it with keen though not sour irony, unperceived by Ross but felt by the silently musing Old Man. The official and public verdict is: the king was murdered by "Those that *Macbeth* hath slaine," the two grooms; they were "subborned," and suspicion rests upon "the King's two Sonnes" because they "are stolen away and fled." Macduff makes no comment when Ross remarks sententiously: " 'Gainst Nature still, / Thriftlesse Ambition. . . ."

As for Duncan, Macduff thinks of him as wrapped in sacred peace. He utters a deeply simple requiem, unlike Macbeth's (II.iii.96ff), for the saintly king. Duncan's body, he says with intense but controlled emotion, has been "Carried to Colmekill," i.e. the holy island Iona,

> The Sacred Store-house of his Predecessors,
> And Guardian of their Bones. 35

For Ross and his like, however, more important now is "Scone," where Macbeth is to be crowned. Ross is disconcerted by his great kinsman's refusal to attend the coronation, but declares: "Well, I will thither." And Macduff plays upon that "Well":

> Well may you see things well done there—Adieu—
> Lest our old Robes sit easier than our new.

Prophetically he discerns that the new sovereign, outwardly so

[37] *Merchant of Venice*, IV.i.197.

promising but hiddenly guilty, may later oppress the very nobles who are supporting him. And now the Old Man also becomes prophetic. In parting with the two thanes he lifts his hands religiously to invoke heaven's blessing upon them—and upon certain others:

> God's benyson go with you, and with those   40
> That would make good of bad, and Friends of Foes.

That final line, like so much else in this drama, is arrestingly ambiguous. To "make good of bad" may mean, as in the case of Ross and the multitude, a politic obtuseness to the question of right and wrong, or an attempt to bring good results out of a bad situation, at the risk of stimulating further evil deeds.[38] Either course calls for the divine compassion. Immediately below, Banquo is shown to be following the second course, unconsciously turning his great "Friend" Macbeth into a deadly "Foe" (41).

e. *my Genius is rebuked* (III.i)

Banquo's conduct here is entirely in accord with the character given him by Shakespeare in the first two Acts: he is a high type of born loyalist. All along he has evinced a sincere, dignified, modest devotion to his two superiors, Duncan and Macbeth, notably in commending one of them to the other (I.iv.54ff, II.i.12ff). He has neither the mediocrity of Ross, Lennox, and their kind nor the rare moral greatness of Macduff, though he is far closer in spirit to the latter, his "Deare *Duff*" (II.iii.94), than to them. But unlike Macduff he has had no inward call to sequester himself from the new regime.[39] He deeply suspects Macbeth of foul play (3); which, however, as indicated in the

---

[38] Cf. "There is *some* soul of goodness in things evil, / *Would men observingly distil it out*" (*Henry the Fifth*, IV.i.4f). The words italicized by me express a qualification regarded by Shakespeare—and no doubt by his Old Man, above—as very important.

[39] Incidentally he has no great estate or fief, such as Macduff's Fife (II.iv.36), to retire to. The ingenious reader may appreciate the greater ingenuity of Shakespeare if he tries to figure out just what course, other than the present one, Banquo could have taken *at the present time*.

two preceding scenes, "the great Hand of God" has so far failed to demonstrate beyond all doubt. He must therefore continue, for the present, his loyal devotion to his leader in arms, so highly esteemed by Duncan, and now regularly chosen by the peers as Duncan's successor.

Moreover Banquo is following a course generally approved in Shakespeare's time and, after various fashions, in all times.[40] A new ruler who like Macbeth has obtained power by dubious means—for instance, a democratic politician who has stabbed the opposing party with falsehoods during the election campaign— is to be supported if outstandingly able and if he refrains in office from further evil-doing.[41] Nor is Banquo blameworthy for having a certain hope of his own: his ambition is without the illness that attends Macbeth's. No whit exulting in his present "Honor" at the new king's court and anxious as ever to "lose none" of the deeper sort (II.i.25-29), he cherishes the "hope" (10) that he may be "the Roote and Father" of "many Kings" if it be true that Macbeth, having done evil, is to be punished by the loss of sovereignty in his "Posterity" (4)[42]—Here his explication, to us, of his present conduct is interrupted by the entrance of the court: it will be continued and completed through his ensuing dialogue with Macbeth.[43]

As Macbeth and his Lady enter, crowned, robed, and richly attended, but with joyless eyes, our twofold suspense is renewed in heightened form: will the new king betray himself? will he show any sign of coming repentance? We perceive in him a restless uneasiness, effortfully controlled. The queen—she whom we last saw carried in a swoon from the stage—is erect now but very pale and reserved; she utters only a single brief speech during the present scene. Her onetime voluble and imperious support of

[40] Hence the theater audience, unless misled by critics, does not normally condemn Banquo here.

[41] In this respect a predecessor of Banquo, though a weak and comic one, is the Duke of York in *Richard the Second*, giving loyal support to the able usurper Bolingbroke.

[42] Such punishment is implied by the word "yet" (3) in its context.

[43] This is an instance of Shakespeare's dramatic economy, so extraordinary in the present play, demanding, and rewarding, the reader's closest attention.

her husband is all gone. This intensifies our suspense in regard
to him. But soon we find that his self-mastery, though difficult,
is remarkably accomplished. Every word he utters is, for his
hearers on the stage, innocent, cordial, and finely appropriate
to the occasion. Eying the solitary Banquo the new king exclaims,
"Heere's our chiefe Guest!" The expressive epithet "Guest"
(its significance will mount as the third Act proceeds) is startling
for us at first. But presently we learn that the sovereign and his
queen have planned for tonight a "great Feast" (12), "a solemne
Supper" (14), already announced apparently to all except Banquo, who takes no part in the ordinary social life of the court.
Now, however, when Macbeth politely but insistently requests
his "presence" at the great function "Tonight," he at once ac-
cedes. "Let your Highnesse," says Banquo,

> Command upon me, to the which my duties
> Are with a most indissoluble tye
> For ever knit.

That is a terse, courageous, and pithy declaration of the principle
that governs his relations with the present king. The secret
prophecy of "the weird Women" (2) ties his destiny to Macbeth's, and his "duties" to the Scottish throne make him quick
to obey all reasonable commands. When counsel has been required of him in important matters he has responded fully: his
"good advice," as Macbeth avers, "still [always] hath been both
grave and prosperous."[44] But he does not regularly attend the
daily meetings of the king's council (21-23); and, more significantly, the former personal intimacy between the two men
has been dissolved, less at Macbeth's instance than at Banquo's
own. He takes long rides on horseback in the afternoons by
himself (19) or with his son Fleance (36). His conduct towards
the king is dutiful and detached, patient and alert, mercifully
but strictly just.

[44] Here and in subsequent passages the dramatist artfully intimates that a long
period has elapsed since Macbeth's coronation. This may be termed narrative
time, different from the stage time in accordance with which this scene (note
the "now" in the opening line) follows immediately upon the preceding one.

All of that has rendered him admirable and helpful, but also deeply distressing, from the standpoint of his conscience-stricken sovereign. During their dialogue the restless Macbeth reveals to us that he both desires, and desires to be free from, his old friend's presence. Surreptitiously he gives him hostile glances; later he determines to destroy him; but he has not yet made up his mind to do so.[45] He wavers long and painfully, as before his murder of Duncan. Certainly he hesitates less now than then, but with a new and fatefully morbid confusion of mind. That confusion is conveyed to us by the dramatist with brilliant skill. When Macbeth says to Banquo, "Faile not our Feast" (28), he *mainly* expects his presence there, even while pondering a plan for secretly disposing of him beforehand. And he yearns to know what Banquo's reaction and advice will be at the council meeting "tomorrow" (33) in regard to the news of "our bloody Cousins" in England and Ireland, "not confessing / Their cruell Parricide, filling their hearers / With strange invention"—concerning his own crime! The possible guilt of Duncan's sons justified Banquo along with the others in crowning Macbeth. So the news from abroad is a crucial "State" matter that craves the joint attention (34f) of the king and his chief councilor. Just what will Banquo think and say of that matter? In Macbeth's tortured and tortuous imagination Banquo will be present tomorrow, and of course tonight. Barring mischance, supposing his "Horses swift and sure of foot" (38), Banquo will not fail—he, so strictly truthful, has promised he "will not" (29) fail—to be present at the feast this "Night" (36).[46] And, in the event, Macbeth's "strange invention" (33), that is his weird imagination, together with his conscience, does not fail to find him there!

Drawing a deep breath after Banquo's departure Macbeth addresses the others with particular graciousness, glancing from face to face, making "every man" (41) feel his cordial regard.

[45] The prevalent contrary opinion contradicts Shakespeare's conception of Macbeth's character and lessens the present dramatic suspense.

[46] The word "night" is iterated more succinctly and significantly during this and the next scene than in the scenes preceding Othello's murder of Desdemona.

The society of each and all of them, he intimates, will be fully as welcome as that of the distinguished Banquo "at Night" (42,36)—indeed, rather more *sweetly* (43) welcome. The "Adieu" and "Farewell" he uttered to his chief advisor (35, 40) are converted, when he dismisses the court, into a heartfelt "God be with you"! His bearing is rightly royal; commanding and dignified yet modest and kind.[47] And it intensifies the compassion elicited from us, along with condemnation, by his ensuing soliloquy. Outwardly he, an able and humane ruler, is "safely" established on the throne—inwardly, not:

> To be thus, is nothing, but to be safely thus:[48]
> Our feares in *Banquo* sticke deepe,
> And in his Royaltie of Nature reignes that   50
> Which would be feared. 'Tis much he dares,
> And to that dauntlesse temper of his Minde
> He hath a Wisdome that doth guide his Valour
> To act in safetie. There is none but he
> Whose being I doe feare: and under him   55
> My *Genius* is rebuked, as it is said
> Mark Antony's was by Caesar. . . .

His fears regarding Banquo do verily stick deep. Piercing his soul, like daggers of conscience and imagination (II.i.33ff),[49] they remain fixed. They may be removed only by penitence. But instead there is increasing, violent, confused remorsefulness. Two sorts of safety are hopelessly confused. We know that Banquo is *not* plotting to overthrow his king; and we feel that Macbeth knows it, or should know it, very well. What he really fears is his friend's noble "being" (55). Externally above him

[47] A comic antithesis is the bearing of Malvolio towards his subjects when he acts, in his imagination, the part of ruler of the realm (*Twelfth Night*, II.v.50ff).

[48] This line is generally divided in two after "nothing" in modern editions. (See notes in the *Furness Variorum* edition, page 179.) But the line as it stands is a rhythmic unit: its movement, hesitant in the first five words, climaxes solidly in the repeated and final "thus."

[49] "Like thorns," says Dover Wilson; but the idea of thorns of conscience is too conventional and weak for the present context.

Macbeth is spiritually "under him": his own "genius," his animating spirit, is tacitly rebuked by Banquo's, as the egoistic moodiness of the ambitious Antony was in the presence of the steadfast Caesar Augustus. Macbeth is too human, however, to hate his friend personally; as he praised the virtues of Duncan (I.vii.16-18) he appreciates here the valor of Banquo and the wisdom that enables him to act in "safety" (54). This word, echoing "safely" above (48), suggests in its present context moral security and equanimity. And Macbeth, still fond of his old friend, hates, though too proud to see and say so plainly, his own loss of that probity which Banquo has. This nobleman is a true loyalist as Macbeth once was, under Duncan, and could have continued to be; and he could have been so, by reason of his great gifts, far more fruitfully than Banquo. But now all the excellence that Macbeth sees in his advisor makes all that is within his own soul condemn itself for being there (V.ii.24f). Macbeth reigns; but over him reigns Banquo's "Royalty of Nature" (50).

And that spiritual ascendancy, at once stinging his conscience and dashing his pride, this king can no longer endure. But also he cannot bear the thought of destroying Banquo. So, submerging that thought entirely for the time being, he tries desperately to picture him as a dangerous political foe.[50] In the lines quoted above he surmises for a moment, vaguely and vainly, that Banquo is planning to "act" (54) against him; then abruptly drops that fancy. Presently, groping in the other's past, he avouches, fantastically, that Banquo "chid the Sisters, / When first they put the Name of King upon me, / And bade them speake to him" (57-59). That is a blatant distortion of his friend's dispassionate and "fair" (I.iii.51ff) words at the time; but it betrays Macbeth's acid recollection of his companion's warning, later, against evil ways of attaining "the Crowne" (I.iii.121), "the Name of King," now so hollow. It is a "fruitlesse Crowne" (he proceeds

---

[50] Thus Macbeth reproduces, in more deeply human and tragic sort, Iago's attitude to Othello, his antipathy to the other's very being and his assiduous search for tangible grievances against him.

to declare), joyless and "barren" of all contentment,[51] now and in the future, with "No Sonne of mine succeeding." In imagination he here sees Banquo as not merely the begetter of *some* kings (I.iii.67,118) but the "Father to a Line of Kings" (60).[52] And he *feels* his "Scepter" being "wrencht" from his "Gripe," as if right now, by "an unlineall Hand"—again that fateful word "Hand"! All of that may not "be so" (64); but he feels it so: and "nothing is, but what is not" (I.iii.141f). Accordingly,

> For *Banquo's* Issue have I filed my Minde,[53]   65
> For them, the gracious *Duncan* have I murthered,
> Put Rancours in the Vessell of my Peace
> Onely for them, and mine eternall Jewell[54]
> Given to the common Enemie of Man,
> To make them Kings, the Seedes of *Banquo* Kings!   70

He has ruined his soul, so he has now come to believe. His hopelessness for the earthly future extends now to that "eternal" life the thought of which he has hitherto shunned (I.vii.7). Worst of all, he, so fond of men, has given himself over to the Evil Power which is the hater of all men. His phrase here, "the common Enemy of Man," is expressive of his innate humanity. He judges himself as a man forever unforgivable.[55] But he is not unforgivable from the standpoint of divine (and Shakespearean) compassion. And the fact that he now sees more simply, plainly, and religiously than hitherto the wickedness of his murder of "the gracious Duncan" (66) is, in itself, promising. Many another ruler who established himself through the destruction of his predecessor (Shakespeare's Henry Fourth, for

---

[51] The reader is of course at liberty to restrict the words "fruitless" and "barren" to the literal meaning, childless. But I think my interpretation is justified by the whole context together with Shakespeare's habit, particularly in this play, of working words for all they are worth.

[52] The dramatist's compliment to King James I should not be allowed to obscure Macbeth's art of imagination here.

[53] Hamlet tainted his mind (I.v.85) but did not defile it.

[54] This recalls Othello's pearl (V.ii.347), alluding to the pearl of great price in Christ's parable (*Matthew* 13:46).

[55] As Othello does, more luridly (V.ii.273ff). In his case, however, despair leads to repentance, signalized by his execution of his criminal self.

instance) has considerably atoned for his crime by endeavoring to govern his realm as ably, justly, and mercifully as possible. And Macbeth, more than the average, is capable of so governing because of his rich humanity. For the same reason, however, he is unable to come to terms with his guilt: his humaneness makes it appear absolute and overwhelming. And his very security on the throne accentuates the remorseful insecurity of his soul.

Clearly his increasing misery can be overcome only by utter repentance. And that prospect, never closed by the God of "Peace" (67), opens widely for a moment upon his complete confession. But pride intervenes, along with that other deadly sin (in the Christian viewpoint) accompanying pride at its worst, namely despairing unbelief in God's mercy. Macbeth resents, instead of submitting to, the divine punishment inflicted upon him through Banquo's aloof and just attitude. He resents that which reigns over him in Banquo's royal nature (50f) and shall reign in his friend's offspring, future "Kings" (70). And so, finally, he discards Christian terms and challenges "Fate" (71) to the uttermost, wildly, vaguely—while still shrinking from the thought of destroying Banquo.

But now that thought begins to press heavily, unhappily, upon him. His extraordinarily long dialogue with "those men" (45) whom he has resummoned to his presence—two fellows as wretched in outward state as he is in spirit—is an elaborate and fantastic attempt to bring about the removal of Banquo without further burdening his own conscience. Sophistically he cultivates the feeling that, in this matter, he can maintain an "innocent selfe" (79). He strives to justify himself in his own sight while doing so in that of his two underlings. Apparently they are quondam and incompetent officials who were more and more demoted, and finally discarded, by decisions of the council instigated by Banquo but approved and carried out by the new king (21-23, 75-84); whom, therefore, they held responsible for their downfall, and heartily hated. Yesterday, however, just yesterday though the interval seems long and dreadful to the brooding, hesitating Macbeth—"Was it not yesterday," he asks them, "we spoke together?" (74)—he explained to them carefully every detail in the procedure against them, blaming Banquo, exculpating himself, and sympathizing with them. And he "went further" (85): he hinted at the possible removal of Banquo—then stopped and dismissed them, overcome by conscience.

And even now, though impelled by the incentives assembled in his soliloquy above, he still hesitates to broach the "point" (86), the need of Banquo's "Death" (108). He argues himself into a firm resolution while manipulating his two wretches, doing this with a fine human insight and political skill worthy of a good cause. Above he had to confess to himself the everlasting wickedness of his *murder* of Duncan (66); but he hopes to escape that necessity in the case of Banquo's "fall" (122), as he terms it. He will merely educe and condone the motives these two creatures already have for taking their opponent off (105). He himself is not to blame, surely, if they find their natures not dominated by Christian "patience"; if they are not "so Gospelled, to pray for this good man" (86ff)—good, really, in Macbeth's consciousness though he uses the word here satirically. And when they intimate that they are not saints but "men" he seizes upon that word to give them a satiric, challenging vision of "men" under the similitude of "dogs": some of them are distinguished from the canine (and human) mass as swift and sure hunters. Have these two men the "manhood" (103) to single out and run down their "enemy" (105)? If so they will be valued (95) highly by their king and grappled to his "heart and love" (106). All of that grips his hearers mightily. It makes these two *underdogs* feel that they have some worth of their own after all; and that they enjoy their sovereign's full sympathy and understanding—expressed with rough, genuine frankness— in regard to "the vile Blowes and Buffets" given them by "the World"; and so they become inspired with reckless, canine fierceness and courage (108-114). For us, however, the elaborate and tumultuous style of the Dog speech displays Macbeth's inward disturbance and moral confusion.

Banquo's very wholesomeness makes Macbeth bitterly aware

of his own soul-disease. We, the king, he declares, must "weare our Health[56] but sickly in his Life, / Which in his Death were perfect" (107f)—a pathetically gross illusion. And presently he goes further. With the unwitting aid of his two accomplices, now murderously hostile to Banquo, he is able to feel that his loyal though aloof advisor—instead of the Common Enemy of Man (69)—is *his* deadly "enemy" (105), "in such bloody distance / That every minute of his being," the "being" feared in his soliloquy (55), "thrusts / Against my near'st of Life" (116ff). Justifiably, from a royal-political viewpoint, he could sweep Banquo from his "sight" with "bare-faced power"; yet "must not,"

> For [because of] certaine friends that are both his, and mine,
> Whose loves I may not drop, but wayle his fall,
> Who I myselfe struck down: and thence it is
> That I to your assistance doe make love,
> Masking the Businesse from the common Eye,   125
> For sundrie weightie Reasons.

Those lines are saturated with a strange, uncanny mixture of policy and humanity. Love and friendship are precious to Macbeth. He "must" bewail—he does not say *seem* to bewail—his old friend's fall. And here his conscience makes him casually confess that it will really be himself, not his two instruments, who shall have struck Banquo down. Incidentally he suggests that these two, along with persons of higher rank, are now close friends of his. He has distinguished them above the "common" (125) run of his subjects. He has given them his sympathy and has evoked theirs for him: he extremely needs their "assistance."

Thus he captivates them, and at the same time drugs his own "Reason" (126, II.iii.117), definitively. They loudly devote to him their "Lives"; he cuts short their words with simple, warm appreciation: "Your Spirits shine through you" (128)—for us,

---

[56] The word "wear," in line with the incessant garment imagery of this play, suggests that without repentance Macbeth cannot have that *inward* "health" which is salvation.

an eerie light! He informs them that "it," the unspeakable deed, must be done this very "Night," and at some distance from the palace. They must keep constantly in mind that he requires "a clearnesse"; and we know that he yearns to keep not just his name but his spirit clear. Therefore it is with elaborate circumlocution that he now announces a further and, to the human heart, a far more shocking horror, the thought of which he has hitherto suppressed: Banquo's "Sonne" and close companion "Fleance" (36, 135), his sole heir, must also "embrace the fate / Of that darke houre." Can the two devoted accomplices stomach that? He tells them to go away, confer upon it together, and inform him later. But they, after a hasty whispering, curtly declare themselves "resolved" (139), fully conscious of the fact that the more they consider this new, inhuman task the harder it will seem: their "Spirits shine" more dimly now. Macbeth perceives their reluctance (hence his Third Murderer in III.iii) but knows it would be merely heightened by additional euphemistic words from him.

Also, he is exhausted: he postpones for a while the giving of explicit instructions to his two Murderers (128-131, 140). Alone again, he draws a deep, shuddering breath. "It is concluded," he breathes. And he thinks of the flight of his friend's "Soul" this very "Night" ("to Night" in the original): the word "night," incessantly repeated, becomes darker each time. He retires to brood upon Banquo's spirit, upon the blackening "Heaven" (142) above him, and upon the past, present, and future— restlessly, alone, as the next scene indicates.

f. *invisible Hand* (III.ii)

"*Banquo* . . . Night": those words in the two last lines of the preceding scene reappear in the first two lines of the present scene, in the dialogue of Lady Macbeth and her Servant. Banquo is "gone from Court" but returns again "to Night," this very night. He, for the new queen as for "the King" (3)—such is the quick suggestion here—is an embodiment of torturing conscience.

But unlike her husband she, soliloquizing now with simple brevity, does not confuse inward and outward safety (6, III.i.49ff):

> Nought's had, all's spent,
> Where our desire is got without content. 5
> 'Tis safer to be that which we destroy
> Than by destruction dwell in doubtfull joy.

Banquo, she knows, does not endanger the throne; but his innocent and noble presence, by day and by night, spoils the peace of two guilty souls. This presence banishes their contentment and renders dubious every touch of royal "joy"—for "all our Nights and Days to come" (I.v.70)!

But when Macbeth enters she instantly puts away all thought of self in her compassion (deepening ours) for the remorseful misery of her "Lord" (8) and "Husband" (II.ii.14). Their love for each other is strong as ever; but she has had to send a servant to request that she may have "a few words" (4) with him. Nowadays he secludes himself continually, even from her; despite his love of human companionship he keeps "alone,"

> Of sorryest Fancies your Companions making,
> Using those Thoughts which should indeed have died 10
> With them they thinke on: things without all remedie
> Should be without regard; what's done, is done.

Taking his hand, smiling haggardly, she pretends for his sake that her own remorse is "done," having died with "them" that "died." The weird series of plurals in that passage conveys her pathetic and fantastic effort to distract him from concentrated "Thought" upon a *singularly* wicked crime: the "Duncan" who haunts his memory (22,III.i.66) should be reduced, she insinuates, to a vague, nameless being among all those that are, just naturally, deceased!

For Macbeth, however (as secretly for her too), that which was "done" (I.vii.1) cannot be felt as ended. The insidious insistence of conscience—the implicit subject of his present speech as a whole (13-26)—is a "Snake" which his "poore" strength has "scorched" (slashed) in vain: he remains exposed to its poisonous "Tooth" (13-15). He speaks those sibilant lines with husky voice and sunk head. Then, rousing himself with convulsive violence, he challenges, instead of "Fate" as above (III.i. 71), the whole constitution of the universe, of the seen and unseen worlds:

> But let the frame of things dis-joynt,
> Both the Worlds suffer,
> Ere we will eate our Meale in feare, and sleepe
> In the affliction of these terrible Dreames
> That shake us Nightly—[57]

Loudly he declaims, shaking lifted fists against the dark sky, against "this Vault" from which his regicide has drained the very "Wine of Life," destroying "Renown and Grace" (II.iii.99-101). "Better be with the dead," he resumes, dropping his hands and lowering his tone,

> Whom we, to gayne our peace, have sent to peace,   20
> Than on the torture of the Minde to lye
> In restlesse extasie.

With awful cosmic irony[58] he has lost, in pacifying his restless ambition, the "Peace" (III.i.67) that passes understanding. He had better lie in his grave than on the invisible rack of frenzied remorse. So now his mind turns to the thought of "Duncan's body" in its "Sacred" rest (II.iv.32-34). And the ensuing lovely verses adumbrate the "Peace" that wraps the spirit, now, of the king who was so just, kind, and "meek" (I.vii.17), so "gracious" (III.i.66):

> *Duncane* is in his Grave:
> After Life's fitfull Fever, he sleepes well—
> Treason has done his worst: nor Steele, nor Poyson,[59]

[57] My dash replaces a colon which, followed (in the same line) by the capitalized "Better," indicates a pause and abrupt change of theme.

[58] Cosmic because it belongs to "the frame of things" (16).

[59] The "fitful fever" echoes *softly* the "restless ecstasy" above. The "poison" recalls the "snake" (13-15) and the earlier poisoned chalice (I.vii.11). And

Malice domestique, forraine Levie, nothing,   25
Can touch him further.

Thus, in Shakespeare's astonishing art, a murderer has been
brought, step by step, to the point of *affectionately*[60] envying his
victim—and just after he has been shown planning the murder
of a still closer friend! The new crime, however, is for the
time being forgotten by Macbeth.[61] He is entirely "lost" in his
"thoughts" (II.ii.71f) of the past. And so his wife, with loving
tact, opposes to "those Thoughts" (10) the happiest event of
the present, tonight's "great Feast" (III.i.12), urging him to
be "bright and Joviall" among his "Guests" (26-28). "So shall
I, Love," he responds, somewhat genially, "and so I pray be
you":

Let your remembrance apply to *Banquo*,   30
Present him Eminence, both with Eye and Tongue—

Vividly he sees in imagination (as he will in Scene iv see dreadfully) the eminent presence there of "our chiefe Guest" (III.i.
10). And we know he could still save his friend's life by counter-
manding his incomplete orders to the murderers (III.i.128-131,
140). Indeed we may wonder how he can now refrain from doing so. How can he proceed to consummate a murderous plot
that must redouble the racking soul-torture which, as he has
just come to believe, nothing but his own death can end?

He can do so only by rendering conscience subservient to
pride. The very thought of Banquo present at the feast, with all
his probity and loyalty, agonizes the conscience, but also the self-
pride, of him who has lost those virtues. "Unsafe the while"

"sleeps well" is of course in simple, beautiful contrast with the "terrible
dreams" that shake Macbeth nightly.

[60] The word "affectionately" is not too strong in view of all the previous
signs of Macbeth's fondness for Duncan. This extremely condensed drama
demands of the reader, in each successive phase, a vivid recollection—not explicitly stimulated by the dramatist, as in *Othello*—of what has preceded.

[61] This stroke of genius on Shakespeare's part is missed by those who assume that Macbeth in his next speech is merely deceiving his wife.

(32), Macbeth mutters abruptly and equivocally.[62] Unsafe as he is *in soul* he knows his *demeanor*, in confronting his chief counselor on this great public occasion, must also be unsafe, far more so than at their preliminary and informal meeting (III.i.10ff). And now regal pride asserts itself mightily. Must the royal host and also his queen, in the very zenith of their power and "Honors," disguise their "Hearts" by pouring forth streams of flattering approval (33-35) upon the very person whose presence is so ruinous for their contentment? Unbearable, he feels, is such humiliation.

She entreats him to "leave" (35) that thought. But he is entirely intent upon his misery; and his murderous project, reviving in his memory, is recapturing his will, enabled to do so effectually now because, as in the case of his first crime, he had allowed it to infect his will and imagination so deeply beforehand. He exclaims: "O, full of Scorpions"—offspring of the "Snake" above (13)—"is my Minde, deare Wife: / Thou know'st that *Banquo* and his *Fleance* lives." She rejoins with forced lightness that they are not to be feared as though they were things eternal in "Nature" (38). But he at once twists that epigram to suit his own dire purpose: "There's comfort yet, they are assailable, / Then be thou jocund"—the very last thing that she or he can in spirit be. He yearns for the comfort of her approval of the imminent "deed": he makes himself feel she will "applaud" it (she never will) afterwards. But now he will keep his "dearest" one "innocent of the knowledge" of it (45). He knows that his "deare Wife" (36) is close to the breaking-point. And his "great Love" (I.vi.23) for her, like hers for him, has been intensified by their present great unhappiness. Moreover, the thing that has to be "done" is even more "dreadfull" (43f) than his first crime, in which she took part. While he speaks of it, vaguely but terribly, she listens in wondering fear. She knows that further "destruction" (7) will be worse than useless. But she sees she cannot now deflect him; she strives in

[62] Hence critics need not opine that some words are omitted here from the text.

vain for words: he says, "but hold thee still" (54). And as she stands cold and rigid with dismay—she who a few minutes ago said "Come on" (26), trying to lead him away—he takes her arm with loving but commanding urgency: "So, prythee, goe with me" (56).

Thus threads of true affection gleam in the black texture of Macbeth's two final monologues in this scene. "Night" here, as not before, becomes an evil *real presence*. It comprises, but is larger and more meaningful than, the "black *Hecate*" (41) whom he cites. Unlike her, and unlike the night so often feminized in poetry, this "Night" (43) is sexless: it is a vast animate but impersonal being. It is secret and swift like the "Bat" flitting in a silent cloister; insensate[63] as the "shard-borne Beetle" that fills the air with mechanic humming, now low, now loud (42f), imposing a deathlike drowsiness upon the "Good things of Day" (52). Macbeth invokes this presence, this "Night," as formerly his wife invoked the evil "Spirits" (I.v.41ff), but with a far more concentrated and *active* horror. "Come," he breathes to this "seeling[64] Night,"

> Skarfe up the tender Eye of pittiful Day,
> And with thy bloodie and invisible Hand
> Cancell and teare to pieces that great Bond
> Which keepes me pale. . . .   50

Macbeth would put a heavy *band* upon the "Eye" of "Pitty" (I.vii.21,24) in his own heart so as to escape the *bond* that keeps his soul pale with fear. This "great Bond" consists of all the invisible ties and understandings by which his conscience keeps him "bound" (III.iv.24) to restless agony (22) regarding past, present, and future, mainly the past (10-26). The "Bond" is personified in Banquo and his son; but "they" (39) are not again mentioned by name in this scene. Macbeth deliberately submerges

---

[63] Insensateness is implied by "shard." Cf. the shards that might have been thrown upon Ophelia's body as that of a suicide (*Hamlet*, V.i.254). See notes on "shard-borne" in the latest editions of the play.

[64] I.e. blinding, particularly by sewing up the eyelids. This word, following upon "drowsy hums" above, suggests a cruelly forced, sleepy dullness.

the thought of them, as he did that of Duncan before his first murder (II.i.49ff)—but now with surpassing imaginational power—under a dark vision of the whole world of evil. In the former case he thought of wicked dreams abusing the curtained sleep (II.i.50f) because he was about to kill the slumbering Duncan in his bed, thus murdering innocent sleep (II.ii.36) and bringing upon himself "terrible Dreames" (18). But now he thinks of the dimming landscape around the castle where two awake and moving persons are to be destroyed: "Light thickens, / And the Crow makes Wing to th' Rookie Wood[65] . . . Whiles Night's black Agents to their Preys doe rowse" (50-53). It is as though all the dark powers, not Macbeth himself, will be responsible for the coming crime: he will not be present. Carefully he keeps himself, as he was not able to do in the previous case (II.i.33-49,57-62), out of the beautifully evil symphony.[66]

His coda, however, alludes significantly though impersonally to his own career: "Things bad begun make strong themselves by ill." He prides himself upon a growing wicked strength felt within; but we, along with his silent Lady, know that he is still extremely vulnerable. His total conduct in this and the preceding scene shows that his project of killing his conscience by *vicariously* killing Banquo is grotesquely hopeless: hence the melodramatic flavor of these two final lengthy speeches. Above all, his sudden, fearful image of the bloody hand betrays him. He has striven to keep the thought of Banquo's blood from his mind; but it obtruded itself once in the preceding scene (III.i.116), and now it obtrudes very awfully here (46-48). It is his own bloody "Hand," not cleansable by the ocean (II.ii.60f), that animates here the "invisible" and impersonal "Hand" of "Night." In quick contrast with the "tender" cruelty of the preceding line comes the gigantic brutality of that "Hand," descending to blot out the script in Macbeth's conscience and rip into pieces the "great Bond."

[65] The twilight forest, ominous with its hidden, restless rooks, is rendered more so by the great "Crow" winging thither in the murky twilight.

[66] His studied omission of the first personal pronoun is accentuated by the intrusion, at the middle of the speech, of a single "me" (50).

But the *spirit* of Banquo stands in the "invisible" (48) "great Hand of God" (II.iii.136-138); and, in the strength thereof, that spirit will fight against the "undivulged pretence" of powerful evil and "Trecherie" (III.iii.16).

g. *the lated Traveller* (III.iii)

Here, as in the opening of the play, three dim figures appear, and the Third, when questioned, utters abruptly the word *"Macbeth"* (2, I.i.7). And here, as there, it penetrates us deeply. That name, displaced in the two preceding scenes (and in the next) by regal titles, was last uttered by Banquo in soliloquy (III.i.7). It indicates that the person "Macbeth," not the new "King" (III.i.1, III.ii.3), is inevitably here in spirit. Outwardly he is represented by the Third Murderer, a mysterious, laconic fellow, sent by him to ensure the complete fulfilment of his plan. But, significantly, the scene adumbrates what must now be going on in Macbeth's mind: his spirit is as active here as Banquo's *ghost* will be in Scene iv.

Macbeth's last speeches, above, are reflected in the following lovely, ominous verse uttered by the First Murderer but inspired, we feel, by the imaginative master-murderer behind the scene: "The West yet glimmers with some streakes of Day" (5). "Light thickens" (III.ii.50) swiftly as the scene proceeds. The air becomes murky, full of oncoming "Rayne" (15)—the rain in which the three Witches loved to meet, hovering through the fog and filthy air (I.i.2,10). Their place is taken here by three more human and immediate instruments of the hell which is at work in Macbeth. "Night's black Agents to their Preys do rowse," while "Good things of Day . . . droope and drowse" (III.ii.52f). One good creature, however, is still active: "Now spurres the lated Traveller apace, / To gayne the timely Inne" (6f). Banquo is spurring but, unwittingly, towards a *timeless* Inn.

His and his son's horses are heard approaching, with rapidly increasing loudness. But a sudden stillness comes; then the clear

voice of "*Banquo within*" calling for "a Light." It is "hee"
(9), the Murderers know, unseen but now very "neere" (7).
Weirdly he remains invisible, and silent,[67] for a few moments,
while the three dim figures before us shrink back, huddling together and whispering (9-14). He has dismissed his horses; we
hear their retreating hoof-beats: they must take the long roundabout roadway. He, from hence to the palace "Gate"—reminiscent of another dreadful "Gate" (II.iii.2)[68]—is following a
short, direct path, making it his "Walke" (which will be completed by his spirit in the next scene).

Banquo appears, preceded by Fleance "*with a Torch*," as in
the former "Night" when he was about to accost his "Friend"
Macbeth (II.i.1,11). Here Macbeth's Three crouch together in
darkness, poised, and muttering "A Light, a Light" . . . " 'Tis
hee" (9,14). He, who in the opening of the second Act noted
that the "Candles" of "Heaven" were all out, exclaims now,
"It will be Rayne To-night"—as he stands there, searching the
sky, with honest face upturned in his small circle of "Light."

"Let it come downe," grunts the First Murderer, leaping
from darkness into that illumined circle, leading the other two
in raining sword-strokes upon that face and head (III.iv.27):
Banquo tries to shield "good *Fleance*" (16), urging the youth
to fly. We see blades flashing for a moment, then darkening: the
First Murderer has struck the torch from the hand of Fleance,
letting him escape. This is the eventuality which the Third Murderer was instructed by Macbeth to prevent. He demands sternly, "Who did strike out the Light?" The First replies, evasively,
"Was't not the way?" It was he who resented, though he dared
not reject, the company of the Third, and who soothed his restless conscience with lovely twilight verses (4-8). And now he
has spared "the Sonne" (19) in compensation for his leading
part in the brutal slaughter of the father, whose throat he cuts

---

[67] In stage performance I think his approaching footsteps should be soundless here, like those of his ghost in the next scene.
[68] This word has not been used in the interval.

after downing him to make assurance doubly sure (III.iv.16).[69]
Thus, as the Second Murderer grumbles, "We have lost / Best
halfe of our Affaire" (20f).[70] That is what Macbeth himself will
feel in the next scene with deep disturbance. The black deed that
has been done is not completely done—and never will be. The
First Murderer closes this scene, and prepares for the next, with
a climactic repetition of the word that has echoed and re-echoed
in this play since its initial utterance (I.i.3), the tragically ironic
word "done."

h. *those eyes* (III.iv)

The occasion is a "great" and "solemne" (ceremonious, even
sacred) "Feast" (III.i.12,14). It is designed, like the earlier offstage banquet (I.vii), to celebrate the peace, well-being, and harmony of the realm under a distinguished and generally approved
sovereign. To be sure the new ruler is not yet possessed of the
entire confidence enjoyed by his predecessor, Duncan. But he is
a legally chosen and "invested" and, presumably, Lord's anointed
king (II.iii.73, II.iv.30-32). So far, moreover, he has governed
discreetly, with the aid of the royal Council, meeting daily (III.i.
21-23, 33-35). He is particularly fortunate in having for chief
advisor his old friend "Noble *Banquo*," who is "knowne" (I.iv.
29f), together with himself, as a savior of the realm from domestic and foreign enemies: the two heroic names have been insepara-
ble in the public mind, "*Macbeth* and *Banquo*" (I.ii.34). All of
that has offset the suspicions attaching to Macbeth in regard to
the murder of Duncan. The lords are content to follow their new
leader in lamenting the late monarch (II.iii.96ff) and in regarding his two sons, now distant and powerless, as guilty of his destruction (III.i.30-35). And so this "*Banquet prepared*"—the
first words of this scene's opening stage direction—has a two-

---

[69] Compare the conscience of the First Murderer in *Richard the Third*
(I.iv.100ff,275ff).
[70] With brutal-humorous emphasis upon the word "Best." Here, as in
III.i.108-111, this fellow with his whining grossness is anticipatory of Caliban in *The Tempest*.

fold signification. It means the kingdom's readiness, after a period of dismay and doubt, to celebrate cheerfully the good order established by the new regime. More importantly it means that Macbeth, because of his human-kindness, cannot be satisfied with a sheerly political supremacy: he yearns to establish himself in the hearts (2,8f) of his people. He is determined to become the vital, as well as the official and sacred, head of "Society" (3)—*with the aid of the spirit of Banquo,* which, before long, he will movingly invoke (40ff).

Ceremonially but with genial gestures the king and queen, entering, pace to a dais at the rear supporting two thrones. The noblemen proceed to a couple of long tables which, conjoined at the middle of the stage in front of the dais, stretch away on either hand, with stools behind them, as thus:[71]

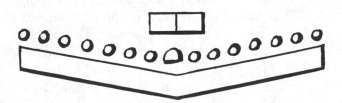

Leaving the central seat vacant, the peers stand in two equal rows (10), right and left of the dais, facing it with heads inclined while the sovereigns sit down. The most important nobles are nearest the thrones; the king, dispensing with the formality of ushering, has permitted them to arrange themselves according to their known "degrees" (1). And now he bids them "sit downe," glancing at each and all of them with warm regard, giving them "the hearty welcome." Unanimously they chorus their "Thankes to your Majesty."

Then, still more graciously, his "Majesty" rising from his throne descends to the floor level, declaring he will "mingle with Society," emphasizing that word—the "societie" he spoke

[71] Note that this arrangement, in contrast with the one advocated by Dover Wilson, renders the central stool the most prominent from the standpoint of the audience.

of so sweetly earlier in the day when he announced he would spend the afternoon "alone" (III.i.41-44). And we, knowing how he has conducted himself in the interval, are aware of an increasing uneasiness in his demeanor as he sets himself to "play the humble Host" (4); incidentally the word "Host" when previously uttered (I.vi.29, I.vii.14) was deeply tinged with irony and omen. However, he diverts the general attention from himself to "Our Hostesse," who remains enthroned; later he will require her to descend and give the company an intimate welcome. "Pronounce it for me, Sir, to all our Friends," she says in a loud, clear voice, trying to steady him, "For my heart speakes, they are welcome." But no sooner has that word "welcome" been uttered, for the third time (2,6,8), than a dreadful object, glimpsed by Macbeth, appears in a doorway at one side in the rear: the First Murderer bespattered with blood.

"See," exclaims the king (seeing what no one else sees, but at once controlling himself) as all the company rise and bow deeply towards the queen—"See, they encounter thee with their hearts' thanks!" He motions them to reseat themselves and attend to the repast. Pointing to the empty stool in the midst he declares he will sit there, presently, and partake of a cup going the rounds, thus identifying himself with all of them; he urges them to be "large in mirth" meanwhile. As ,he speaks he steps backwards and away, towards the door, while the guests properly refrain from turning their heads to watch him. Evidently the ruler has suddenly bethought himself of one or another "cause of State" (III.i.34) demanding a few moments of private attention.

He, confronting the First Murderer, recoils in horror. Not only are the fellow's hands and garments gory: "There's blood upon thy face!" This is the blood which Macbeth had carefully planned to keep invisible. The fellow, hitherto unaware that his very face is streaked with it, declares, " 'Tis *Banquo's* then." And Macbeth, mastering himself with a convulsive effort, mutters in cryptic haste, " 'Tis better thee without, than he within" (14) —better that his blood (this word he avoids repeating here and in the rest of the colloquy) should appear on you so horridly than that he himself should appear within this room. Macbeth has a feeling, swiftly intensifying, that his friend Banquo *may* appear "within." Therefore he adds, "Is he dispatched?" and later comes the still more urgent query, "But *Banquo's* safe?" (25). For meanwhile he has learned of Fleance's escape and is still more deeply disturbed:

> Then comes my Fit againe:
> I had else beene perfect;
> Whole as the Marble, founded as the Rocke,
> As broad, and generall, as the casing Ayre:
> But now I am cabined, cribbed, confined, bound in
> To sawcy doubts, and feares.   25

His fears, we perceive, are not mainly due to Fleance; this lad is too small a cause for the magniloquent complaint of those great lines. As he says in his next speech, "the worme that's fled" is no present danger: his thoughts are obsessed by "the growne Serpent"—literally Banquo but really "the Snake" of awful remorse which "the frame of things" has fastened upon his soul and which he has tried in vain to kill (III.ii.13ff). He had hoped to surmount his inward division, to become a "perfect" (entire) man, whole and firm like the rock-built earth, intact and free in scope like the air that encases it—a really "Royall" (19,32) sovereign. But now he feels as though imprisoned in a hovel (cribbed), shackled and tortured, "bound in" far more than ever before to importunate, bitter doubts and fears.

His condition is the worse, moreover, because he cannot picture Banquo as at peace like Duncan in a distant and "sacred" grave (II.iv.34, III.ii.19ff). His friend's grave, a nearby ditch, is a gory horror devoid of peace, presently to be associated in Macbeth's mind with "Charnell-houses," and with the still more horrible image of human bodies devoured by birds of prey, buried thus in the "Mawes of Kytes" (71-73). Banquo, treacherously slaughtered, is surely not sleeping well, out there in a trench, with "trenched" (27) gashes in his head and slashed throat, doubtless still bleeding.

"Thankes for that"—those ghastly thanks Macbeth blurts out, shuddering. He can bear to hearken no more now. He will hear more when he shall be himself again "to-morrow"—that normal tomorrow (cf. III.i.33) which will never come. Dismissing his bloody companion he moves towards the feasting company with blind, entranced mien. His Lady, watching him anxiously from her place of vantage, speaks studiously pointed, rousing words (32-37): she urges him to provide constant cheer and welcome for "the Feast," else the occasion is a mere "Meeting." But another sort of meeting and ceremony have been provided by the invisible "World" (III.ii.16). In the doorway from which the First Murderer vanished another gory figure suddenly, motionlessly, appears, seen only by Providence and by us, while Macbeth, inclining his head towards his queen, mutters "Sweet Remembrancer"! And now the unsweet remembrancer, *the Ghost of Banquo*," advancing slowly and steadily, "*sits in Macbeth's place*" (in the words of the stage direction) while the king himself is pacing unsteadily, nervously, to the far end of the table, mechanically wishing "good digestion," "Appetite," and especially "health" to his guests, who this time are watching him wonderingly.[72]

As Macbeth returns towards the center, Lennox pressingly invites "your Highnesse" to sit. And the king, coming to a standstill, utters a speech wonderfully and pathetically mixed in its motives:

> Here had we now our Country's Honor, roofed,   40
> Were the graced person of our *Banquo* present—[73]
> Who, may I rather challenge for unkindnesse,
> Than pitty for Mischance!

[72] The modern view of the Ghost as sheerly a figment of Macbeth's imagination weakens the drama very much. That view, held by Lady Macbeth and eventually but dubiously adopted by the hero himself, is contravened by the fact that the specter appears to us (and in a very significant manner) *before* it is discerned by him. Certainly he is carefully prepared by Shakespeare to be the sole person on the stage to perceive it. But the apparition is not merely psychological: it is religiously sent to punish Macbeth.

[73] Here as elsewhere, but with special effect, a dash is substituted by me for the Folio's colon.

As after his first murder, he is assailed by a yearning that his victim could suddenly come alive again (II.ii.74). He feels anew that "Renown and Grace is dead" (II.iii.99): Banquo like "the gracious *Duncan*" (III.i.66) is a "graced person" (41) in Macbeth's remorseful memory. His eyes rove the table staring at the guests, one after another, with vague intentness. This noble company which he had hoped to delight in, all loyally assembled under the royal roof, "our Country's Honor," is sadly incomplete without "our *Banquo*"; he ought to be here: indeed he seems in some strange way really to be "present." Gripping himself the *kind* host expresses the hope that his friend's absence may be due to *unkindness*, not pitiable "Mischance." But the compassion that seizes him here, like an earlier onset of "Pitty" (I.vii.21), unmans him further and makes him still more acutely aware of the presence of Banquo's spirit, somehow, in this room.

And that awareness is intensified when Ross reminds him of Banquo's "promise" (44), that solemn, unfailing promise (III.i.28f), to be present here, and urges him to sit and "grace us"—echoing Macbeth's "graced" above (41)—with "your Royall Company." But this, exactly, is what the guilty host cannot do. He knows he does not deserve the regal and gracious terms applied to him by the company. He cannot take part in this fellowship with real regality and real grace of spirit; he cannot take seat among the innocent and noble guests. But Banquo could—and must in fact have done so! "The Table's full," the king exclaims, glancing wildly from one seated figure to another, dreading, but finally constrained, to fix his gaze intently upon the place to which the nearby noblemen are pointing, termed now by Lennox "a place reserved" (46). This is the place designated by Macbeth for himself (10). But it became a place reserved, he thinks, for a "graced person" (41) with "Royalty of Nature" (III.i.50); and Banquo, acting as ever boldly and wisely, has assumed the seat, with the collaboration, doubtless, of other courtiers. Macbeth's face is contorted with dread and suspicion. Hoarsely he demands, "Which of you have done this?" But that fatal word "done" causes the apparition to turn upon Macbeth its accusing face, the face that has been haunting him, marked with gore—the blood which his own hand could not and did not shed. The wretched man cries out:

> Thou canst not say I did it—never shake 50
> Thy goary lockes at me!

The guests rise and stare. But the queen, descending from her chair of state because required by the king, though otherwise than he meant, induces them to reseat themselves and attend to their repast, ignoring him. Her manner with their "worthy Friends" (53), imitative of the manner her husband had wished to use constantly, is properly royal, familiar but not in the least condescending, at once friendly and firm. The tragedy is sharpened by the fact that the two of them, if free from evil, would have supported each other excellently in a very human kind of sovereign sway (I.v.71). And her explanation of his present state of mind, "my Lord is often thus, / And hath beene from his youth," is truthful enough. Always, by reason of his intense humanness, the inward contemplation of inhuman projects has filled him with fearful imaginings. Only by violently banishing such contemplation, with the aid of various and strange devices, has he been able to nerve himself to do his crimes and to achieve self-control afterwards.

But obviously his self-control before (II.i) and, in public, after the murder of Duncan (II.iii) far surpassed that exhibited just before the murder of Banquo (III.ii) and immediately afterwards, in the opening phase of the present scene. The very elaborateness of his latest scheme for circumventing his conscience foreshadowed its failure. His meticulous persuasion of the Murderers (III.i.74ff) made the crime more vivid to him than if he had, as in the case of Duncan, done it quickly and secretly himself. In imagination he *staged* (III.iii)[74] this "deed of dreadfull note" (III.ii.44) and continued to do so, with mounting horror, while listening to the First Murderer's account

---

[74] Hence, of course, Shakespeare's decision to present the second murder, unlike the first, on stage. In witnessing it we can *feel* Macbeth witnessing it too.

of it, increasingly unable to submerge his awareness of himself as the real protagonist. Hence his initial, agonized, vain outcry to the Ghost, quoted above. In spirit he knows that his friend's spirit knows all his dreadful guilt: his genius, more than he foresaw, is rebuked "under" Banquo (III.i.49-57). And so, for a while (52-58), he stands facing the specter in a silence as deeply significant as its own. Through the providential medium of this *outward* apparition he contemplates *inwardly* that which he feels "might appall the Devill" (60), his own accumulated wickedness.

His raptness here is the climactic sequel of that which he experienced at the first (I.iii), also in the presence of Banquo and others. Then, he was obsessed, function was smothered, by the "horrid Image" of a murder he might commit in the future: "nothing is, but what is not" (I.iii.135ff). Now, nothing is but what has been: the horrid image of it is in him, and before him. Then, it was Banquo who recalled the "Worthy *Macbeth*" (I.iii. 148) to himself and to a genial awareness of the presence of his admiring companions. Now, with great dramatic irony, Banquo's spirit obliterates the king's awareness of the festive company around him, by means of which he had hoped to bury all thought of Banquo except for gracious memories. The austere apparition makes the no longer "Worthy" Macbeth betray himself irreparably to others while summoning him to face, directly and fully, his own sinfulness.

So now occurs a battle more awful than that which opened the play but, like that, initially "Doubtfull" (I.ii.7): the crucial battle between the pride and the conscience of Macbeth.[75] His conscience is abetted by the spirit of his best friend; his pride, by his beloved wife. She indeed (as will be shown definitively in V.i.) has no disbelief in conscience, and she no longer cherishes any

[75] This episode is the tragic acme of a situation recurrent in Shakespeare's works. For combined depth, concision, and vividness it surpasses the Temptation scene in *Othello* (III.iii). There the hero's pride is elaborately, but somewhat factitiously, abetted by a false friend, Iago; his conscience is stirred by Desdemona's appearance, but not so dramatically and deeply as Macbeth's by the ghost of his most intimate friend.

hope of inner "content" (III.ii.5) for herself and her husband; but in his presence, trying to alleviate his ruinous misery, she suppresses her own remorse. That was what she did after his first crime with mighty resolution (II.ii.13ff); before his second, with weary, gentle quietness (III.ii). And now, summoning all her remaining strength, she does so once more, this time with preternatural force and skill, seemingly inspired again by the demonic world (I.v.41ff), desperately trying to enable him to overcome the preternatural disturbance that bids fair to ruin his rule of his kingdom, now, as well as his rule of himself. Whispering at his ear she appeals, as at the first (I.vii.46ff), to his manly courage (58-68): "When all's done"—this fateful word again—"You looke but on a stoole!"

But during her speech the specter slowly rises from that stool, to more than mortal height, while Macbeth watches with fearful gestures (63) and contorted visage (67). And when it silently inclines its head towards him (70) he recoils violently, pulling his wife back with him, whispering to her and to it, urging her to "see" and it to "speake"; but its silence, better than words, is speaking to his soul. She, looking and seeing nothing, and pierced by his ghastly ejaculation regarding birds of prey (71-73) —recalling an earlier dreadful speech that silenced her (III.ii. 50ff)—cannot help shuddering, though quickly she regains self-control. He with a mighty effort banishes the specter, or his sight of it, for the time being,[76] but stands trembling, "quite unmanned," she says, "in folly." But he knows that this vision is far from folly. Whatever may have been the nature of "the Ayre-drawne-Dagger" (62) ridiculed by her, he is certain of the supernatural reality of the present apparition. "If I stand heere," he avers with solemn certitude, "I saw him" (74). And

---

[76] The Folio has no stage direction here regarding the Ghost. Originally perhaps, instead of utterly disappearing through a convenient opening in the floor, or otherwise, it retreated to the doorway by which it entered, and stood there visible to the audience and ready for reappearance to Macbeth. On the modern stage, by means of a dimmed spotlight and other devices, it can be made to remain obscurely visible to us, indicating its continued presence in Macbeth's mind.

so, staring into space and ignoring her bitter word "shame," he
declares *loudly*:

> Blood hath bene shed ere now, i' th' olden time   75
> Ere humane Statute purged the gentle Weale:
> Ay, and since too, Murthers have bene performed
> Too terrible for the eare. The times have bene
> That when the Braines were out, the man would die,
> And there an end—But now they rise againe   80
> With twenty mortall murthers on their crownes,
> And push us from our stooles. This is more strange
> Than such a murther is—

That speech, if he had continued it, could have been a full,
public confession of his wickedness. Here the word "murder,"
generally shunned by him, notably at the ensemble after his first
crime (II.iii), is uttered thrice, for all to hear, in a context awfully significant. The twenty deep "gashes" (27) on Banquo's
head mentioned by the First Murderer have become in Macbeth's vision twenty "murthers" destroying the very "Braines"
of his friend—but not the spirit that was therein resident. This
spirit has pushed him away from the royal seat gained by secret
and "terrible" slaughters which have violated the "humane" and
"gentle" commonweal fostered by the preceding king and loved
by the better self of Macbeth. He had planned to celebrate that
commonweal by the present grand feast, leaving behind him,
rising in spirit above, his very "strange," unnatural crimes. But
the unseen "World" (III.ii.16) has taken action even "*more
strange*" than the horribly brutal "murder" of his friend "is"—
He stops short on the word "is": *must* this deed still exist in
his mind, unnerving and humiliating him, keeping him from being the king that he *is*? Complete and plain confession is balked
by his pride—with the aid of his wife, she too now speaking
loudly, in a firm, clear tone: "My worthy Lord, / Your Noble
Friends do lacke you." Surely he *is*, and can more and more be,
a worthy and noble "Lord" in the midst of his worthy and noble
supporters. He apologizes to "my most worthy Friends"; he

attributes his amazing conduct to "a strange infirmity" (86), thus transforming the context of his word "strange" above (82), and trying to make himself believe that his awful vision is "nothing." With loud geniality he exclaims: "Come, love and health to all, / Then I'll sit downe"—significantly adding the word "love" to the "health" he wished them above (39)— "Give me some Wine, fill full."

But now, as all rise to drink that wine with their king, the "Wine" that means to him a new and free and humane life, we perceive the Ghost again in the midst, this time *standing*, like the others. We see it with swiftly increasing clearness because Macbeth is thus seeing it in his mind. And this vivid inward vision obscures for him the faces about him, which he will not again see clearly till later (115). They are very dim to him as, with goblet in hand, he surveys the company, which he finds tragically incomplete. He knows that Banquo should be here; without his noble presence how can the harmony and "joy" (89) of this great occasion be real and full?

> I drinke to th' generall joy o' th' whole Table,
> And to our deere Friend *Banquo*, whom we misse—   90
> Would he were heere—to all, and him, we thirst,
> And all to all.

This is the "Measure" the king was about to "drinke" (11) when interrupted by the First Murderer with Banquo's blood on his face. And all the lords, with a strange uneasiness reflecting his, raise their cups. "Our duties," they exclaim in desultory chorus, "and the pledge," the pledge directed very particularly to the missing guest, "our *Banquo*" (41), now "our deere Friend *Banquo*" (90). But the pledge the king so thirsts for is not drunk. His magnificent goblet falls crashing; so do the cups of the others, some onto the floor, some onto the table: the wine of vital and general joy is spilled.

For Macbeth's gaze has concentrated, slowly, fearfully, upon a spectral face confronting him, and his eyes glare into "eyes" which responsively "glare" into his (95f). Entranced he speaks spasmodically:

> Avaunt, and quit my sight, let the earth hide thee:
> Thy bones are marrowlesse, thy blood is cold—
> Thou hast no speculation in those eyes   95
> Which thou dost glare with.[77]

Thus he tries to regard "him" (74), the spiritual person animating the apparition, as a mere cadaver, a lifeless thing belonging underneath the senseless earth. But "those eyes," which he knows so well, which have so often regarded him intently and intimately, are not lifeless though so dreadfully fixed. Devoid of "speculation," of natural human sight, they are aflame with supernatural judgment of him. And now for a few moments he stands as still and speechless as the Ghost itself, not hearing the queen as she, again on her dais, entreats the forbearance of the "good Peeres" (96-98), undergoing the awful condemnation in the eyes of his "deere Friend"(90).

But again his pride forestalls confession and penitence. He stirs and, stepping back a little, rouses his self-will. "What man dare, I dare" (99)—a fateful reproduction of the boast that immediately preceded his first crime (I.vii.46). He proceeds to proclaim his bravery to the specter, and to its supernatural world, with a fantastic magniloquence in striking contrast to his hushed averment of his courage above (59f). He adjures the spirit to take the form of some ferocious but *natural* creature; or to assume its own body again and "dare me" (104), sword in hand, to a combat in the "Desart," the fearfully dangerous and lonely but natural wilderness. Thus, summoning up all his great natural courage, he strives to overcome his great moral "trembling" (103,105) brought about, climactically, by the supernatural light streaming from "those eyes" in the murdered face of his friend. Finally he applies to his own daunted and humili-

---

[77] This passage is parallel in situation to the one in which the ghost "glares" at Hamlet (III.iv.125-130), as it did not do when it first appeared to him (in I.iv and I.v). In both cases the dramatist reserves for a great crisis the look in the specter's *eyes*.

ated self a term surpassing in bitter scornfulness all of his wife's
reproachful words: "The Baby of a Girle." Then, with a surpassing effort of arrogant will, he manages to make himself believe that the "thou" (100) whom he has been addressing all
along is an impersonal thing; that this real spirit is just a horrible mocking fantasy unmanning him. And so, suppressing his
conscience violently, he is able to dismiss the vision effectually:
"Hence, horrible shadow, / Unreall mockery, hence!—Why so,
being gone, / I am a man againe.—Pray you, sit still."

He himself dare not sit, nor glance again at the vacant stool
in the midst. He surveys the nobles blankly. Now "the mirth"
(109), as the queen points out, is all gone: he has ruined "the
good meeting" with his amazing conduct. And suddenly he
realizes that no one else has felt, in the least, that which he has
suffered. All the others are "naturall" (115): his own "disposition" is, for a "man" (108), strangely unnatural. He, guilty,
is also utterly solitary. He speaks with a pathetic simplicity at
the opposite pole from the melodrama of his preceding speech:

> Can such things be,   110
> And overcome us like a Summer's Clowd,
> Without our speciall wonder? You make me strange
> Even to the disposition that I owe,
> When now I thinke you can behold such sights,
> And keepe the naturall Rubie of your Cheekes,   115
> When mine is blanched with feare—

Can he refrain, now, from telling his friends how different his
awful vision was from the transient shadow of a pleasant sum-
mer-cloud?

But he reads in the flushed faces around him a suspicious aloofness which his conscience immensely magnifies: these faces accuse him, he thinks, as much as did Banquo's visage rubied (115)
with its blood. And now his mind is flooded with the memory of
his self-betraying exclamations to the specter in regard to blood
and murder. His own blanched face (116) flushes heavily; and
he starts back as from a very ghost when Ross, close at hand,

inquires sharply, "What sights, my Lord?" He can make no reply of any kind. He is dumb with confused passions, remorse, fear, suspicion, and, above all, proud rage: "he growes worse and worse" (117f), as his queen notes. She dismisses the guests in haste. Lennox, despite her injunction to "speake not," says with cool irony: "Good night, and better health / Attend his Majesty." Remote from majesty is the king's present mien; and the "health" together with "love" (39,87) which he had wished for the company, including himself, is very far from attending him. While his Queen haggardly speaks "A kinde good-night to all" he, unkind, remains as silent to all as the Ghost was to him.

And now that silence, like the specter's, means utter and fearful (116) condemnation of himself. Alone with his wife, he ejaculates desperately (122):

> It will have blood, they say—
> Blood will have Blood:[78]

The "It" and "they" are suggestively inclusive: "they," all human beings, including those he has just been confronting, know that "It," "the frame of things" (III.ii.16), provides "judgement here" and "Bloody" retribution (I.vii.8f) for murderous deeds. And the same testimony, he proceeds to aver, is given also by natural objects, inanimate and living, "Stones . . . Trees . . . Rookes," the last two recalling his ominous "Rookie Wood" (III.ii.51). All persons, all things, all happenings conspire to bring forth, to exhibit to himself and others, the "secretest man of Blood" (125f). Public exposure and "torture" of conscience have now, in his case, combined to render his restless ecstasy (III.ii.21f) no longer bearable. What shall he do? We know there is no real escape for him except through repentance; and here, as in so many similar crises in Shakespeare's works and in the Elizabethan drama at large, a penitent motion on the part of the protagonist would be in order.

[78] In modern editions the two lines have become one, with loss of emphasis and often with misleading punctuation: "It will have blood; they say, blood will have blood." Properly the "It," as I indicate above, is not identical with "Blood" in denotation; its meaning is far more comprehensive.

For Macbeth the "Wine of Life" is not merely all drawn (II.iii.100), that "Wine" (88) for which he has been yearning so ardently at the feast: it has now been turned into "Blood." This time no device, no fine sentiment or gesture, can serve to veil the fact announced by him with new plainness: "It . . . will have Blood." His present speech differs from all his previous monologues in its intensity of moral conviction. He cannot comfort himself, as before, with the feeling of something in his soul that is really above his evil deeds, a spirit of "Love" (II.iii.116) and human-kindness which, cooperating with "worthy Friends" (85-92), can live down those deeds. He knows now, as never before, that he has become, simply, a "man of Blood" (126)— and of darkness. "What is the night?"[79] he exclaims to his wife, who, far more exhausted than in their previous private conference (III.ii), is listening to him with climactic, yet hopeless, sympathy and horror in preparation for her next and final appearance in V.i. She replies laconically, and significantly: "Almost at oddes with morning, which is which." Darkness and light are warring in his soul now: he must choose between them. He could revive and obey the abortive motions of humility and penitence that he experienced under a series of providential admonishments in the darkness after his first crime (II.ii). His need now is far greater than then; it has been rendered definitive by the workings of the powers of light. But the powers of darkness cunningly persuade him to revive and strengthen his defiant pride.

His sense of utter guilt causes him to recall the fact that the innocent and great Macduff has not yet appeared at court. Suddenly, and startlingly for his Lady (129) and for us, he declares: "How sayst thou that *Macduff* denies his person / At our great bidding" (128f).[80] This speech, ostensibly a question to his wife, is really an exclamation to the world of darkness. "How sayst thou"—i.e. thou art telling me in some strange manner—recalls and opposes "they say," above (122). "They" (representing the

---

[79] The word "night" is the quick sequel of the word "secretest" (126).
[80] A question-mark, supplied by modern editors, is conspicuously and rightly absent here in the Folio text.

world of light) have brought his wickedness home to him; and he knows that Macduff has a great nobility forfeited by himself. If his remorse is to be converted into penitence he must, at the very least, refrain from hostile feelings towards that nobleman. But he does not refrain. He yields to the sudden, strong impulse to believe that his sovereignty has been positively repudiated by the Thane of Fife. This, as we know (II.iv.20ff), is not the case; and presently we are informed that Macduff has not yet plainly disobeyed a specific royal summons (130). But now he embodies, in place of and more powerfully even than Banquo, the conscience of the king. Conclusively the conscience of Macbeth is requiring repentance; otherwise, as he now knows, it will utterly undermine his sovereignty, outward and inward—unless by utter egoism he can undermine his conscience. And he initiates this evil process by refusing to bear the humiliation of Macduff's aloofness. He must force this person, under whom his "Genius" is supremely "rebuked" (III.i.56), to support him in mastering, greatly (129), his kingdom and his remorse.

Thus Macbeth is impelled into further and worse evil-doing by a diabolic but very human mixture of pride and conscience, hell's masterpiece. Accordingly he determines to consult the special instruments of hell and of darkness, the Witches, "to-morrow . . . betimes" (132f)—in the early hours of this "morning" (127) which could have "brought forth" (125) new light and life for him. Here he is far closer in spirit to "the weyard Sisters" than ever before, and we foresee that this time, as not at the first (I.iii.70ff), they will abide his questioning and tell him more.

> More shall they speake: for now I am bent to know
> By the worst means, the worst, for mine own good,[81]　　135
> All causes shall give way. I am in blood
> Stept in so farre, that should I wade no more,
> Returning were as tedious as go o'er—

[81] The modern full stop after the second "worst" stops the full flow of the sense. The words "for mine own good" have floating power as an adverbial phrase modifying the preceding and following predicates.

Tragic irony is in his new phrase "mine own good," following immediately upon the repeated word "worst," and ushering his resolution to scorn all the "causes" that all along have importuned him, especially in the present scene, to seek his own *real* good. He will make them "give way" (136), as at the first the brave Macbeth carved out his passage through hostile ranks, so bloodily (I.ii.16ff). He will "wade" ahead "in blood," the innocent blood which has now rendered all the waters of his imagination indeed one "Red" (II.ii. 63)—towards no discernible shore but, he fancies, "farre" (137) away from conscience. With satanic arrogance he avers that "Returning,"[82] i.e. repentance sought with religious patience, would be equally "tedious." Really he is stepping, for the first time deliberately, into the awful tedium which (as in Dante's *Inferno*) characterizes hell.

Into it, but not into its utmost depths. We cannot believe he will succeed in utterly annulling his "great Bond" (III.ii.49) of human-kindness. Just now it prevents him from definitely visualizing further deeds of "blood" (136); this word, a main theme of the present scene, does not recur in his concluding lines (139ff). Suddenly clasping his temples he mutters wildly: "Strange things"—not "Bloody things," as hell's logic would require—"I have in head, that will to hand, / Which must be acted ere they may be scanned." He dare not here (as once he did) look upon that "hand" so very much incarnadined. He stands silent for a moment in abstraction so nightmarish that his queen ventures to urge: "You lacke the season of all Natures, sleepe"—a lovely ironic echo of his own lines upon sleep (II.ii. 39). Now less than ever may he hope to "sleepe" in "peace" (III.ii.17ff). But, taking his wife's hand, with acute awareness of her selflessness and exhaustion, he promises that "wee" (in emphatic contrast with her "You") will together achieve some sort of sleep:

[82] This word is a well known Christian synonym for repentance, derived from Isaiah 30:15, "In returning and rest shall ye be saved."

Come, wee'l to sleepe.—My strange and self-abuse   142
Is the initiate feare, that wants hard use:
We are yet but young in deed.[83]

Certainly those monosyllabic lines have a simple, surpassing dreadfulness. Devilish pride has enabled him to convince himself that all the admonitions given him by the just and merciful heavens, from his initial "Fears" (I.iii.137) to the great panic inspired by the ghostly "eyes" (95ff) of Banquo, were merely delusions due to "a strange infirmity" (86) of his singular "disposition" (113)—"strange" self-deceptions (142), to be overcome by the more terribly "Strange" things (139) he will now proceed to perform: thus he will unify his now radically divided "self" (142). Such is his design. But we have every reason to doubt its success. He managed before his first crime to get himself evilly "settled" (I.vii.79); but afterwards came a tremendous unsettlement (II.ii). And his prediction immediately before his second crime, "Things bad begun make strong themselves by ill" (III.ii.55), was shatteringly refuted in the present scene, so his reaffirmance now of that prediction may have a similar sequel. His words here are extremely evil, but their very extremeness suggests that his present mood may lapse and change. His mood is nightmarish, and his plans are uniquely vague. In striking contrast with his designs against Duncan and Banquo he here (if we refrain from reading Act IV back into the present situation) formulates no actual murderous plot against Macduff. And we wonder just what "hard use" (143) he may give to his evil will. Can the very human person that he is become other than "young" in inhuman conduct? The possibility of his eventual repentance is preserved here by Shakespeare's Christianity and by his deep dramatic instinct: both, in this matter, demand suspense. Of course if Macbeth proceeds actually to wade in blood (137), he may succeed in drowning his awful remorse; but,

---

[83] The Folio has "indeed," which may very possibly be what Shakespeare wrote, with a characteristic *double-entendre*. But even so the "in" and the "deed" must each be slow and emphatic like every syllable in this short and heavily significant final line of the scene.

on the other hand, increasing remorse and further punitive visions[84] may finally overwhelm his proud ambition. In short, this scene as a whole is so designed by Shakespeare as to leave us, not in less, but in greater suspense than ever.

[84] Shakespeare's dramatic wisdom postpones until later Macbeth's exclamation, "no more sights!" (IV.i.155). But even there the possibility of further visions is not absolutely ruled out.

THIRD PHASE

THE POWERS ABOVE

(ACT THREE, SCENE FIVE—ACT FIVE)

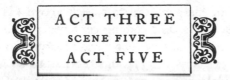

a. *such Artificial Sprights* (III.v)

SCENES v and vi are for relief and transition. Macbeth, brought
so intimately close to us above, is now viewed in ironic distance,
first from the standpoint of the evil powers, then from that of
the realm of good.

The present scene is very different from the rest of the play
in style. It and two later passages (IV.i.39-43,125-132) were in-
terpolated, probably by Thomas Middleton, possibly with the
consent of Shakespeare, to lighten the atmosphere for the sake
of the spectators in the theater. Certainly relief is needed now
even more than when it was provided after the first crime by the
drunken Porter. But such broad humor as his would be out of
place here; and the somber wit of Scene vi, though very pertinent and intriguing, does not afford sufficient diversion for all
of the audience. Hence the insertion of this fantastic Scene v. Its
fairylike protagonist is not the weird Hecate that invaded Macbeth's imagination before each of his two crimes, in the second
case (III.ii.41) more blackly than in the first (II.i.52).

Nevertheless the scene adumbrates the conception of evil that
is basic in this drama as a whole. In the world beneath the
"Moone" (23) a single, secret spirit of evil, a "close contriver of
all harmes" (7), is constantly at work, with ambitious and zest-
ful art, behind all the particular forms of wickedness. It was this
spirit that inspired the initial meeting of the Witches "with *Macbeth*" (4, I.i.7). And now that spirit, embodied in Hecate, prepares for a second and far more decisive meeting. But the danc-
ing lightness of her style, together with our knowledge of Macbeth's character, prevents us from taking seriously her assurance
that her magical sprites shall inevitably "draw him on to his
Confusion," his utter ruin (24-29). The triple "I will" and

ninefold "I" of his penultimate speech above (III.iv.130-140) still ring in our ears. His coming conference with the Witches, willed by himself, is a very subordinate feature, so far, of his designs, "his owne ends" (13); and the nature of its effect upon him shall be determined, not by this Hecate and her servitors, but by his own "wayward" (11) will.

Suggestive, however, are Hecate's tone at the beginning of this scene and her dire words near the end. At the first she vents an arrogant anger (1-9) that mimics the mood exhibited by Macbeth in the climax of the preceding scene. And we know he will open himself fatally to the influence of the evil powers if he allows his soul to be *entirely* swayed, as he has not yet done, by wrath and pride. In such case his doom will be that which Hecate predicts when her tone, for a moment just before the fantastical close of the scene, rises to tragic:

> He shall spurne Fate, scorne Death, and beare   30
> His hopes 'bove Wisedome, Grace, and Feare. . . .[1]

b. *such grace* (III.vi)

Young Lennox is a wary and watchful timeserver with good intentions. His first lines here show that he has carefully tested (off stage) and is still testing his listener before trusting him "farther" (2). In the course of his long speech his irony, veiled in the presence of Macbeth (II.iii.106, III.iv.120f), becomes increasingly open and bitter. From his initial hint, "Things have bin strangely borne" (3)—echoing his word "strange" in earlier scenes (I.ii.47, II.iii.61)—he works up to the declaration, "He has borne [i.e. done] all things well" (17). This gibe at Macbeth in the middle of his career, with disaster looming ahead, alludes to the people's adoring praise of Christ at the height of His career with crucifixion imminent, "He hath done all things well" (Mark 7:37): thus it throws Macbeth's poetic pity for

---

[1] Every *noun* in those two lines may recall to us one or another utterance of Macbeth himself in the previous scenes of Act III. For an effective method of representing Hecate on the stage see *Shakespeare Quarterly*, Autumn 1954, page 403.

his victims into deadly contrast with the words and deeds of divine charity, combining sympathy with uprightness.

But that charity is lacking in Lennox himself. On the one hand it requires a sympathetic realization of the great agony of spirit evinced by Macbeth in the Feast scene; on the other hand, immediate dissociation from him on the part of an upright courtier who now deems him a murderous "Tyrant" (22). Lennox, however, will remain subservient to his "good Lord" (III.iv.48, IV.i. 143)—so he addresses Macbeth when in his presence—until the opposition in Scotland and England becomes powerful enough to induce him to fight for justice "so much as it needs" (V.ii.29). At present he compensates his failure to take decisive action by uttering a private and elaborately clever hostile oration. In its close, having unwarily allowed his voice to rise a little, he glances fearfully about—"But peace!"—and whispers a bold question to his hearer (21-24). The charitable irony which he lacks, Shakespeare has for him!

Lennox is quite typical of the noblemen who thronged the royal hall in the Feast scene. In striking contrast his companion here, a new[2] character, a nameless Lord—not a courtier, apparently, but a rural thane intimate with Macduff—is simple, outspoken, and sincerely religious. He feels deeply the present contrast between the Scottish and English courts. In the English court Malcolm, the maligned and powerless heir to the Scottish throne, is entertained by "the most Pious *Edward* [the Confessor] with such grace" (27) as negates all merely politic considerations. Moreover the true charity of that "Holy King" (30) has inspired him to take righteous action. He has been so moved by accounts of the sufferings of the neighbor nation that he is preparing for "some attempt of Warre" (39) against Macbeth

---

[2] In this paragraph and the next I have indicated what seem to me Shakespeare's good reasons for introducing a new character here. Dr. Johnson's different opinion (see Furness Variorum edition, page 236, note 2) has naturally been agreed with by many actors—less naturally by a number of critics. Incidentally my treatment of this scene as a whole may serve to show that its various inconsistencies, so much emphasized by Joseph Quincy Adams in his edition of the play (1931), are natural enough when regarded from a dramatic standpoint.

before being entreated by Macduff to incite Northumberland to invade Scotland (29ff). So there is good hope that Macduff, who has now (unlike Lennox and the other courtiers) openly refused obedience to the tyrant, and has set out for Edward's court, may save his country "by the helpe of" the northern English forces, "with Him above / To ratifie the Worke" (32f).

The speaker regards that "work" as not only patriotic but divinely ordered and blessed. And Lennox, though not deeply holding that belief, chimes easily with it. So, after characteristically hoping for "a Caution" and safe "distance" on the part of Macduff, he vents a magniloquent precation that "Some holy Angell / Flye to the Court of England, and unfold / His Message ere he come. . . ." (43-49). But the other and nameless Lord, in the scene's final line, says of Macduff simply and devoutly, "I'll send my Prayers with him."

That line points at the main purport of this scene as a whole. "Heaven" (19), having punished and warned Macbeth climactically in the Feast scene, through the spirit of Banquo, is now working through various human agents to dethrone him. At the outset we are reminded (3-20) that he himself began his downfall when he committed his first crime, to which his destruction of "the right valiant *Banquo*" (5-7) is here, significantly, subordinated. This misdeed, sequel of the other, would not have taken place if real repentance had succeeded his remorse for his regicide. The horridness of that crime was accentuated by its pendant, his ignoble, brutal slaughter of the two helpless grooms, poor "Slaves of drinke, and thralles of sleepe" (13): the humane dramatist wishes his audience not to forget this episode, so vividly recounted by the present speaker, Lennox, just after its occurrence (II.iii.106ff). But chiefly recalled, now, is the graciousness of "Duncan," less as king (his title is deliberately omitted here) than as human person and father (3,10,20). That aspect of him prepares for the signalizing of the "grace" of "Edward" of England (27ff).

Implicitly we are reminded that what Macbeth lacks and desperately needs is openness to the divine grace. And ominously, though with brief parenthetic generality, we are told that at present he is going from bad to worse: "the knife" which he once shrank from using but did use against a royal guest (I.vii. 16) has generated the many "bloody knives" of his hired assassins threatening the guests at "Feasts and Banquets" (35). He has launched upon a career of wide-roving suspicion and murderous treachery *before consulting the Witches* (III.iv.131-133). In the second half of the play, as in the first half, the extent of their influence upon him shall be determined by his own *graceless* will.

c. *Lion-mettled, proud* (IV.i)

The silent "Prayers" attending the heroic Macduff in the close of the preceding scene are succeeded now by low thunder and the weird noises of hellish spirits, topped by the wild scream of the Third Witch's Familiar: "Harpier cries, 'tis time, 'tis time." His name, not given at the first (I.i.8ff), and apparently Shakespeare's invention, suggests the harpy-like mode in which the Three hover around and over their "charmèd pot" (9). Each, in turn, stoops into the surrounding blackness to seize upon horrid ingredients (34); then throws them into the cauldron with clawed hands glimmering in the red and yellow light of the hell-fire underneath.

The fire leaps up when the pot receives the venomous "Toad," chill and dank though still living, that has hibernated long "under cold stone" (6-8). Deadly cold and fierce heat conjoin and live in the heart of hell. Such is the keynote of this scene. But the fierceness is subordinated, for the time being, in the soft, insidious verses of the first two Witches. The ingredients of the pot as listed by them, from "poysond Entrailes" (5) to "Howlet's wing" (17), represent the secret venom of the evil heart. Its "Sting" may be mild in outward form; its rancour is concealed in its quick-shifting variety of trivial manifestations (12-17): it seems weak. But essentially it is a "Hell-broth" causing "powrefull trouble" (18f).[3]

[3] Compare the masterly account of the concealed malice of Frank Innes ("Mephistopheles") in R. L. Stevenson's *Weir of Hermiston*, Chapter VII.

And those powerful terms, in the close of the Second Witch's speech, prepare for the very different ingredients manipulated by the Third. To the First's soft "Wooll of Bat, and Tongue of Dogge" (15) she adds "Scale of Dragon, Tooth of Wolfe" (22). Towering above her sisters she flourishes and hurls into the cauldron, successively, twelve objects emblematic of violence, black magic, blasphemy, pagan wickedness, and unnatural, beastly cruelty:

> Finger of Birth-strangled Babe,   30
> Ditch-delivered by a Drab,
> Make the Grewell thicke, and slab.

With dreadful irony that first line recalls Macbeth's "Pity, like a naked new-born Babe" (I.vii.21); and it alludes darkly to his coming slaughter of Macduff's hapless "Babes" (152). And brutal ferocity is in the very sound of "a Tiger's Chawdron" (viscera), the Third Witch's final contribution to the pot: it comes full circle upon the First Witch's initial item, "poisoned entrails," thus enduing deep venom with savage feline strength. Here the nether fire leaps its highest, as though to devour all.

But the flames subside into ghastly flickering when the Second Witch, with mocking laughter, cools the contents of the pot "with a Baboon's blood" (37), signalizing the grotesqueness which, an essential feature of evil, pervades the present scene as a whole. This scene is the full and heightened sequel of the brief opening scene of the play. There the lightning flared in dark mist. Here the hellish blackness (48) is flaringly illuminated by wayward fire, rising, sinking, wavering, rising again, consonant with the luridly fantastic utterances of the Witches and of Macbeth himself.

His original encounter with them was preceded by their announcement, "*Macbeth* doth come" (I.iii.31); and in their ensuing speeches to him they iterated and reiterated his name. In the present scene they never once pronounce it;[4] suggestively it is first uttered, and then iterated, by evil spirits in the form

---

[4] Except in the non-Shakespearean line 126.

of apparitions. The Second Witch announces his approach as though he were no longer a human person: "Something wicked this way comes" (45). Like the "deed" they are doing he is now "without a name" (49)—and so are they for him. In the first Act they were mystic persons addressed and described by him in deferential and poetically charming words. Now he accosts them as "secret, black, and midnight Hags" (48)—ugliest and worst of "Night's black Agents" (III.ii.53). And the hellish confusion symbolized by the "ingredience" (34) of their cauldron reappears in his wild speech of conjuration to them (50ff).

The mood of destruction and disorder (III.ii.16, III.iv.110, 135f) which has been gradually increasing in him culminates in this scene, entirely mastering his will. Therefore his imagination, for the first time, can enter fully into the warfare of the powers of evil against civilization—particularly against religion, on which all human values depend: Macbeth's present speech begins and ends on that theme. First the Witches (and the evil spirits inspiring them) are pictured as using brute nature to fight "Against the Churches" (53); and their ultimate aim is to confound "the treasure / Of Nature's Germens," the precious seeds of growth by means of which, according to ancient Christian belief, God at the beginning transformed chaos into orderly "Nature" (59). In Scotland all hell is striving to bring chaos again by means of an irreligious king who is becoming a murderous tyrant. Hence the murderous quality of the two potions now cast by the Witches into "the Flame": the blood of a sow that had devoured her own numerous brood and, worse, the accumulated death-sweat of many gibbeted "Murderers" (66).[5] The fire, towering, illumines the first *"Apparition"* rising in the murky vapors of the cauldron, *"an Armed Head"*—the head of the nation severed from its body, supreme power used for purely selfish purposes, designed by hell to bring about the "destruction" (60) of the realm and of the tyrant himself.

In the last Act the spectator will discover that the manner of

---

[5] By using the singular case here, *murderer's* instead of *murderers'*, editors have weakened the symbolism.

Macbeth's ending—his beheading by Macduff after the conquest of his forces by young Malcolm's army—is foreshadowed by the three apparitions. But here their literal meaning, hidden by the lying fiends who enact them, is submerged by Shakespeare in large and multiplex suggestiveness. The second apparition, "*a Bloody Childe,*" whose relation to Macduff is not made plain until the end (V.vii.41-45), is here a "potent" (76) image of the increasing bloodiness (III.iv.136-138) of Macbeth. It is the sequel of the "Birth-strangled Babe" above (30). And it tells us that Macbeth's original capacity for pity (I.vii.21) and dread of "blood" (II.ii.60) wrongly shed are now being overcome entirely by his evil will. His "thought" (69), conscious and subconscious, known to the first fiend, is apparent also to the second, who interprets and encourages it thus:

> Be bloody, bold, and resolute:
> Laugh to scorne
> The power of man. For none of woman born   80
> Shall harm *Macbeth.*

But there are "Powers above" (IV.iii.238), above the "power of man" (80), as Malcolm will declare in the close of the present Act. And now he is obscurely represented by the third apparition, "*a Childe Crowned, with a Tree in his hand.*" What strikes us immediately, however, is the great contrast between this child and the bloody one above. The intimation is that the bloody and unnatural disorder of the realm cannot be cured until the "Sovereignty" (89) is given to innocence of heart in harmony with that living and growing "Nature" (59), symbolized by the "Tree," which is divinely designed: the child's "hand" clasping the "tree" must displace all the evil hands that we have seen distorting the kingdom.

That idea is unfolded further—after the foul cauldron has sunk and sweet, weird hautboy music has risen (106)—by "*A shew of eight Kings,*" future rulers of the realm, descended from the innocent and temperate Banquo. In appearance they are, for the abashed Macbeth, "too like the Spirit of *Banquo*" (112), whose figure appears at the end of their procession, smiling now (as not in III.iv) upon Macbeth, in serene triumph, while he "points at them for his" (123f). The implication is that they will inherit his unstained, noble nature; this will enable them successfully to govern Scotland and, in time, larger realms beside (121). And these eight "shadows" (111), each with the bright "hair" of vigorous young manhood over "Gold-bound-brow" (113f),[6] are the sequel of the "Child" with crowned "Baby-brow" (88): his vital "Tree" has matured and fruited in them.

In absolute contrast to that background is Macbeth's third[7] and most viciously unnatural crime, the slaughter of Macduff's innocent family. His "thought" of it attains full and clear form in a sudden "moment" (146,149). But, as the dramatist shows in many ways, it has long been forming in his soul subconsciously. It is the result of his whole evil career, though particularly of his experiences in the present scene. These, very significantly, could have forestalled that crime if he had so willed. For, since deity can make evil subservient to good, the four successive visions—the three apparitions and then the show of kings—though produced by the devil, provide Macbeth with heavenly and mounting warnings.

Accordingly the immediate result of the first two apparitions is a strikingly humane impulse on his part. He exclaims, "Then live, *Macduff*: what need I feare of thee?" (82). This informs us that, secretly and reluctantly, he has considered destroying that great aloof thane instead of merely disgracing him (III.iv. 128, III.vi.23). The good impulse, however, passes quickly:

> But yet I'll make assurance double sure,
> And take a Bond of Fate: thou shalt not live,
> That I may tell pale-hearted Feare it lies;   85
> And sleepe in spight of Thunder.   *Thunder*[8]

[6] The word "bright" is of course my guess: it seems to fit the context and to explain the otherwise nonplussing reference to their "hair."

[7] That is, his third *particularized* crime. It is prepared for by the many assassinations alluded to vaguely in the preceding scene (III.vi.35).

[8] This stage direction, displaced in modern editions, echoes tellingly Macbeth's final word.

This "Feare" (85) is greater than the "feare" (82) he has just dismissed. Still ignorant of Macduff's flight to England Macbeth has a dread of him that is far more spiritual than physical— like his earlier fear of Banquo, but much heavier than that. His accumulated remorse for his crimes becomes a desperate burden when he contemplates the serene and strong integrity of "the Thane of Fife" (72). Macduff's character is a supernatural "Thunder" that renders him "pale-hearted" (85f): these confessional images outdo in simple intensity any that he has previously uttered. In destroying Macduff he hopes finally (but, as ever, vainly) to conquer his unsleeping (86, III.ii.17-19), unrepentant remorse.

Therefore the evil powers exult; they foster his self-deception increasingly. The second fiend had urged Macbeth to be "bloody, bold, and resolute," and scornful (79f). Now the third tells him to be "Lyon-mettled, proud" (90), recalling the "Tiger's Chawdron" above (33). And in his next speech his pride mounts to a fantastically evil height. He pictures himself as "our high-placed *Macbeth*,"[9] quite unconquerable; and blasphemously (cf. line 26) he regards his career as in harmony with the laws of the divinely ordered "Nature" (99,59) which he has so flagitiously disobeyed and disdained. But soon his arrogance is dampened by the vision of the future kings. He watches it with throbbing heart (100f); with eyes seared and starting (113,116), with impotent wrath at first, but finally with horrified dismay that culminates when the image of his second crime reappears, the "Bloodboltered *Banquo*" (123). A few moments ago he had exclaimed proudly, "Rebellious dead, rise never," (97) but now they, Banquo and his royal progeny, have risen again, in his soul and before his eyes. Crouching he flings his arms across his eyes, overcome with remorse and despair, and for a few moments he is broodingly silent.[10]

When he lifts his gaze again the Witches, together with the

[9] Compare Satan in the opening lines of Milton's *Paradise Lost*, Book II.
[10] The First Witch's ensuing speech (125-132), though not written by Shakespeare, indicates that in the original performances of the play Macbeth at this juncture stands "amazedly."

vision of the kings, have vanished. And now, reversing the mood in which at the close of the Feast scene he determined to consult them (III.iv.132-135), he curses "this pernicious houre" (133f). That anathema is propitious; and his expressive face tells us that again, as so often, but now climactically, he is swaying between good and evil. "What's your Grace's will?" (135). So speaks the entering Lennox, for the first time applying to him that suggestive title, and voicing the question that is in our own minds. Which way is Macbeth's "will" going to turn?[11] Suspense is intensified (as in III.iii) by the sound of the "gallopping of Horse," rising upon the vanishing of the Witches, growing ever louder, stopping for a moment, then resuming and gradually dying away in the distance.[12] And Macbeth harbors a weird and confused fancy of "the Weyard Sisters" (136-140) riding away through the air on horseback. He recalls the murky air in which he first saw them and into which they vanished, and he has grace enough to declare:

> Infected be the Ayre whereon they ride,
> And damned all those that trust them. . . .

Properly he would now proceed to distrust that which they have fomented, especially during the past "pernicious" hour, his own pernicious desires.

But while he still temporizes he learns from Lennox with immense dismay that Macduff has "fled to England"—an immediate, surpassing threat to his crown and life. "Fled to England?" he echoes, hating to believe; then he slowly advances to the forefront of the stage, facing us, and the future. Now he speaks the most terrible of all his soliloquies. He is deeply aware

[11] The notion that it must inevitably turn to evil is a modernism entirely out of keeping with the Elizabethan Christian outlook and with Shakespeare's fine art of dramatic suspense.

[12] The sound of galloping should be heard, I think, upon Macbeth's exit in I.iv (though not mentioned there) to signalize the suspense before his first crime. See the equine allusions in I.iv.49, I.vi.22f, I.vii.22-28, III.i.19-39, III.iii.6-12. Thus the present galloping of "Horse" (horses) is climactic; and the sounds off stage should be far more fully rendered here than elsewhere in the play when it is performed.

that the latest of his "dread exploits" (144), his proposed destruction of Macduff, was postponed by his humaneness, like the
"terrible Feat" (I.vii.80) of stabbing Duncan and that "deed
of dreadful note" (III.ii.44), the butchery of Banquo; and he
knows that this time, as not before, the delay may well prove
fatal to himself. So he is confronted with an ultimate crisis: he
must either discard his ambition utterly or utterly crush his humane dreads and remorsefulness. And gradually in the course
of the speech, with visage more and more horribly working, he
adopts the second course.

At the first he asserts in general and vague terms that hence-
forth every quick ("flighty") "purpose" (145) he entertains
shall be enacted at once: "The very firstlings of my heart shall
be / The firstlings of my hand." Immediately he will take Macduff's castle by surprise and subdue all of "Fife" (151); here he
hesitates[18] for a brief instant, and we know that a prudent, less
emotional tyrant would be content with that "purpose."[14] But
this "firstling" of Macbeth's "heart" cannot assuage the present
despair and violent turmoil of that heart. A few minutes ago he
had a vision of Banquo's "Line" of descendants continuing till
doomsday (117). Shall Macduff's "Line" (153), too, flourish and
reproach him till the end of time? His evil "will" (150) sweeps
him along. He will "give to th' edge o' th' Sword," not only all
who oppose him in Fife on Macduff's behalf, but also

> His Wife, his Babes, and all unfortunate Soules   152
> That trace him in his Line. . . .

That conventional "unfortunate," following hard upon "Babes,"
indicates how little remains here of Macbeth's "Babe" of "Pity"
heralding a storm of "tears" (I.vii.21-25).

And this time his wicked purpose does not need to be bolstered,
as in the close of the Feast scene, by preliminary "boasting,"
which now seems to him the utterance of "a Foole" (153f). His

---

[18] But Dover Wilson replaces with a comma the semicolon after "Fife."
[14] In the middle of Chapter 22 of Scott's *Quentin Durward* the brutal tyrant
William de la Marck is prevented by prudence from carrying his butchery to
an extreme that would (like Macbeth's) have been ruinous for himself.

bloody intentions there (III.iv.135-140), so vague and possibly
transient, have concentrated here and hardened into the will to
do a single, and singularly bloody, "deed" (154,146, III.iv.
144). And this volition is sustained by his rearoused and here, as
never before, unmitigated arrogance. It is now indeed terribly
feline (90,33) in its strength and stealth. It incites him to "surprise" (150) and overcome all opposition, especially that which
is offered by his own heart. Not a word does he say here of the
outward dangers signalized in the speeches of the three Apparitions above. We may assume he hopes that his slaughter of his
chief thane's helpless family, an extreme of brutality not expected of him, shall dismay the other thanes and prevent them
from following Macduff's example. But the fact that this point,
which would engross the thoughts of an ordinary tyrant, is here
not mentioned throws into relief his main aim: to dismay and
vanquish his own humaneness. Abandoning his sophistical attempt to feel himself in harmony with "Nature" (99) he will
now make war against it, mainly in his own soul. Thus his pride
attains a hellish height, prefigured in the beginning of this scene
by the aspiring deadly fume of the Witches' boiling "Hell-
broth" (19). And we know it will double and redouble toil and
trouble not only for others but for himself. But now he exults
in the power of his devilish will to vanquish that troublous "pale-
hearted Fear" (85) occasioned hitherto by his remorse. In
slaughtering innocent human beings he will slaughter in himself,
so he believes, every inkling of humaneness.

But his humanity throbs again in the dramatic close of the
soliloquy:

> This deed I'll do, before this purpose coole,
> But no more sights!—Where are these Gentlemen?   155
> Come bring me where they are.

The repeated "this" betrays the effortfulness, less than in the
case of his previous crimes but still real, with which he bends
himself up (I.vii.79) to the immediate doing of the appalling
"deed." He knows his purpose will "cool" if he lets himself

envisage that deed. And the hand raised determinedly while he utters the first of those three lines covers his eyes swiftly[15] at the beginning of the second. The term "sights" is comprehensive. It comprises all the spectacles, some more or less actual, some entirely imaginary, that from the outset have providentially warned him against the way he was going (II.i.42). His evil ambition was able to repress them or distort them to its own advantage, only, however, after an inward struggle that divided his will sharply. Here he is resolved to annul that self-division by utterly banishing all such "sights." And he aids himself, very humanly, by turning his mind outward to that which he always loves, the presence of loyal friends. After his initial struggle against "horrible Imaginings" he turned with great relief to three "Kind Gentlemen" (I.iii.129,150). And now, abruptly ending his hellish soliloquy and dropping his hand from his eyes, he craves the sight of the "two or three" (141) nameless but loyal persons whom Lennox left outside. Though they might be commoners, for all Macbeth knows, he divines they are friendly "Gentlemen" (155) of some importance who have hastened (140) to bring him word of Macduff's flight; and he yearns to go quickly, together with the still (supposedly) loyal Lennox, to "where they are."[16]

And we can easily imagine him greeting them with gracious warmth of appreciation, hiding from them and from himself a will which has continually, and now climactically, rejected heavenly grace. Far more dreadful than the hellish cauldron upon which this scene opened is the human "heart" (147) of Macbeth at the close, seething with all the manifold evil that the contents of that pot symbolized. Nevertheless, as the next scene shows, he will finally shrink from taking any physical part in the ensuing crime. Above (150-154) he was resolved to lead in person the

---

[15] But the comma after "cool" is generally replaced by a full stop in modern editions.

[16] Macbeth's eagerness for their company is emphasized by the omission of punctuation after "Come" and by the repetition of "Where" and "are." Of course we may assume that he wishes to cross-examine the messengers; but that point, explicitly stated on similar occasions elsewhere in Shakespeare's plays, is here not mentioned.

assault on Macduff's castle and to superintend the slaughter.[17]
But in Scene ii he is conspicuous by his absence: his very name
is not mentioned and there is no indication that he is anywhere
in the neighborhood. The suggestion is that he keeps himself as
far from it as possible. The crime is committed by hired Murderers, as in the case of Banquo, where, however, Macbeth carefully refrained from saying what he has deliberately asserted
here, "This deed *I'll* do." Eventually he finds he cannot bear
any "sight" of it (154f) at all.

d. *my Father* (IV.ii)

By his flight to England Macduff has become, legally and
publicly, a "Traitor" (4,82) to his native "Land" (1). He, the
greatest of the thanes, is the sole one who has so far dared to
incur that odium. We know he has done so for the sake of Scotland, which he has perceived the present king is likely not merely
to oppress but utterly ruin. So far, however, he has confided his
purpose only to one close friend, a "Lord" of obscure station
but, like Macduff himself, noble in character (III.vi.23-37).
He has concealed it from all his kinsmen—notably the timeserv-
ing Ross, to whom he was ironically reticent at the first (II.iv.
20ff)—great-heartedly refusing to implicate them in his dubious
adventure. For the same reason he has hidden it even from his
wife, trusting that her obvious innocence will protect her and
her children from the royal anger when Macbeth, in accordance
with custom, deprives the "traitor" of his "Mansion and his
Titles" (7). But Macduff's resolve to keep *her* entirely ignorant
of his plans must have cost him a hard effort of sacrificial self-
control. That fact is evident from the present scene.

The emergence here of the play's second woman recalls the
initial appearance of Lady Macbeth (I.v). Their demeanor is
ironically similar, with an essential contrast underneath. Both
are remote from and ignorant of public conditions; both are temperamentally passionate, forthright, and impatient. Each, intense-

---

[17] Of course that passage may be read differently. But I have chosen what
seems the most *dramatic* interpretation.

ly devoted to her absent husband, is sharply critical of his ambiguous conduct. Lady Macbeth blames her lord's extreme human-kindness; Macduff's "Wife,"[18] her lord's extreme lack of the same.

His secret and apparently senseless flight, news of which has just now been brought by Ross, dismays and angers her. She cries out, "He loves us not, / He wants the naturall touch" (8f). Unaware of the crucial nature of his refusal to attend the royal court (III.vi.39-43) she thinks he has "done" (1) nothing that would necessitate his flight. This, therefore, must have been caused by his succumbing to a sudden and entirely irrational (13f) "feare" (4). And that fear, she thinks, was shockingly selfish. For his very forebodings, though baseless, would normally have constrained him to remain at home protecting his wife and "his Babes" (6), especially the babes. Even the tiny "Wren" in the face of horridest danger will fight to save the "young ones in her Nest." But that high instinct was apparently overcome in her husband's heart by the base instinct of self-preservation. In his case "All is the Feare, and nothing is the Love" (12). And so, just because she loves him intensely and has hitherto admired him unreservedly, she is appalled by his present conduct: her tone and gestures convey supreme perturbation.[19]

Presently, however, she succeeds in calming herself with the aid of Ross. His first adjurations (2,4f) are brief, cautious, and conventional. But soon (14ff) his pity and affection inspire him to urge warmly the one consideration that can really help her: she must "schoole" herself into relying upon what she knows of her husband, ceasing to brood upon the mystery of his procedure in the present convulsed time. Here Ross suddenly checks himself—like his friend Lennox above (III.vi.21)—glancing about

[18] Only thus is she denominated by the Folios in this scene and elsewhere (notably V.i.47); the designation "Lady Macduff" is a modern convenience. The term "Wife," like the term "Mother" (32), emphasizes her dependence, devotion, and pathos.

[19] To regard her as merely querulous is to miss the dramatic quality of the scene and, incidentally, her contribution to the passionately intense atmosphere of the play as a whole.

him fearfully. He dare not breathe a word against the king or even name him. Instead he laments in vague terms the "cruel . . . times" in which "we" (18-20)—himself and all the other ordinary thanes—may become "Traitors" unawares. They, swayed by fears and rumors, not knowing what to do, "floate upon a wilde and violent Sea / Each way, and move." They move only as the billows move them. But not so Macduff; such is the implication: moved by his own superior will he is taking decisive action against Macbeth on behalf of Scotland. Ross dares only to hint at that aphoristically: "Things at the worst will cease, or else climbe upward" (24). Soon, hastily and emotionally, he takes his leave. But Lady Macduff's demeanor shows she has now regained her better self. She believes along with Ross that her husband is acting for the "best" because she knows he "is Noble, Wise, Judicious" (16).

That is the faith too of Macduff's young "Son"[20] and heir, who, after listening with silent intentness to the speeches of the other two, takes now the center of the stage. He, as the dramatist deftly makes us realize, has in him the very spirit of his father.[21] His mother, facing the fact that her husband's death may result from his flight, finds relief in bandying words with her boy in seriocomic vein: "Sirrah, your Father's dead"—she knows he knows the contrary (27)[22]—"And what will you do now? How will you live?" (30f). We might expect boyish heroics in his answer, or at least some emotional excitement. But he replies quietly, "As Birds do, Mother," in allusion to Christ's sayings on that theme.[23] Thus he evinces in his very first speech

[20] He is nameless; such being the case in this scene with Macduff himself, who is referred to only, and continually, as "Husband" and "Father." Cf. note 18 above.

[21] Obviously the effect would be ruined if the boy himself were shown to be conscious of that fact like his more mature forerunner, Orlando: "the spirit of my father, which I think is within me . . . [which] grows strong in me" (*As You Like It*, I.i.24,73f).

[22] Of course it may be claimed that she speaks line 27 aside to Ross and that the boy has not heard the preceding dialogue. But this interpretation seems more conventional than Shakespeare's art in this play is.

[23] See Matthew 6:26; and, perhaps more pertinently, Matthew 10:29: "one of them shall not fall to the ground without your Father." Cf. Luke 12:6.

the simple piety characteristic of Macduff (II.iii.71-74, IV.iii. 223-227). So that when he declares, "My Father is not dead" (37) we feel that in the Son's nature (as the close of the scene will demonstrate in action) his "Father" is very much alive. And in the rest of the present dialogue (38-64) something of the ironic nonchalance displayed by Macduff in his last appearance on the stage (II.iv.21ff) reappears in the Son. For this precocious young aristocrat has, along with simple-heartedness and courage, the desire to cover up his feelings in a crisis, with efforts, still childishly crude in his case, at wit and apothegm. However, when "*a Messenger*" rushes in the boy becomes silent and watchful again, as he was in the first half of the scene, and remains so (65-82) until near the end. But now his mute watchfulness is so intense and alert that our attention remains fixed upon him.

The Messenger has a strikingly "homely" (68) and honest visage. Unknown to Lady Macduff, yet fully acquainted with her rank and situation, he is doubtless one of Macduff's most obscure yet also most devoted tenants.[24] He has noted the evil mien of certain armed men approaching the castle; and though he cannot be certain of their intentions his heart suspects the worst. Secretly and swiftly he makes his way hither and blurts out breathlessly, "Be not found heere—Hence, with your little ones." Then, smitten by Lady Macduff's frightened looks, he terms himself "too savage" but warns her that "worse" is "nigh," possibly "fell Cruelty," from which he could not protect her: "Heaven preserve you. . . ."[25]

Alone again with her silent Son, and not knowing whither to fly, Lady Macduff exclaims, "I have done no harm!" (This recalls for us the fact that Macduff by his prudent secrecy has kept her mind free from any touch of disloyal thought towards the present regime.) But then, with the bitter and excited wordi-

[24] Compare Gloucester's "Old Man" in the contemporary *Lear* (IV.i.13ff). For a different view of the Messenger see the Furness Variorum edition of the play, page 273.

[25] Compare Albany's prayer for Cordelia just before her brutal murder is revealed (*Lear*, V.iii.256).

ness she displayed in the opening of the scene, she reflects that innocence may be no protection "in this earthly world" (74-79). Thereupon the *"Murtherers"* enter; and in their looks all the worst evil of "this earthly world" seems incarnate. Their faces, topped and encompassed by shaggy locks of hair, are utterly debauched and brutal.[26] With deep, simple horror she whispers, "What are these faces?" And when their leader demands the whereabouts of Macduff the thought of the noble character (16) and mien of her "Husband" (80), over against the brutality confronting her, irradiates her mind and countenance. In spirit now, as not in any of her previous speeches, she is completely with him. She answers boldly:

> I hope in no place so unsanctified
> Where such as thou may'st finde him.

(We know he has gone to a place *not* unsanctified, III.vi.30.) "He's a Traitor," declares the leading murderer, raising his dagger to kill the Wife. But the little Son rushes between, crying out, "Thou liest, thou shagge-eared Villaine!" The astonished brute exclaims, "What, you Egge? / Young fry of Treachery?" and stabs the boy to the heart. The "Mother," urged by the child's gasping last words (84f), runs off stage *"crying Murther,"* yearning to save, actually to die with, the rest of her "little ones" (69). The murderers pursue her, dragging away the small body of the "young fry"—the true Son of his Father.

e. *healing Benediction* (IV.iii)

"Let us seeke out some desolate shade, and there / Weepe our sad bosomes empty." Thus Malcolm utters, unawares, a coda for the preceding scene, accentuating our pity for his companion, Macduff. He, ignorant of his dreadful loss, has been recounting off stage, and now continues to emphasize, Macbeth's destruction of Scottish men—*not* women and children; all these,

---

[26] On the stage they are the same three actors as in III.iii but made up far more horridly.

so far as the speaker knows, are allowed to live, bewailing their husbands and fathers (5). Their sorrows

> Strike heaven on the face, that it resounds
> As it felt with Scotland, and yelled out
> Like Syllable of Dolour.

But Macduff knows that tearful sympathy (2) with the sufferings of his country can cause martial hands to tremble. "Let us rather / Hold fast the mortall Sword": they must now fight to rescue their native land, their "Birthdome," from its abject misery.

But though force must be employed against evil it cannot by itself remedy evil: that ethical and Shakespearean conviction underlies the whole of the present scene.[27] Providence, according to Christian faith, distils good from evil[28] by making use of tyrants to signalize and punish human sin; as Macduff himself will see and say later on (223ff). Therefore any touch of self-righteousness in the opponents of the tyrant is fateful; their primary need is humility. Much else, however, is desirable in a new leader such as Malcolm who is called upon to overthrow the tyrant and to rule in his stead. So the normal audience[29] is keenly interested in finding out how well qualified for that task the young prince is and, also, whether the relations between him and his chief supporter, Macduff, are likely to be sound and fruitful.[30] At the outset the artful dramatist fills us with doubts which, as the scene proceeds, he gradually resolves. Certainly neither of the two men is free from defects. But in the end Malcolm and Macduff are seen to complement each other very well: together they appear providentially designed not only to make

[27] The present-day audience, like the Elizabethan one, may have been taught by recent history to take that conviction somewhat seriously.

[28] See note 38 to Second Phase, above.

[29] This does not include those who accept the Romantic tradition that this scene is hopelessly dull. Exceptionally good actors can make it interesting in the theater by bringing out its intense psychodramatic quality.

[30] The political literature of the Renaissance stresses continually the fact that of almost equal importance with the prince is his chief adviser: to know how to choose and use him is a main feature of an excellent ruler.

war against Macbeth effectually but also to remedy, so far as possible, the evil he has done.

At first, however, Malcolm seems weak and wavering, and abnormally distrustful of his visitor (8-17). He is willing to "waile" elaborately the sorrows of Scotland (1f, 8) and to "redresse" what he can at some future and opportune but very indefinite time. As for the others' claim that *now* is the time to use the sword: "it may be so perchance." He speaks with much hesitancy, eying his companion furtively. The "Tyrant," Macbeth, whose name he emotionally refrains from blistering his tongue with (12), was formerly "thought honest" and was well "loved" by Macduff, who, unlike many other thanes, has apparently not "yet" been injured by him. And very possibly Macduff, deeming Malcolm too "young" and "weake" (14,16) to rule Scotland, has made a secret covenant with the present king: Macbeth will end his outrages if Duncan's heir, the main center of disaffection (III.i.30-35), shall be lured by Macduff into Macbeth's grasp. This would be accomplished if Malcolm could be persuaded to head in person a Scottish rebellion, supported ostensibly by the chief thane, Macduff, but eventually betrayed by him into captivity and almost certain death. That outcome, not stated by the speaker in those plain terms, is indicated when he says to his companion: "something / You may discerne[31] of him [Macbeth] through me." Macduff may well believe that patriotism and piety demand such conduct from him on behalf of the peace of Scotland; which, he hopes, may now have nearly completed its tale of providential sufferings for its sins. He may be convinced that it would now be wisdom to sacrifice an "innocent Lambe [Malcolm] / T'appease an angry God."[32]

---

[31] Such is the reading of all the Folios. Theobald's emendation, generally accepted, of "discerne" to "deserve" ignores the fact Malcolm carefully refrains from suggesting that Macduff's chief aim is material advancement for himself. Malcolm means: "You may believe that Macbeth will rule better if I am disposed of."

[32] The word "God," decapitalized in modern texts, is regarded as referring to Macbeth. But Shakespeare may intend a vivid dramatic allusion to the *Old Testament* Jehovah.

But the audience, knowing Macduff well, is critical of Malcolm for not knowing him better. And when the noble thane declares with simple intensity, "I am not treacherous," we feel that Malcolm should be convinced by his mien even if strangely ignorant of the character of Duncan's intimate friend and adviser (II.iii.51ff). The prince's next speech, however, demonstrates that he does know Macduff's character but that he also knows, realistically, the mighty power of temptation in the political realm: "A good and vertuous Nature may recoyle / In an Imperiall charge." And as for Macduff's present mien:

> Angels are bright still, though the brightest fell.
> Though all things foule would wear the brows of grace
> Yet Grace must still looke so.

Like his father, but better, the son knows that there's no art to find "the Mind's construction in the Face" (I.iv.11ff). Whereas Duncan was deceived in Macbeth his son will not quickly trust even the far more ingenuous countenance of Macduff: it looks as if illumined by divine "Grace" but may merely "wear the brows of grace."

Here, and increasingly hereafter, we appreciate the "modest Wisedome" (119) of Malcolm, extraordinary in one so young. He has steadfast prudence, that homely virtue without which all the loftier endowments of a prince are ineffectual. And the dramatist gives the audience the satisfaction of perceiving that fact while Macduff remains blind to it. He ignores the reasonableness of the other's suspicion that his departure from his dear ones without any "leave-taking" (28) may indicate collusion with Macbeth. The prince invites him to give the "rightly just" (30) explanation, which is known to us,[33] but which Macduff is now too indignant to utter. Warmly and confusedly he attributes Malcolm's hesitancy to two motives that contradict each other: a lack of courage to fight tyranny (32f) and a conviction that Macduff is a "Villaine" (35). The second accusation is patently unfair; Malcolm has shown that (unlike Macduff) he

---

[33] See the first paragraph under section d (*my Father*) above.

has been able to refrain from passing any final judgment upon his companion (20f,30f). But our sympathy with Macduff, too, is increased because we know that his glowing patriotism is entirely sincere. And his prudence was displayed earlier in several ways. Mainly, he postponed as long as possible a resort to armed rebellion against the present, and duly anointed, king of Scotland. Now, however, his duty is to arouse others to warfare. But Malcolm, upon whom rests the ultimate responsibility, must refrain from "over-credulous haste" (120). Thus the dramatist secures our appreciation for each of these two so different men; and he deepens it with every subsequent speech.

Malcolm succeeds in preventing a precipitate departure (34) on the part of Macduff, whose assertions, he gently suggests, have been too "absolute" (38). And the very nature of those assertions, at once so emotional and so uninformative, justify Malcolm in maintaining his suspicions of his visitor. So he now tests him definitively by means of a very dramatic pretense which, though penetrated by the audience, outwits the great thane completely. First, Malcolm declares his readiness to fight Macbeth to the death, fully confident of conquering him with "my Sword" (39-46), thus echoing nicely, and making his own, "the mortal Sword" (3) advocated by Macduff. Then he avers that he himself shall prove to be an even worse king than "blacke Macbeth" (52), who, in contrast with his successor, shall seem "a Lambe"—alluding with dramatic irony to the "innocent Lambe" above (16). Macduff exclaims violently:

> Not in the Legions   55
> Of horrid Hell can come a Devill more damned
> In evils, to top *Macbeth*.

For us those lines, recalling the "horrid" Cauldron scene (IV.i), signalize the world of evil, the "Legions" of "Hell," warring against Heaven, and working ambitiously through Macbeth to reduce the human world to chaos. But also that histrionic passage is precisely what the speaker would declaim at this juncture if he (an accomplished actor) were trying to conceal his secret understanding with Macbeth. And so Malcolm proceeds with his own histrionic pretense, gradually heightening his self-disparagement.

But in that process he reveals to us unconsciously a virtue that would cease to exist if he were highly conscious of it: his constant humility, his "Lowlinesse" (93), deep underneath his royal prudence. He has pondered Macbeth's career with the aim of rightly guiding his own. That tyrant, formerly "honest" and lovable (13), has now become "Bloody,"

> Luxurious, Avaricious, False, Deceitfull,
> Suddaine, Malicious, smacking of every sinne
> That has a name. . . .   60

But every man who examines himself humbly and closely must perceive the germs of all sins in his own nature; and Malcolm knows that supreme power is the climate wherein they can terribly flourish. He hopes to avoid that fate by magnifying, for the purpose of full and clear scrutiny, his own potential wickedness.[34] Accordingly his long confessional speeches in the presence of Macduff have very much the quality and tone of soliloquies addressed to the audience and to "God above" (120).

His first and most obvious danger when he becomes king will be the temptation of luxuriousness (58), i.e. lust. Later in the scene he states that he is "yet / Unknown to Woman" (125f). But that "yet," emphatic as end-word of a verse, betokens his awareness of a sovereign ruler's tendency to "Voluptuousnesse" (60-66). Macduff, much abashed, declares that "Boundlesse intemperance" in that regard is indeed a fateful sort of "Tyranny," akin to Macbeth's sort; it has ruined "many Kings" (66-69). He hopes, however, that the new king will keep his lasciviousness within bounds. But Malcolm, without speaking to that point, hastens to accuse himself of boundless, staunchless "Avarice" (78ff). Macduff, more disturbed, exclaims that this sin,

---

[34] In this respect he resembles his great forerunner, the crown prince of Denmark. Note that Hamlet in his confession to Ophelia is semi-soliloquizing (III.i.122ff) as Malcolm is now.

from the political standpoint, is more "pernicious" (85). But even avarice, added to lust, will not render Malcolm a real tyrant if outweighed by good qualities, by "King-becoming Graces" (90f). Now, however, Macduff's persistent eagerness to gloss over his companion's faults has become very suspicious. So the prince heaps opprobrium upon himself. He can do so with intensity because of his intense devotion to the royal graces he disavows:

> As Justice, Verity, Temperance, Stablenesse,
> Bounty, Perseverance, Mercy, Lowlinesse,
> Devotion, Patience, Courage, Fortitude—
> I have no relish of them, but abound   95
> In the division of each severall Crime,
> Acting it in many wayes. Nay, had I power, I should
> Poure the sweet Milke of Concord into Hell,
> Uprore the universall peace, confound
> All unity on earth.   100

Macbeth spoke eloquently of "Love" (II.iii.116,123). But that word, here omitted by Malcolm, may denominate an emotional and imaginative mood rather than a virtue. Real love is present and active, though undeclared, when "Bounty" (kindness and generosity) is controlled by "Justice" and "Mercy," these two tempering and preserving each other, nourished by devoted, patient humility, and productive of true "Courage" and "Fortitude." Macbeth's "Milke of humane kindnesse" (I.v.18) has dreadfully soured. Malcolm cherishes "the sweet Milke of Concord" that nourishes "peace" and "unity" in the human world, preserving it from the chaotic world of evil which is "Hell" (98), "horrid Hell" (56).

As poetry the prince's speech is far below Macbeth's magnificent soliloquy upon "Justice" and "Pity" (I.vii.10,21). But that great poetic passage, exploiting the speaker's self-deceptive warmth of heart, prepared the way for a crime devoid of any tinge of justice and mercy. Malcolm, so distrustful of his own heart, finding in himself the potentiality of every "Crime" (96), has unawares evinced a deep "Verity" (92) which in itself is poetically beautiful. The meekness that Macbeth contented himself with admiring in Duncan (I.vii.17) is fully evident in Duncan's son. Macbeth's speech preceded the murderous theft of a throne and the misuse of power. Malcolm's speech prepares for the fair though forceful winning of the crown by one who by piercing self-criticism has tried to render himself "fit to governe" (101). And in the second half of the scene, which begins at this point, his utterances and actions will show that fitness positively.

He watches and hearkens keenly while Macduff gives vent to a passionate despair caused by the prince's self-condemnation. And here the thane's sincerity becomes indubitable. It is sealed by the closing lines of his speech. This time his farewell (111), which above could have been a feint (34), is entirely desperate in tone and authentic in context. It is preceded by extraordinary praise of Malcolm's parents and followed by definite rejection of the son who is, apparently, so full of "Evils." These have "banished" Macduff from his beloved "Scotland" (113,100), to which, if he were in collusion with Macbeth, he would wish to return, after making some specious excuse to his companion. Instead, with bent head and hands on "breast," he moves blindly away, an entirely hopeless (114) exile. Here he completely captures our sympathy at the expense of Malcolm, who, however, quickly regains it.

After assuring the "Noble" (114f) thane that he no longer doubts his "integrity" Malcolm reveals a fact which justifies his "blacke" (and, otherwise, too cruel) "Scruples": the "Devillish" Macbeth has often tried to get the prince into his power by the very "traines" Macduff seemed to employ. And now, while unspeaking his self-blackening, Malcolm makes amends to his friend by putting himself under his "Direction" (122): "What I am truly / Is thine, and my poore Country's, to command" (131f). Thus the dramatist calls attention to the fact that these two men, both free from Macbeth's pride, complement each other admirably for the service of their "Country." Macduff, too naïve for sovereignty, will be an honest, devoted, and strong supporter of the throne. Malcolm, not forceful but pure, unselfish, and politically wise, will know how to test, conciliate, and employ his counselors; in this connection the reader may recall speeches made by the prince early in the play (I.ii.3-7, I.iv. 2-11). But in the close of his present long monologue he shows that, though not forcible like his friend, he has firm courage and resolution. Previously, while testing his listener, he stated that the king of England had offered him help, which he might accept at some future time (10,41-44). Now he reveals the fact that, before Macduff's arrival, he had determined to set forth *immediately* for Scotland with "Old Siward" and "ten thousand warlike men" (133-137). He concludes, finely and strongly, grasping Macduff's hand: "Now wee'll together. . . ."

The main source of Malcolm's resoluteness and all his other royal virtues is his Christian faith. But since the essence of it is humility he cannot expatiate upon his possession of it, so the dramatist causes him to manifest it casually in various ways. When Macduff declared, above,

> . . . Thy Royall Father
> Was a most Sainted-King: the Queene that bore thee,
> Oftner upon her knees than on her feet,   110
> Died every day she lived. . . .[35]

the prince, bowing his head, listened with feelings too deep for words. Presently by way of sequel he exclaimed to his friend, in Biblical idiom, "God above / Deale betweene thee and me!" (120f). And later when he speaks reverently and beautifully of the "good King" of England (147)—more than Duncan a "Sainted-King"—it is clear that Malcolm, without saying so explicitly (and priggishly) is taking this monarch as a model for himself. Certainly, in the background, the dramatist is suggesting a contrast between this Christian sovereign, with his "holy Prayers" (154), and the present king of Scotland, whose prayers at the outset failed to be holy (II.ii.27ff). In the foreground,

---

[35] There is no suggestion of those traits in Holinshed's *Chronicles*: Shakespeare deliberately invented them and couched them in the strongest possible terms for present purposes.

however, is the fact that Malcolm has "often" (148) watched worshipfully while the good king performed his wonderful deeds of healing, and is now eager to watch him again (140-145). The suggestion is that the prince himself "solicites heaven," constantly and humbly, on behalf of his own "strangely visited people" (149f), hoping that he himself may be the instrument (239) of a "healing Benediction" (156) for them. Significantly Malcolm declares that the "gracious" king of England (43) is not only a healer of "the Evill" (146): he is the source of "sundry Blessings" that "hang about his Throne" and "speake him full of Grace" (158f). Malcolm hopes to provide such a throne for his own country. And when his "Countryman" Ross enters the scene the prince breathes a fervent petition that his own exile from Scotland will be ended by the "Good God betimes" (160-163).

Ross utters an equally fervent "Amen." And strikingly in harmony with the gracious atmosphere disseminated by Malcolm's speeches is the present demeanor of Macduff's "ever gentle Cousin" (161). Ross, devoted to Duncan (I.ii.45ff), shared his high approval of the martial Macbeth (I.iii.89-107). And he condoned this warrior's enthronement, albeit with misgivings of conscience and despite the emphatic aloofness of his admired "good . . . Cousin" Macduff (II.iv.20,36). In the Feast scene Ross was charitable enough to sympathize with Macbeth's initial ghostly perturbation, deeming him "not well" (III.iv.43-45,52). Nor in the immediate sequel did he revolt from him; but unlike his dramatic opposite, the cleverly satirical Lennox (III.vi. 1-20, IV.i.135ff), he did not again appear in intimate attendance upon the guilty tyrant. He risked a visit to Macduff's lonely and distraught wife, comforting her greatly and promising to come again soon (IV.ii.23). On his return, however, he was confronted with a horrible scene that turned the timeserver into a rebel and sent him, after interment of the butchered bodies of Macduff's dear ones, to England posthaste. But now he enters slowly, with a mien of deep grief. And the perfect tact with which he leads up to his dreadful disclosure is not only the product of

an "ever gentle" (161) heart (and, incidentally, very dramatic):
it seems inspired by that divine grace and pity of which Malcolm
has just been speaking.

First, Ross tries (avoiding direct reference to the murderous
Macbeth) to preoccupy Macduff's thoughts with the general
grief of Scotland. That "poore Country," he avers, should now
be called not "our Mother, but our Grave,"[36] that earth, so
vivid in the speaker's memory, wherein he had buried his cousin's
wife and babes—gone like "the Flowers" worn happily by
"good men . . . in their Caps" for a while, then perishing prematurely (164-176). Such is Ross's unspoken vision. Aloud he
compares the "good men" themselves to those flowers, impelling
his listener to think of their untimely "Dying" and of their fami-
lies' "violent sorrow," each "newest" grief being swiftly followed by another. And Macduff, deeply sharing that common
sorrow, broods upon it silently for a moment (173-176).

Then, aware of a solemn reticence in the narrator, Macduff
inquires abruptly about his own family. Like everyone else, before the event, he has never thought the present Scottish king
capable of murdering women and children.[37] Nor can the good
Macduff think so now, despite the evil extremes to which he
knows Macbeth has gone in other respects (55ff). But he does
think that the tyrant, hardened by incessant slaughter (so heavily emphasized by Ross) of men, may have exhibited some harsh-
ness towards Lady Macduff, and even his children, assailing
their innocent peace.

MACDUFF   How does my Wife?
Ross   Why, well.
MACDUFF   And all my Children?
Ross   Well too.
MACDUFF   The Tyrant has not battered at their peace?
Ross   No, they were well at peace when I did leave 'em.

[36] The noun "grave," not used in previous accounts of Scotland's misery,
was reserved by Shakespeare for the present occasion.

[37] There is no indication anywhere in the play that Macbeth ever purposed,
much less perpetrated, this sort of crime except in the case of Macduff's family.

They have *well*-being, in a peace beyond any tyrant's power, beyond the "violent sorrow" suffered by other women and children in Scotland (165ff), beyond all the ills that they themselves may have suffered. Ross declares with peaceful firmness that he "did leave 'em"[38]—as he wishes Macduff presently to do —"well at peace." Thereupon in quickly rising tones the speaker dilates upon that which he knows will help Macduff most: his country's crucial need of him at the present instant. A "worthy" rebellion is rising there—such is the cheering and hopeful news which Ross has withheld until now—and Macbeth is preparing to suppress it: "I saw the Tyrant's Power afoot" (185).

> Now is the time of helpe: your eye in Scotland
> Would create Soldiers, make our women fight,
> To doffe their dire distresses.

More than those bereaved women, so the speaker implies, Macduff must be able to doff "dire" distress, albeit a distress far more dreadful than theirs (192-195,201-203). Ross (still not naming it) emphasizes its fearful and, at the same time, its communal nature: every "honest" person "shares some" of the "woe" which mainly pertains "to you alone" (197-199). Macduff, called upon to restore his beloved country's weal, is the chief representative of her woe—in a way which he can now "guess at" (203).

Accordingly Ross abandons the circumlocution which, so well employed beforehand to alleviate the coming blow, would be torture for his listener now. But a far worse torture would be a description of the "manner" (205) of the massacre. He must tell Macduff the exact truth, but briefly and without any precise details: "Your Castle is surpriz'd; your Wife and Babes / Savagely slaughter'd." A softer statement would have been cruelly false; a longer one, cruelly graphic. Ross makes his next two speeches as short and plain as possible, then refrains from further speaking. His significant silence during the rest of the scene expresses his

[38] The abbreviation of the pronoun emphasizes the word "leave." But the culminant stress, in this rising and falling pentameter line, is on the phrase "well at peace."

sympathy for his stricken cousin even more graciously than the careful monologues preceding his awful disclosure.

Macduff, struck dumb at first with horror, is presently able to whisper: "My Children too?" (211). His grief for his "wife" (213) is equally deep. But he finds it almost impossible to conceive Macbeth as a slayer of babes:

> He has no Children—All my pretty ones?[39]
> Did you say All? Oh Hell-Kite! All?
> What, All my pretty Chickens, and their Damme,
> At one fell swoope?

The tyrant's childlessness, passingly recalled, is at once dismissed: it cannot account for his "fell" slaughter of all those "pretty" and helpless little ones together with the mother who, as implied by the metaphor—for us the sequel of Lady Macduff's simile of the "poor Wren" (IV.ii.9-11)—would fain have protected every single one of them. In Macduff's horrified vision Macbeth, now worse than the worst of hell's devils (55-57), has become a hellish, inhuman, foul bird of prey. And for us the term "Hell-Kite" signalizes the nadir of Macbeth's deterioration from his onetime vaunted humanity (I.vii.45-47).

In contrast, Macduff's next speech (quoted below) gives conclusive expression to his religious and, therefore, growthful humanity. Macbeth's human-kindness, instead of growing, has withered more and more; it entirely gave way, in the case of his third crime, to subhuman, kitelike cruelty. His natural humaneness was infirm because devoid of supernatural support. The religious *feelings* that shook him immediately before and after the murder of Duncan (I.vii.19-25, II.ii.25-33) were transient and ineffectual. But Macduff's bearing, upon the discovery of that crime, was at once warmly human and truly religious (II.

---

[39] "He" is Macbeth, not Malcolm, to whose preceding speech Macduff has not listened. The dash is my insertion, displacing a period. Modern texts decapitalize the second and fourth "All" while wrongly stressing Ross's "all," above (211), by making it the end word of a verse. Ross said: "Wife, Children, Servants, all that could be found." Macduff echoes that "all" emphatically with his fourfold "All."

iii.68-85). That episode prepared for the full unfolding of his character in the present scene. His passionate, unselfish, religious devotion to his country and to righteousness is displayed by the dramatist in the first half of the scene, culminating in his final adjuration to Malcolm (102-114). This long and significant speech is followed by a long period of comparative silence no less significant and intense (114-159): here we are to picture him as meditating deeply upon his prince's "welcome" (138) apologia, and then upon the story of the English monarch's "healing Benediction" (156) for "wretched Souls" (141).[40] Such a benediction is needed by Macduff himself in the second half of the scene. And blessedness indeed touches (143) his final reaction to his great calamity. He will strive against his overpowering grief "like a man" (220):

> But I must also feele it as a man;
> I cannot but remember such things were
> That were[41] most precious to me. Did heaven looke on,
> And would not take their part? Sinfull *Macduff*,
> They were all strucke for thee—Naught that I am!   225
> Not for their owne demerits, but for mine,
> Fell slaughter on their soules: Heaven rest them now![42]

That prayer is the sequel of Ross's "well at peace" (179). Also it recalls Malcolm's "Merciful Heaven" (207); also his account of the good English king soliciting heaven (149); and, most significantly, Macduff's cherished memory of the saintly queen, Malcolm's mother, humbling herself in prayer as a human sinner in the sight of God (109-111). Macduff himself—no saint,

---

[40] Obviously this lengthy peaceful interlude provides for the audience (along with Macduff) a relief that heightens the emotional effect of Ross's ensuing utterances.

[41] Compare the instantly repeated "were" in *Measure for Measure*, II.ii.73.

[42] The two exclamation points are mine, displacing a comma (225) and a period (227). The parallel capitalization of "Heaven" and "Naught" throws the last four words of those two lines into strong contrast. The final "Heaven," moreover, is emphatic over against the first and uncapitalized "heaven" (223). The three cited lines are similar in caesura but otherwise subtly differenced in rhythm.

certainly, but a Christian reverer of holiness—does the same now.

And thus he becomes the complete antithesis of his enemy. Macbeth's deep remorse after his first crime (II.ii) could have brought him to repentance. But it was stultified, though because of his natural kindness it could not be extinguished, by his pride: hence his increasing desperation. Finally, torturing remorse (III. ii.15ff) and hardened pride (IV.i.90ff) drove him to commit the crime that is the immediate cause of his undoing, the brutal, senseless slaughter of an innocent woman and her children: here, and here only, he suppresses absolutely the better motions of his "heart" (IV.i.147ff). And that same dire deed serves wonderfully, in fact awfully, to bring out the very best in the "heart" (210) of Macduff. He rises by humility while the other declines through pride. Sorrowfully but penitently he submits to the "Heaven" (227) defied by the remorseful but impenitent Macbeth. Macduff, in obedience to Christian teaching,[43] accepts as punishment for his human failings, for his "demerits" in general, a calamity he has not in particular deserved.

Now therefore, and not until now, he is entirely qualified for the act of justice he is called upon to perform.[44] His recognition of heaven's chastening in his own case fits him to be heaven's chief "Instrument" (239) for the punishment of Macbeth. Accordingly, while he wipes away his tears, he must also check the natural impulse to proclaim boastfully (231) what he intends to do.[45] He entreats the "gentle Heavens"—a significant sequel of his previous references to heaven (223,227)—to bring him "Front to Front" with "this Fiend of Scotland." Then, if the tyrant escape, "Heaven forgive him too!" (234). Such is Macduff's ironic and modest mode[46] of expressing confidence that

---

[43] See for instance *Luke* 13:1-5.

[44] This situation recalls Hamlet in his final phase. See my *Scourge and Minister*, page xxv.

[45] Note the ironic echo of Macbeth's "No boasting like a Fool" (IV.i.153). In reality he is there the fool of the powers of evil. But Macduff, now in the service of the powers of good, the "gentle Heavens," will not "play the . . . Braggart with my tongue."

[46] Compare his irony and modesty in II.iv.21ff.

his weapon, wielded against that "Fiend," will be the "Sword" of "Heaven" too. Profound dramatic irony (rooted in Christian doctrine) resides in the fact that Macbeth, who never calls himself sinful, is to be overcome by a noble human person who terms himself "Sinful Macduff" (224).

Malcolm, who opened the scene with doleful words, closes it with a strong and hopeful speech prepared for by his preceding utterances. His immediate reaction, above, to Macduff's unspeakable sorrow was the strong, simple, heartfelt sympathy of one man for another (207-210). But presently, as prince and statesman, he must (unlike the silent Ross) turn his friend's disaster to public advantage while at the same time urging that this will provide for Macduff himself consolation and strength, both comprised in the old full sense of the word "comfort."

> Be comforted.[47]
> Let's make us Medicines of our great Revenge
> To cure this deadly griefe.   215

The plural pronouns intimate that this deadly grief, not confined to Macduff, is deeply shared by all supporters of the "great" cause together with their prince; and the word "cure" recalls the supernatural power of "Cure" (142,152) evinced by the English king, the patron—the patron saint virtually[48]—of their great enterprise. But Malcolm leaves that religious intimation in abeyance while he appeals to the manly fortitude (220)

---

[47] The period and long pause (contrast modern texts) are very expressive. "Be comforted" sums up Malcolm's preceding speech. Silently and with appropriate gestures he emphasizes his *particular* sympathy for Macduff before proceeding to a *general* consideration indicated by the "us."

[48] Such suggestion is surely intended by Shakespeare. The very fact that Saint Edward the Confessor, "the most Pious *Edward*" (III.vi.27), is never referred to *by name* in the lengthy course of the present scene accentuates that mystical aspect of him which is established by continual allusion to his invisible, powerful presence "heere" (43). In the central episode he seems about to appear on the stage (140) but does not: he is close at hand but unseen, exerting his miraculous gift of healing. And in the climax of that episode he is said to have also "a heavenly gift of Prophesie" (157). This stands out in contrast with the hellish, misleading prophecies made to Macbeth in the Cauldron scene. It assures the success of Macduff (IV.i.71,82) and, above all, of Malcolm, the young, pure, and vital "issue of a King" (IV.i.87).

of Macduff and stresses the need of converting great grief into great wrath against the tyrant (228f) in response to the exigencies of the present time: "This time[49] goes manly" (235). Then his final words resume the religious motif and summarize it strikingly:

> Come, go we to the King; our Power is ready;
> Our lacke is nothing but our leave. *Macbeth*
> Is ripe for shaking, and the Powers above
> Put on their Instruments.—[to Macduff]Receive what
>   cheere you may.—
> The Night is long that never findes the Day.   240

In uttering that closing line the speaker, facing the theater-audience, looks prophetically beyond.[50] Obviously he is thinking of Scotland's present sufferings; but his words allude dramatically to "The Night" characteristic of this play as a whole—the "secret, black, and midnight" powers (IV.i.48f), the "Night's black Agents," hitherto predominant over the "Good things of Day" (III.ii.52f). And now the powers of "Day" (240), the "Powers above" (238), are taking the ascendancy: they are putting on, i.e. are instigating, their human "Instruments."

Those heavenly Powers, far above "our Power," are represented by "the King" who will bless the departing Malcolm and his forces (236f). In the course of this scene the military might of that English king (43f,134,189f) is made to appear entirely subordinate to his spiritual powers (140-159). A previous scene informed us that he was preparing for "some attempt of War" against Macbeth, but only because the tyrant's treacherous cruelty aroused the righteous indignation proper, and indeed essential, to a "Holy King" (III.vi.30,39). Like the deity he is at once righteous and merciful. In the present scene his deeds of mercy are emphasized; these stand out in mighty contrast with the deeds of Macbeth and utterly condemn them. But

---

[49] This word, changed by Rowe to "tune," may of course be a misprint; but "time" is more comprehensive and suggestive than "tune."

[50] As Macbeth does, with very different intent, in the final lines of III.i. and III.iv.

it is never suggested that this so-merciful monarch condemns utterly (unlike the deity) the *person* Macbeth. The dramatist relegates to Malcolm and Macduff that sort of condemnation, humanly natural under the circumstances but impossible in "this good King" (147) so "full of Grace" (159). None the less he approves and supports the now entirely necessary war against the tyrant "ripe for shaking" (238)—a war as of "Christendom" (192) against one who has newly allied himself with the hellish powers that "fight / Against the Churches" (IV.i.52f). Consequently Malcolm's final injunction is, in its total context, richly suggestive: "Come, go we to the King" (236)—the supreme, unseen ruler silently working, close behind the scene, like "God above" (120), on behalf of mercy and justice and "the Day."[51]

This scene, much longer than the others, has not their quick, intense emotional effect. But it has a meditative intensity of its own which, so far from disrupting, deepens the whole tone of the tragedy. For the underlying theme of the scene, steadily developed and lending interest to even its most conventional lines, is, simply, *valid humanity*; and this is the criterion applied by Shakespeare throughout the drama to Macbeth. Here it is fully and effectively displayed just before Macbeth's catastrophe in Act V. His great humanness, if he had not misused and stultified it, might well have developed into real human greatness. His emotional and imaginative power is thrown into high relief by contrast with the deliberately plain, often prosaic style of this scene; and though rivalled at the close by Macduff he is far from equalled by him in rich and striking human appeal. But just for that reason we are made to sense more acutely the ruinous nature of his pride. His less gifted opponent obtains, in large measure,[52] the gift of humility, fundamental for true humanness, from which Macbeth has insulated himself more and more —extremely in the final phase of the Cauldron scene (IV.i.90ff,

[51] Thus the closing rhymed couplet is not, as some critics have assumed, a redundant tag.

[52] Of course far from perfectly; else he would not be human; and the same is the case with Malcolm.

135ff). There he is suddenly confronted with disastrous news, as Macduff is in the final episode of the present scene (200ff), but with an opposite result: thus the dramatist brings out climactically the contrast between the two protagonists. Larger, however, is the antithesis of those two scenes in toto. Retrospectively the evil displayed so luridly in the Cauldron scene appears comparatively (far from absolutely) unreal over against the plain goodness shown in the present scene. The world of evil, so "bloody, bold, and resolute," has at its center dubiety and "pale-hearted Fear" (IV.i.79-86): its power is real, and terrific, for the time being, but much less real than arrogant and ostentatious. The Cauldron scene means that the *nature* of evil is essentially *unnatural*, i.e. irrational and unhuman. The Benediction scene (so to term it) means that "goodness," though apparently weak at first (33,136), has a natural and supernatural gradually growing strength. The world of good here—in contrast with the other scene's world of evil with its pride, panic, and occultism—centers in humble, rational, religious humanity.

f. *a wife* (V.i)

That true humanity appears in the good Doctor who now enters; but at the same time the long "Night," dispelled prospectively by "Day" in the final line of the preceding scene, re-enters and resumes its sway. Its unnaturalness and dubiety are indicated by his opening words: "I have two Nights watched with you, but can perceive no truth in your report. When was it shee last walked?"—as though "shee" (nameless throughout the scene) were a ghost of the "Night."

No direct reply to his question is given by the "*Waiting-Gentlewoman.*" We are not told how long it is "Since his Majesty went into the Field" (4, cf. IV.iii.185): many days and many long nights may have elapsed since then. The time is vague, endless, monotonous during which his wife has been impelled, continually, to "rise from her bed, throw her Night-Gown upon her, unlocke her Closset, take forth paper, folde it, write upon't, read it, afterwards Seale it, and againe return to bed; yet all this while in a most fast sleepe." That moving-picture is etched on sheer blackness (the sleep-walker's candle does not yet appear): the night enwraps her more than the "Night-Gown" she hastily throws upon her; and the careful detail, centering in the word "write," conveys the dark urgency of the "written troubles" of her brain (V.iii.42).

Her "slumbery agitation," so the Doctor comments, denotes a "great perturbation in Nature" (10-12). This, for us, is reminiscent of her own last speech, her final *conscious* utterance in the play: "You lacke the season of all Natures, sleepe" (III.iv. 141). Soon thereafter her husband, to whom those words were spoken, declared in the Cauldron scene his resolve to "sleepe in spite of Thunder" (IV.i.86): this outcry—his final utterance in the play upon the incessant theme of sleep—was his ultimate defiance of the awful voice crying, in the night, after the murder of Duncan, "Sleep no more." But she who defied it at the first for his sake (II.ii.44ff) cannot now defy it on her own behalf. The dreadful fact is that her "most fast sleep," to which her weary wakefulness gives way sometimes, is very different from the sleep that is "the Balme of hurt Mindes" (II.ii.39). The deeper her sleep, the deeper the affliction of "terrible Dreames": she lies on the torture of the mind in restless ecstasy (III.ii.18-22).

Hence she cannot lie still in her bed; she has to rise and walk. And she must write *to everybody* a remorseful confession which, for her husband's sake, must be seen by nobody: the papers are sealed and locked in her closet, and in the closet of her spirit. Thus her abortive efforts for relief augment the sick burden of her "mind" and "heart" (V.iii.40,45). Consequently her heart yearns for *oral* confession; the dire words she writes and reads in secret clamor to be spoken aloud. This urge is repressed by the strength of her will in her waking hours, but only with such efforts as intensify it subconsciously. Therefore in the course of her somnambulations she is likely, "at any time"

(14),[53] to give voice to some of those words, the ones that prey most dreadfully upon her soul. And so terrible are they that the Gentlewoman, who alone has overheard them, dare not repeat them. She has given the Doctor a "report" (2) of her mistress's *actions* (13f) but "will not report" (16), though importuned by him, any of her *utterances*: "Neither to you, nor any one, having no witnesse to confirme my speech" (20f).

At the word "speech" Lady Macbeth enters silently; unseen at first by the two speakers; carrying "*a Taper*" in one hand while the other gropes forwards. The light of the candle illumines her "open" but sightless eyes (28f): she is indeed "fast asleep" (23). At the front center of the stage, vacated hastily by the two watchers (24), she sets the candle on a table, lifts her hands, then dips them suddenly—

DOCTOR	What is it she does now?[54]	30
	Looke how she rubs her hands.	
GENTLEWOMAN	It is an accustomed action with her, to seeme thus washing her hands: I have knowne her continue in this a quarter of an houre.	

And she *may* "continue" in this silent action for many minutes *now*, thereafter departing speechlessly. Our suspense is therefore extreme. But presently her lips begin to work terribly in the upslanting candlelight. We lean forward, like the two stage-listeners, to hearken (36). She whispers with wrenching agony: "Yet heere's a spot"—the "damnéd spot" that will not "out" (35,39). And presently we learn that spot's *central* meaning for her. The very heart and center of her ensuing confession is the wild, moaning outcry: "The Thane of Fife had a wife—where is she now?" (47f).

That allusion to Macbeth's third crime comes immediately and startlingly after her allusions to his first (39-45). Primary in her recollection of the regicide is the sharp sound of the little

---

[53] This phrase is parenthesized in the original text for emphasis.
[54] This dramatic pause wherein Lady Macbeth begins to rub her hands (contrast the unbroken flow of the Gentlewoman's ensuing speech) is eliminated by the modern printing of the Doctor's two lines as one.

bell she struck, once, twice, when it was "time to do't." The "time," the silent "murky" midnight, was then (and is now) very appalling to her. But she was able to help her husband by scorning his fear together with her own, even when she had to handle, unexpectedly, the dripping daggers: "what need we feare? who knowes it [i.e. fear],[55] when none can call our power to accompt—yet who would have thought the olde man to have had so much blood in him!" Obviously she *did* know fear, and she knows it now more deeply. For there was one who could "call our power to account," namely a slaughtered "old man": the dead Duncan has exacted retribution increasingly. The blood which at the first she fancied could be quickly forgotten, with the aid of "A little Water" (II.ii.67), has clung to her husband's soul and to her own ever more thickly—"so much blood." Here her low tone takes on a rising horror. Then suddenly, for all to hear, comes the agonized cry (quoted above) regarding Macduff's wife; while her lifted, trembling hands invoke the night: "where is she now? What, will these hands ne'er be cleane?"—recalling her husband's outcry, "What Hands are here?" (II.ii.59), after the murder of the king.

The clinging blood of Duncan, who resembled her father as he slept (II.ii.14), has been awfully freshened by the blood of a woman who was a lonely, devoted wife like herself, but innocent and helpless like Duncan. Accordingly her imagination has leapt from the first to the third crime, skipping the murder of Banquo. This, no doubt, is alluded to passingly by her next words, her adjuration to her husband not to "marre all with this starting" (50). But his "starts" (III.iv.63) due to Banquo's ghost were not very much more violent than those occasioned by the *ghostly* knocking at the gate after the regicide while his wife implored him to regain his constancy (II.ii.68) before the arrival of observers. And now "this starting" associates itself, in her nightmare vision, with his slaughter of Macduff's family— all the more vividly because he kept her in complete ignorance

[55] Modern editions read "what need we fear who knows it. . . ." But the original, though less obviously syntactical, is more dramatic and suggestive.

of this deed. It has horribly fulfilled his vague prediction to her of "Strange things" to be "acted" as he waded forward "in blood" (III.iv.136ff). And, brooding upon it in her solitude, she imagines that his discomposure after each of his first two murders must be evincing itself, still more violently, after his third and most ghastly crime, marring "all" (50) his efforts to maintain his throne.

She would fain have prevented that completely brutal and *ruinous* deed; but she knows it resulted from his first crime, which she herself instigated and abetted as much as she could. She did so because of her intense, blind love for him. And now that love, no longer blind but intenser than ever, *makes her take upon herself the whole of his wickedness.* "Heaven knowes," exclaims the Gentlewoman, "what she has knowne" (55); and thereupon Lady Macbeth lifts her hand (not to "Heaven" but) to her face with climactic horror. "Heere's the smell of the blood still":[56] the odor of it is deeper in her spirit than the sight of it; and here her moaning is deepest (58f). Her phrase "this little hand" echoes her husband's "this my Hand" (II.ii.61) but with new and ultimate poignancy. The blood on *his* hand after the regicide, which all the ocean could not wash away, has been thickened immeasurably by his subsequent crimes. And so her efforts to cleanse *her own* hand are utterly futile; they merely accentuate "the *smell* of the blood": the distilled essence (so to speak) of all his guilt saturates her soul along with his. His hand has become increasingly great and powerful in evil; hers, after the first crime, lost its evil strength. But she feels that, equally with his, her own small and feeble hand reeks of blood, especially the blood of which she herself is (formally) guiltless, that of the other lonely and helpless wife. So, "all the perfumes of Arabia will not sweeten this little hand."[57]

---

[56] Claudius declared, "Oh my offence is ranke, it smells to heaven" (*Hamlet*, III.iii.36). Lady Macbeth omits the "Heaven" invoked by her Gentlewoman but waived by herself at the beginning (I.v.54f). The ranker, therefore, is in her case "the smell of the blood."

[57] Obviously the adjective "little" throws her small *human* hand into contrast with the vast *inhuman* Arabia. But it connotes much more.

Shudderingly she lowers that hand; her heavy sighing ceases, leaving her "heart" more "sorely charged" than ever. For a moment she stands silent (59-67) in the candlelight with white, rigid countenance, like one who has "died." Then, stirring a little, she whispers to her husband as though he were present "now" (48), in this "murky" (41) night, with the blood of *all* his murders on his "hands" (68ff). "Wash your hands, put on your Night-Gowne, looke not so pale: I tell you yet againe *Banquo's* buried; he cannot come out on's grave." Here her voice, which has gradually loudened, fails abruptly: she senses the fact that her lifted hand, admonishing her husband, smells "still" (56), i.e. constantly,[58] of the blood of the Thane of Fife's wife. So her confused references here to the first two murders are not followed by any further allusion to the third. The *unspeakable* horror of it overcomes her completely now; and she stops, significantly, upon the word "grave."

That word, emphasized by her pause and the Doctor's whispered "Even so?" (72), anticipates the deathliness of her ensuing and final speech: she yearns for the final sleep. "To bed, to bed: there's knocking at the gate—Come, come, come, come, give me your hand—What's done, cannot be undone. To bed, to bed, to bed." Originally she heard "a knocking at the South entry," increasingly noisy, which warned her and her husband to "retire," not to bed, but to "our Chamber," there to make ready for meeting and mastering others in the oncoming dawn (II.ii.65-72). But now "there's knocking," soundless, mystic—she hearkens with bent head and hand to ear—summoning her to the gateway that leads to the grave.[59] In the night at the close of the Feast scene she could still expect, though fearfully and wearily, another "morning" after "sleep" (III.iv.127,141f). But now her fatigue and despair are ultimate. She has learned that "what's done" can *never* be "without regard" (III.ii.12). Her

---

[58] This is the common Elizabethan meaning of "still."

[59] Note the contrast in whole tone and rhythm between the two lines cited above: "I heare a knocking at the South entry. . . ." "To bed, to bed: there's knocking at the gate."

husband knew that better than she at the outset (I.vii.1ff), but now she knows it better than he; so she precedes him in being "aweary of the Sun" (V.v.49). Beckoning him to "come" with her out of the light, and out of life, she moves off, *without her candle,*[60] the "light" which she has hitherto kept "by her" constantly (25-27). Later her husband will disdain the light of life as a brief candle (V.v.23) while still unwilling to relinquish it. Here she feels his reluctance and entreats him to "come," far more for his sake than for her own, though longing to have him with her always, in death as in life. She gropes her way into the rear darkness with one hand; with the other she feels for his: "give me your hand . . . to bed."

The Doctor, like the one in the preceding scene, pities extremely the wretchedness he has witnessed and knows that the malady, far beyond the reach of his art, is within the "Cure" of "Heaven" (IV.iii.141-145). The "unnaturall troubles" bred by "unnaturall deeds" (79f)—the double and redoubled "toil and trouble" of the Cauldron scene—need supernatural remedy. He believes that this tortured queen could die "holily" in her bed (67) if, with the aid of a "Divine," she would confess her "Secrets" to "God" instead of to her "deafe" pillow (80-83). But he perceives with deep dismay that she is very unlikely to do so; for (along with us) he knows, "but dare not speake" (87), the fact that penitence on her part is obviated by her loving loyalty to her unrepentant husband. (Here there is no "good King" who, unlike the present king of Scotland, will solicit heaven to dispel "the Evil," IV.iii.146ff). But he hopes the divine mercy may save her, and her husband too, among "us all." Here he is acutely aware—like Macduff in the preceding scene (IV.iii.224-226)—of his own defects. He is timid, wary, and helpless in the presence of great evil and misery; and so he prays, "God, God forgive us all!"

That fervent prayer stands out in strong contrast with the Gentlewoman's cold, sanctimonious remark above, "Pray God it

---

[60] In the usual interpretations she takes it with her. But why?

be [well], sir" (64); to which he made no rejoinder. But gradually his gentle goodness penetrates her self-righteous "bosome" (62). In the climax of the scene she is for the most part silent; gone is her flair for sharp animadversions. After answering his final question with a single quiet word (78), she listens respectfully to his last speech, so lengthy and troubled, centering in his petition (quoted above) to the deity. "So, good night," he concludes, moving off slowly, hands clasped on his breast, his head bowed in mute "remembrance" (37) and meditation (87). His humble benevolence shines in the darkness of this night. And the Gentlewoman, taking up the now guttering candle, will attend upon her mistress (83-85) with new sympathy. Ardently she exclaims: "Good night, good Doctor!" His goodness has made this black "Night" (1) good. And those closing words of hers prepare for the next scene.

g. power (V.ii)

"Night" yields to "Day" (IV.iii.240) here. And a "Drum"—which portended at the first the rising strength of the world of evil (I.iii.30)—signalizes now the gathering of the powers of good. The "many worthy" Scottish rebels (IV.iii.183), entering with their national "Colours," are enheartened by good tidings. "The English power is neere, led on by Malcolm, / His Unkle Siward,[61] and the good Macduff"—in the service, as Malcolm has averred, of "the Powers above" (IV.iii.236,238). And it is significant that the young prince's "deare cause" (3) is supported by "Siward's Son" and "many unrough[62] youths," eager to demonstrate "their first of Manhood" (9-11). They together with him fulfil the providential meaning of the Third Apparition in the Cauldron scene, "a Child Crowned, with a Tree in his hand." True "Sovereignty" is related to all that is fresh, inno-

---

[61] The term "Uncle" (grandfather in Holinshed) brings him into close relationship with Malcolm. Previously he was "good Siward" (IV.iii.190); but here the adjective is reserved for "the good Macduff"; cf. II.iv.20.

[62] The "unruffe" of the Folio means, literally, beardless; but the implication of the word is larger in its present context.

cent, healthy, and growthful in nature, symbolized by "Great Birnam Wood" (IV.i.89,93). Near that wood the allied forces are to "meet" (5f). And Malcolm is termed, in the close of the scene, "the Medicine of the sickly Weale . . . the Sovereigne[63] Flower," displacing "Weeds" (27,30).

Against that wholesome background the unnaturalness of Macbeth's condition, alluded to near the end of the preceding scene (V.i.79f), stands out vividly. The "Tyrant" has much might: "Great Dunsinane he strongly Fortifies" (11f), i.e. his castle on "high Dunsinane Hill" (IV.i.93); and he is full of "valiant Fury." But his power is decadent, for his "cause" is "distempered" (15), i.e. diseased and disordered.

ANGUS   Now does he feele
           His secret Murthers sticking on his hands;
           Now minutely Revolts upbraid his Faith-breach:
           Those he commands move only in command,
           Nothing in love. Now does he feele his Title   20
           Hang loose about him, like a Giant's Robe
           Upon a dwarfish Theefe.[64]

MENTEITH   Who then shall blame
           His pestered Senses to recoyle, and start,
           When all that is within him does condemne
           Itselfe for being there!   25

Taken together those two speeches constitute a single passage wherein the dramatist, using for mouthpiece the enemies of Macbeth, depicts his final state with extreme objectivity. The two speakers have no sympathy for that which Macbeth "does . . . feele" (16,20); but just for that reason they can recount it with sharp succinctness. "Now," more than ever, he knows that all his crimes have sprung from his breach of the "Faith" he owed, and avowed, to his gracious sovereign, Duncan. Angus, who conducted him in the beginning to "our Royal Master"

---

[63] Here this term denotes both royal status and sovereign remedy.
[64] The simile is more striking than the passage in which Claudius is termed a thief who stole and pocketed the precious diadem (*Hamlet*, III.iv.99-101).

(I.iii.101), heard him pledge his loyalty and service to that king with utmost fervency (I.iv.22-27). And now "even-handed Justice" (I.vii.10) is bringing about the defection of thanes who pledged loyalty to himself. "Now minutely," therefore, his conscience upbraids him for that worst of all "Revolts," his own. "Nothing in love," moreover, characterizes the motions of those who still obey him; and that phrase is ironically and bitterly true of his own motions when he professed love, fancying he still had it, for his murdered king (II.iii.114ff).

At the first Macbeth was garmented by Duncan with "New Honors" (I.iii.144f) which, together with the "Golden Opinions" he had won from "all sorts of people," could be innocently and happily "worn now" (I.vii.32-34). But "Now" (16,18,20) —the iteration of that word insists upon the fearful passage of Macbeth's time—his honors, stolen and unfit, are very unhappily worn; the royal "Title" hangs loose about him. He feels like a dwarf arrayed in a gigantic and gorgeous purloined "Robe," which, however, he will not doff; so all his "Senses" (faculties) are embarrassed and disconcerted (23). That image is blatantly comic: evil, essentially absurd because unnatural, appears in the upshot very grotesque.[65] Thus the image condenses the bizarre strain that runs through this play as a whole. But outright laughter is of course prevented by the tragic context.

The last two lines of the passage (24f) express concisely the inward tragedy of Macbeth; and, together with the first two lines (16f), they recall for us the preceding scene. Like his wife Macbeth feels his murders "sticking on his hands"—"these hands" that will never be "clean" (V.i.48f). His "heart" like hers is "sorely charged" (V.i.59f) but, as the next scene will show, even more fully and heavily: "all that is within him does condemn / Itself for being there." His *outward* might is declining; the scene ends with his enemies resuming their confident "March" (31). But his real tragedy is the decadence of his *inward* "power" (1).

[65] This idea is prominent in medieval and Renaissance art and literature, notably in Shakespeare's tragic and tragicomic plays.

h. *sick at heart* (V.iii)

"Bring me no more Reports." Macbeth's outcry as he enters here, followed by *"Doctor, and Attendants,"* echoes his exclamation at the close of his preceding appearance on the stage: "But no more sights!" (IV.i.155). There he determined to shut out from his imagination all visions that could weaken his will. Here he tries to banish from his mind the continual revolts of his thanes upbraiding his own "Faith-breach" (V.ii.18). Vehemently he exclaims, "let them flye all . . . fly, false Thanes" (1,7), endeavoring to forget his own treason and falseness. This recollection makes him "taint with Feare" (3); it corrupts his *inward* strength.[66] So he strives to concentrate his mind upon his *outward* power, relying on the prophecies of the "Spirits" (4) in the Cauldron scene and, above all, bolstering his "Lion-mettled" pride (IV.i.90):

> The minde I sway by, and the heart I beare,
> Shall never sagge with doubt, nor shake with feare.   10

But instantly he turns pale when a "cream-faced Loone" (11) appears, a "Lilly-livered Boy" (15), trembling, and at first dumb, with terror. For this sudden apparition—like Banquo's ghost though in a different manner—reflects the conscience of the king, causing his cheeks to blanch with fear (III.iv.115f). The lad's white cheeks are "Counselors to feare" (17) in a double sense. They abet the "secret" and awful condemnation of Macbeth by his conscience (V.ii.17,24f); and they can infect his followers with dismay in regard to the "ten thousand" (13) oncoming English soldiers. Presently he orders Seyton to send out more horsemen who, scouring "the country round," shall "Hang those that talke of Feare" (35f). This brutal military measure will help him control his own "pestered Senses" (V.ii. 23). By suppressing all signs of fear around him he can repress, he fancies, the "fears" that "stick deep" (III.i.49f) in his own soul and that keep his murders "sticking on his hands" (V.ii.17).

---

[66] Compare the innuendo of "taint" in the ghostly warning to Hamlet, "Taint not thy mind" (I.v.85).

The fear with which his conscience plagued him before his first crime (I.iii.135ff) has continued to torture him (III.ii.21) throughout his career in ever new ways, ways varying in accordance with the dire expedients employed by him to banish that fear. It drove him to desperation in the fourth Act. He embarked upon a series of "dread exploits" in order to subdue it: "That I may tell pale-hearted Feare, it lies, / And sleepe in spite of Thunder" (IV.i.85f,144), the thunder of heaven's justice. But his slaughters, striking heaven on the face (IV.iii.6), have occasioned those wholesale revolts of his thanes which, unlike every previous portent, can reduce his proud "heart" (9) to *complete* despair.[67] "I am sick at heart," he moans, / "When I behold" (19f)—he stops short, covering his eyes and sinking his head. His imagination sees his revolted thanes joining the advancing "English Force" (18); and it sees much else that he shrinks from giving voice to. Raising his head he declares distractedly: "this push [crucial attack by his opponents] / Will cheere me ever, or disseate me now." For a moment he harbors the fancy that a glorious victory, maintaining his throne against great odds, would render him happy for the rest of his life. But he knows that such a victory, alienating more than ever his onetime followers, now his enemies, would merely intensify his misery. And so the vision which his sick heart beholds is poured forth intensely, now, and with piercing elegiac beauty:

> I have lived long enough: my way of life
> Is fallen into the Seare, the yellow Leafe,
> And that which should accompany Old Age,
> As Honor, Love, Obedience, Troopes of Friends,   25
> I must not looke to have—but in their stead,
> Curses, not lowd but deepe, Mouth-honor, breath
> Which the poore heart would faine deny, and dare not.

In that soliloquy Macbeth attains, at long last, a plain veracity regarding his "way of life." The diction, for the most part mono-

---

[67] Pride resulting in great despair is a main theme of Renaissance literature from Dante to Milton. See Spenser's *Faerie Queene*, I.viii and ix.

syllabic, is extremely simple. Here are no magniloquent tears drowning the wind and no self-glorifying image of vaulting ambition overleaping itself and falling (I.vii.25-28). Here the grief is too deep for airy tears, and the fall, now actual, is very different. The journey of his life, like the earth's brief year of seasons, "Is fallen into the Seare," into the last phase of autumn, so seared and sere:[68] no autumnal glory, nor winter's healthy whiteness—just the scorched and withered yellow leaf. In the beginning of the Feast scene he cherished the illusion that, having ended his evil-doing, he could become—with the aid of his kindly feelings towards his murdered friend Banquo —the healthy-spirited (III.i.107f) leader of a well-ordered and genial "Society" (III.iv.3). But now he knows that ahead of him is a seared "Old Age" void of "Honor, Love, Obedience, Troops of Friends." Formerly he had real and great honors (I.iii.104, 144; I.vii.32-34) consonant with the "Love" and "Honor" he owed to his rightful sovereign (I.iv.27). Now his own kingship is "Mouth-honor," mere "breath" with deep curses underneath it. And his sickness of "heart" (19) in receiving such honor makes him sympathize with "the poor heart" (28) of his people giving it to him perforce. The misery of his spirit is replete.

Thus his human-kindness, under the working of the powers above, has supplied the ultimate punishment of the ambitious evil in him. All along he had intimations of this outcome; and from the outset he knew he ought to heed them "holily" (I.v. 22), i.e. reverently and entirely. But he would not do so; and before his second crime he defied the "eternal" unseen "World" from which they came, thus renewing crucially the rancors in the vessel of his "Peace" (III.i.67-72, III.ii.16); and now the "poisoned Chalice" (I.vii.11) has proved to be far more deadly than he foresaw. In the Cauldron scene he defied death, asserting that "our high-placed *Macbeth*" (IV.i.98) would live out

[68] Surely both these meanings are implied by "Seare" (cf. IV.i.113), which however is altered to "sere" by some editors. For the substantive use of this word see Kenneth Muir's edition, page 152. Incidentally the word "fallen" alludes to "fall" as synonymous with "autumn" (season of fallen leaves and the year's decline), an old usage now uncommon in England but preserved in America.

the natural span of his life triumphantly. And many a guilty tyrant has done exactly that, submerging all remorse for his evil deeds, but Macbeth's humanity prevents that denouement. After strenuous efforts to conquer his great remorse, he is eventually reduced by it to fatal unhappiness. The death that threatens his body in the present scene is the superficies of the death that is overcoming his soul. He "must not look to have" the least "breath" (26f)—this word is sequel to the breathless "yellow Leaf" (23)—of the amity and comity that constitute, for him, the reality of life. And so, reversing his blind, arrogant dictum in the Cauldron scene (cited above) he now confesses that, even if he triumphs in the coming battle, he has "lived long enough."

The undertone of the speech is suicidal. But now the thought of suicide is overwhelmed, as it will be till the end (V.vii.30-32),[69] by his resurgent pride. Abruptly, loudly, he shouts, "*Seyton?*" (29). And this new personage, entering reluctantly after being thrice summoned, gives laconic mouth-honor to his "Lord." The disaffected Lennox—the last speaker in the preceding scene—did so earlier (IV.i.135ff); and his first words there, "What's your Grace's will?" are echoed by Seyton's here, with an ironical difference: "What's your gracious pleasure?" His Grace's ungracious pleasure is to "fight till from my bones my flesh be hackt"—a violent picture reminiscent of the battle with which the play opened. There the "brave Macbeth . . . carved out his passage" through hostile ranks (I.ii.16-19) and made "Strange Images of death" (I.iii.97); here he makes *himself* into such an image, a fleshless skeleton, emblem of death. But he will not descend to the abject act of self-destruction: he will invite death in battle valiantly.

As ever he is no whit afraid of physical death. But this brave "Soldier" *is* "afeared" (V.i.41f), here more than ever, of death in his spirit—the doom that is "too like the Spirit of Banquo" (IV.i.112); death in ghostly "shape" condemning him for all

[69] Contrast the final words of Brutus and of Othello; in killing themselves they condemn the pride that has misled them.

the "terrible . . . murders" he has perpetrated (III.iv.102,77f), and now, finally, death in the form of autumnal, deathly despair. This, really, is that which he will violently fight. "Give me my Armor" (33). And though it is "not needed yet," as Seyton curtly reminds him, he insists on donning it: he will armor himself against his lethal thoughts. But these continue to assail him; and complete protection from them is, he knows, impossible. And so in the second half of this scene (no episode in the play is more suggestive) he fitfully and testily puts on, with the aid of the silent Seyton, one piece of armor after another, while (seeking relief that armor and battle cannot give) he unbosoms himself in a fitful, indirect manner to his humble Doctor.

The silent presence of that "good Doctor" (V.i.87) in the background during the first half of the scene suggests the constant presence in Macbeth's mind, since his return from "the Field" (V.i.4), of the sorrowful anxiety regarding his wife which now comes to the fore. "Give me mine Armor"[70]— / How does your Patient, Doctor?" (36f). She can no longer help with valorous words to armor his spirit; but his affection for her, like hers for him (in V.i), is intenser than ever because of the loss of all other "Love" (25). Their devotion to each other is the sole health of two hearts "sick" (19, 37) with despair. The Doctor, who has been watching and listening to the king with discreet intentness, knows well what he dare not say: that "my Lord," like the sleepwalking Lady, is sorely "troubled with thicke-comming Fancies." And Macbeth's ensuing plea on her behalf is also a veiled confession of his own disease. He exclaims tersely and longingly, "Cure of that?"[71] (What is the cure for her trouble—and mine?) He pauses a moment and then, when the Doctor remains gravely silent, pours out a rising torrent of appealing images:

[70] The tone of this repeated demand is strengthened by "mine" replacing the previous "my" (33).
[71] The question mark, substituted by me for a colon, is parallel to the one at the close (45) of the succeeding lines. F2 and F3 insert "her" after "Cure," which however may be a noun here.

> Canst thou not Minister to a minde diseased,   40
> Plucke from the Memory a rooted Sorrow,
> Raze out the written troubles of the Braine,
> And with some sweet Oblivious Antidote
> Cleanse the stufft bosome of that perillous stuffe
> Which weighes upon the heart?   45

The yearning murmur in the low-toned opening line, persisting as undertone throughout the whole passage,[72] yields more and more to loud sibilance. The penultimate verse is spastic.[73] Here the speaker's hands, after rising to entreat "some" (vague and remote, impossible in nature) "sweet Oblivious Antidote,"[74] clasp his breast convulsively. The fingers of his spirit would fain pluck out or raze out (41f) the stuff that stuffs the bosom of himself and his wife—the multiplex stuff[75] that comprises: thick-coming fancies (38); more deeply, sorrow and trouble rooted in the memory, inscribed in the brain; most deeply, the secret evil weighing upon the uncleansed "heart" (44f)—the "heart . . . sorely charged," aching to confess and be made "cleane" (V.i.49,59f).

That secret yearning pervades the speech: the thematic query is "Canst thou not . . . Cleanse . . . ?" The good Doctor replies significantly: "Therein the Patient," man or woman, "Must minister to himselfe"[76]—he knows that his Lord, like his Lady, needs penitence and penance; that "God" can "forgive us all"; that even the wickedest person may, through confession and full

---

[72] The m's and n's that dominate the first line are less prominent in the rest of the speech; but the murmuring tone is sustained also by l's and r's.

[73] This effect, at once bizarre and tragic, is missed by critics who object to the repetitiveness of "stufft" and "stuffe."

[74] The idea of line 43f returns upon that of 39f. Suggestively the long high vowel of "sweet" and the first syllable of "Antidote" echo in reverse order the ee-sound of "diseased" and the "an" of "Canst."

[75] The very sound of the end-word "stuffe" conveys the sense of a vague and large comprehensiveness, like the end-word "air" in a previous passage: "As broad and generall as the casing Ayre" (III.iv.23). It denotes an atmosphere of thick-coming fancies at one extreme; at the other, a large burden of oppressive stuff upon the heart.

[76] In sequence to the previous question and answer (37-39) the Doctor *might* have said here "*my* Patient" and *her*self."

repentance, die "holily" (V.i.67,82f). And we know that Macbeth at the outset was capable of willing "holily"[77] (I.v.22), and that after his initial crime he yearned to pray to "God" (II.ii.25-33). So now when he remains silent for a moment, pondering "himselfe,"[78] contemplating his own diseased soul, there is the very dramatic possibility, real if remote, that he may unburden his stuffed bosom to his companion—as his wife did unconsciously in the opening scene of this Act: the wretched monarch may confess, to this lowly but sympathetic subject, the good Doctor, all within him that condemns itself for being there (V.ii.24f).

But his pride is too great for that. Presently he exclaims, in violent reaction from his confessional mood: "Throw Physicke to the Dogs," to the mongrels that formerly symbolized for him the "worst rank of Manhood" (III.i.93,103). And feverishly, and symbolically, he proceeds with the armoring of himself, his sinful self. But he cannot help blurting out pathetically that which in the present situation sickens his heart most, and which in the scene's opening speech he endeavored to disdain: "Doctor, the Thanes flye from me" (49). He declares he would applaud the physician loudly, again and again, if his science could find the "Disease" of "my Land" and "purge it to a sound and pristine Health." Such was the "Health" (III.i.107, III.iv.39) he vainly envisioned for his land and for himself at the dark height of his career, on the eve of his plunge into ruinous tyranny. Now he knows well that the wholesale desertion of his thanes is the inevitable result of his own evil doing; that his "diseased" (40) self is his land's "Disease" (51): that no "Medicine" procurable by him can purge "the sickly Weale" (V.ii.27f).

But he desperately strives to hide from himself that catastrophic conviction. Wrenching his thoughts from the rebelling

---

[77] This adverb occurs only in the two instances cited above, though Shakespeare might easily have used it elsewhere in the course of this play.

[78] A considerable pause is indicated by the suspension of the rhythm here (46). The line "Must minister to himselfe"—(the dash is mine) remains metrically incomplete, in contrast with the preceding verse: "Which weighs upon the heart? Therein the Patient. . . ."

thanes—while roughly bidding Seyton to pull off a wrongly placed piece of armor (54-56)—he concentrates his ire upon "these English,"[79] those "English Epicures" (8). He tells himself that at least one emotion of his heart is right and healthy: the patriotic desire to expel from his land an invading foreign army.[80] But covertly he is aware of that desire's unsoundness and of the impossibility of fulfilling it: "what Purgative drugge / Would scowre these English hence?—hear'st thou of them?" He would like to have the comfort of his physician's disapproval of them. But the truthful, wary Doctor gives an evasive reply (57f). And Macbeth, turning from him impatiently, begins to move off stage, at the same time repulsing Seyton's attempt to put upon him a final piece of armor: "Bring it after me." He who at the first, battling triumphantly in a good cause, was completely armed, "lapped in proof" (I.ii.54), is not so now. But just before he disappears he vaunts:

> I will not be affraid of Death and Bane,
> Till Birnam Forrest come to Dunsinane.   60

Immediately that vaunt is mocked by the prudent[81] Doctor's closing couplet; he has perceived that, despite Macbeth's "Royall Preparation" (57), Dunsinane is doomed:

> Were I from Dunsinane away and cleere,
> Profit againe should hardly draw me heere!

Thus the last four lines of the scene, taken together, exemplify Shakespeare's continual conjunction of the wicked, the tragic, and the ludicrous.[82] Macbeth's extreme mood of bravado is

---

[79] The speed of this sentence and the covert connection of ideas are indicated by the punctuation of the original: "Pull't off I say, / What Rubarb, Cyme, or what Purgative drugge / Would scowre these English hence?" The English army in Scotland should be pulled off and scoured hence.

[80] Compare the English villain Edmund's *noble* patriotism in defending "our land" against the invading forces of France (*Lear* V.i.25-28, 51-54).

[81] The classic and Christian virtue of prudence, rather than timidity, characterizes him in the two scenes of Act V in which he figures; and prudence, like his greater virtue, charity, requires a sense of humor. In his present speech he might be Prudence appearing as Chorus at the center of the play's last Act. Notice that his humor would be out of place either earlier or later in this Act.

[82] See note 65 above.

fantastic, but tragedy is underneath. He is deeply "affraid" of the "Bane" (59), the "Seare" (23), in his breast. His soul's despair is lethal: he has rightly named it "Death."

i. *Bough* (V.iv)

"Cousins," Malcolm's opening word, addressed to the Scottish rebels who have joined him and his English army, signalizes the comradeship and good will pervading the whole "Host" (6), in contrast (as the prince intimates presently) with the spirit of the "constrained" creatures who still "serve with" Macbeth; whose "hearts are absent too," i.e. are as alienated from him as the hearts of the many "more and lesse"—persons of all ranks, high and low—who already, at every opportunity, "have given him the Revolt" (11-14).

So Malcolm is confident that Macbeth shall be overthrown quickly; soon "Chambers will be safe" (2): Scottish homes shall be free from the tyrant's murderous spying. But that thought leads him to reflect, silently, upon the fact that Macbeth's spies, scouring the country roundabout (V.iii.35,49), will try to ascertain the size of the opposing army.[83] Consequently the prince, contemplating the forest just ahead of him—while Menteith is informing Siward that "this" wood "before us" is "The wood of Birnam" (3)—has a sudden, odd, but valid inspiration:

> Let every Soldier hew him downe a Bough,
> And bear't before him; thereby shall we shadow   5
> The numbers of our Host, and make discovery
> Erre in report of us.

Those straightforward and casual lines (so carefully casual on the dramatist's part) give the theater audience a mystic thrill. Here the invisible world of good, by means of natural and human "Instruments" (IV.iii.239), is manipulating the world of

---

[83] Macbeth knows that the "English force" is "ten thousand" (V.iii.13,18; cf. IV.iii.190); but he does not know to what extent it has now been augmented by secretly revolting natives. The dramatist envisages the military situation with graphic precision.

evil.[84] Unconsciously and providentially, Malcolm is fulfilling quietly the vision that came to Macbeth in "*Thunder*," the "*Apparition*" of "*a Childe Crowned, with a Tree in his hand*" (IV.i. 86ff). The phantasm told Macbeth merely that he would not be vanquished till Birnam wood should "come against him." But that statement was expanded by his own deceptive imagination:

> Who can impresse the Forrest, bid the Tree
> Unfixe his earth-bound Root? Sweet bodements, good. . . .

In the upshot the "Tree," true (like Malcolm) to nature's laws, keeps its root firmly fixed in the earth. But the prince is impressing (conscripting) the forest; and the "bodement"[85] is wholesome and gracious, "sweet" and "good," in a higher way than Macbeth expected. The miracle here is a natural one, supernaturally inspired.

Our sense of providential guidance here is accentuated by the ensuing speeches. The soldiers shout enthusiastically, "It shall be done" (7). And the "many . . . youths" (V.ii.10) in the army, each bearing a fresh green bough, represent a healthy and vital humanity arrayed against a diseased, baneful tyranny emblemized by "the yellow Leaf" (V.iii.23,40,51,59). But the buoyant confidence of the young prince and his youthful followers needs to be tempered—so Siward and Macduff proceed to intimate—by the prudence of age. Old Siward reminds them that the "Tyrant," on his part, has reason to be "confident": his opponents shall have to besiege him (cf. V.v.3) in his great stronghold of Dunsinane (8-10), high on its "Hill" beyond "Birnam Wood" (IV.i.93). Macduff concurs (14-16): rightly "we" must concentrate our minds upon "Industrious Soldiership," setting aside for the present mere "Censures" (opinions). He states his point with characteristic conciseness. But it is taken up and elaborated

---

[84] The word "hew" (4) may remind the reader of Hamlet's "divinity that shapes our ends, / Rough-hew them how we will" (V.ii.10f).

[85] This word in its total context (IV.i. and V.iv) is finely right; such terms as omen, prodigy, portent, augury would be out of place.

by Old Siward with rhetorical loquacity in the scene's closing
speech: "The time approaches. . . ."

His words here, like the final speech of the preceding scene,
though in a different manner, give the audience a passing touch
of relief. And here too the relief is closely related to the main
action. Siward is certain that the "issue" of the imminent and
hard contest shall be decided entirely by warlike "strokes." He
declares with clumsy magniloquence, "Thoughts speculative
their unsure hopes relate." Unsure, he means, are Malcolm's
two hopes: that all of Macbeth's present adherents are ready to
desert him, and that the carrying of the boughs by the prince's
army will prove to be of considerable importance. Both those
hopes, however, are fulfilled in the sequel. Siward, one of the
best and most experienced generals in Christendom (IV.iii.191f),
looks on with silent, disdainful irony while the soldiers perform
the strange maneuver of cutting down the branches and marching ahead, each with a bough held before and above him. But
in the close of the next scene the irony will be reversed. The
tyrant whom Siward regards, from the military standpoint, as
justifiably "confident" of enduring a long siege will unexpectedly give up his "maine hope" (8-10): deserting his great stronghold he will issue into the open because of the providential
boughs that "shadow" the oncoming "Host" (5f).[86]

j. *aweary of the Sun* (V.v)

Macbeth re-enters the scene even more vauntingly than he
left it. Now he is completely accoutered in armor, as not before
(V.iii.58), and attended by the "*Soldiers*" of his garrison "*with
Drum and Colours.*" He shouts, "Hang out our Banners on the
outward Walls"—not on the donjon merely, but on the outmost
ramparts. That loud call with its iterated "out" denotes the
speaker's increasing but hollow effort to circumvent his inward
fears by means of outward bravery. "The Cry is, still, they come

---

[86] The end word "shadow"—in contrast with the synonymous "shade" (see
Love's Labour's Lost IV.iii.43) which would here be metrically possible—is
emphatic and mystically suggestive. And its "o" is echoed by the "o" of Host."

—our Castle's strength / Will laugh a Siege to scorne." His thronging fears are laying siege to his spirit, but he will deride them scornfully. His proud soul, armored and castled,[87] flaunts the strength of its defenses. But its confidence is destined to be undermined in the rest of the scene.

Here as previously (V.iii) the most immediate occasion of his inward misery is the defection of his thanes. It causes him to utter now an airy and fantastic brag in defiance of the mighty English army. (The fact that it is led by the Scottish prince Malcolm—a fact previously alluded to with scorn by Macbeth (V.iii.3ff)—is here, in the presence of his soldiers, omitted by him carefully.) He asseverates that "We" could have met those forces darefully in the open field, and "beate them backward home," if they were not reinforced "with those that should be ours" (5-7). But now he has to learn of the death of the one person who *is* entirely "ours"—she who would fain have reinforced him with all her heart and soul in his final struggle. No sooner has his vaunt terminated in the word "home" than a fearful sound comes from the very heart of his own dwelling, "*A Cry within of Women.*"

Controlling himself he exclaims, "What is that noyse?" Seyton, departing to investigate, replies smoothly, "It is the cry of women, my good Lord."[88] But the outcry, renewed and continuing for a moment, is very far from smooth. Its preternatural "Direnesse" (14) reminds Macbeth of horrid shrieks in the "Night"[89] and "dismall" discourses which, in earlier days, would make the hair of his head "rouse and stirre" like a living creature; so vitally empathic, then, was his imagination. But now such direness, he avows tragically, cannot "once start me" (15), not even at this crucial instant when he expects, fearfully (9),

[87] The representation of the soul as a "Castle" is common in allegory. See *The Faerie Queene*, II.ix; but Spenser's Alma has the "Temperance" lacking in Macbeth.

[88] This verse, in contrast with the movement of Macbeth's preceding speech, is even and unemphatic; notable is the decapitalization here of the stage-direction's "*Cry*" and "*Women.*"

[89] This word, in its context, reinstalls the play's atmosphere of dreadful "Night" culminating in V.i.

the worst news of his beloved wife. In proportion to his intense
love for her is his intense dismay that the fateful wailing of her
women, penetrating his heart, cannot make his "senses" shudder.
We remember his violent starts at the first (I.iii.51) and later—
"this starting" (V.i.50) reprehended by her because of her love
for him! But now (with keen dramatic irony) he is able to obey
her by refraining from starting when he hears the portentous cry
that probably announces her death, so dreadfully has evildoing
dulled his senses. He has "supped full with horrors," this phrase
being the "full" sequel of his foretaste of a poisoned cup
(I.vii.11f): direness has become "familiar to my slaughterous
thoughts." Thus he confesses, in soliloquy, that appalling burden of remorse which he is trying to dismiss from his "thoughts"
while hiding it from his soldiers under loud bravado—the burden which fully, and in the main vicariously (V.i.47ff), assumed
by his wife, and in her case entirely unrelieved, became a fatal
disease[90] of her mind and heart (V.iii.40-46). Therefore "that
cry" (15) of her women (his final reference to it is a fearful
whisper) is also the cry of his own conscience. And when his pre-
monition regarding her is confirmed by Seyton's formal announcement, "The Queene, my Lord, is dead," he is speechless at first
with deep, remorseful grief.[91]

Rousing himself he mutters broodingly: "She should have died
hereafter; / There would have been a time for such a word"—a
word such as "dead" but with a sense far more awful than that
expressed by Seyton's word. His wife's premature and dreadful
ending is better than the living death she would have had hereafter, along with him—even if, indeed especially if, he maintains
his throne—she as "Queen" still, he as royal "Lord" (16), both
of them more and more sick at heart with a remorse which their
intense love for each other would day by day intensify. When we
last saw them alone together as king and queen in the close of

[90] The later and natural enough rumor that she committed suicide (V.vii.98-
100) is untrue: she dies of a broken heart.
[91] Compare Romeo's incapacity for words of overt grief when he learns
of the death of Juliet (V.i.17ff). Very wrong is the notion that Macbeth's
sorrow here is shallow or even non-existent.

the Feast scene (III.iv.122ff) they were miserably unhappy and apprehensive: he turning to "slaughterous thoughts" (14), vainly hoping for relief through further wicked deeds; she doomed to inaction, soul-stifling memories, and eventual death from heartbreak. Deadly ennui was in her final words of all, addressed to her absent husband: "Come, come, come, come . . . To bed, to bed, to bed" (V.i.74-76). And now the same ennui but deadlier is heard in his next lines, addressed to his absent wife, present to him in spirit, present in their dual despair:

> To morrow, and to morrow, and to morrow,
> Creepes in this petty pace from day to day,   20
> To the last Syllable[92] of Recorded time—
> And all our yesterdayes have lighted Fooles
> The way to dusty death. Out, out, breefe Candle!
> Life's but a walking Shadow, a poore Player,
> That struts and frets his houre upon the Stage,   25
> And then is heard no more. It is a Tale
> Told by an Idiot, full of sound and fury,
> Signifying nothing.

"Creepes"—is creeping *now*! The present tense of those first three lines comprises also all the future. In "this" (20) present and seemingly everlasting moment of great grief and despair he perceives, as never before, the utter pettiness of his career, despite all the "Banners" on its "outward walls" (1). He feels his soul creeping, crawling wormlike,[93] in the dust towards death, now and through morrow after morrow, "from day to day," one day trailing after another with deathlike monotony. And he hears the innumerable voices which, after his demise, will utter, syllable after syllable, the record of his horrorful (13) yet trivial life, to the very end of "time." All along he has been warring against "Time" by means of what he grandly termed—but does not now—"my dread exploits" (IV.i.144). Time has been win-

---

[92] His fivefold syllable "to" repeats the threefold "to" in *her* last words, quoted above.

[93] Not snakelike. No touch here of the evil grandiosity of his lines concerning a mighty "Snake" (III.ii.13-15).

ning covertly, more and more, and shall win overtly and absolutely in the days ahead. "And all our yesterdayes have lighted Fooles. . . ." The future throws back a quick and livid light upon the past. His "slaughterous" (14) and foolish yesterdays, together with the creeping morrows, are present at this moment in his memory and imagination, in his very soul.

In the first half of the speech he is thinking mainly of his wife and himself: of "our" dreadful past days and of the deadly "time" (18,21) they would have experienced together if she had not died now. Her taper, guttering and then disappearing at the end of the Sleepwalking scene, flickers again in the mind's eye, Macbeth's and ours, when he, staring off weirdly into void time, exclaims: "Out, out, brief Candle!" But his nightmare vision, unlike hers, widens to comprise all persons whose evildoing and remorsefulness have ruined their lives in Time: "all our yesterdays," the yesterdays of himself and his wife and all those others, "have lighted Fools / The way to dusty death." This "way of life" (V.iii.22) is the way of death: it falls into the withered "yellow Leaf," then crumbles into dry, lifeless dust. And so, for such persons, "Life" is ultimately a wavering "walking Shadow" cast by candlelight. It is a pitiable "Player" walking the "Stage" (the theater's and the world's) for his hour, strutting and fretting—as Macbeth is doing in this last Act—then "heard no more," like a foolish tale that is ended, an insanely meaningless tale. Indeed that life is "a Tale / Told by an Idiot, full"—like the opening speech of this scene—"of sound and fury, / Signifying" (his voice sinks to a slow whisper) "nothing."

That last word of his final great speech upon the way of his life fills the blank left at the end of his first great speech upon the same subject (I.vii.1-28). There he saw his vaulting ambition overleaping itself and falling "on the other"—that vague, grandly disastrous "other" side which now is seen to be, simply, "nothing." In the earlier speech, waiving the life after death, "the life to come," he predicted with elaborate eloquence a tremendously dramatic retribution which would overtake him "here" on earth, "upon this Bank and Shoal of time." He did not foresee that time itself, present, past, and future, would become for him an arid monotony; that his life "here" would eventually be a "dusty death" in life, that his whole career would in the end seem to him, not at all grandly tragic, but— and this is the essence of his tragedy—a loud, egotistic, idiotic "Tale" signifying blank nothingness.

Such is the confession of his inmost self. But soon his outward self speaks again, "full of sound and fury." When "*a Messenger*" totters in, speechless, with a countenance of fearful amazement, Macbeth angrily demands "thy Story quickly" (29). The word "Story" is a quick echo of "Tale" above (26);[94] and the fellow's strange tale is a dramatically ironic sequel of his master's soliloquy. The weird unnaturalness of Macbeth's career is matched by that of the moving forest.[95] The Messenger, stationed "upon the Hill" (33) to watch the country roundabout (V.iii.35), "looked toward Birnam, and anon, methought, / The Wood began to move." He stared until his incredulous eyes were convinced (*not* until he could discern the soldiers carrying the boughs before them). "Within this three Mile may you see it comming"—this verse moves strangely, like the forest itself— "I say, a moving Grove."

Macbeth's resounding "wrath" (35f), ostensibly intended to check the dismay of his garrison, covers his own deep, secret fear; which, however, is now so strong that it betrays itself to his companions in his concluding speech. He declares loudly to the Messenger:

> If thou speak'st false,
> Upon the next Tree shall thou hang alive
> Till Famine cling thee—If thy speech be sooth,   40
> I care not if thou dost for me as much.

[94] The Folio text reads suggestively:
> And then is heard no more. It is a Tale
> Told by an Ideot, full of sound and fury
> Signifying nothing.   *Enter a Messenger.*
> Thou com'st to use thy Tongue: thy Story quickly.

[95] His phrase "a walking Shadow" recalls Malcolm's word "shadow" in the preceding scene (V.iv.5). See note 86 above.

That word "Tree," not previously used since the Cauldron scene,[96] recalls the vision of the crowned child with a *"Tree"* in his hand, "the Tree" (IV.i.95) regarded by Macbeth as a propitious bodement, which it really was, and is, though not for his sinful will. Here the mysteriously moving grove of trees is an ultimate sequel of all the providential signs which from the outset have moved his throbbing "Heart" (I.iii.136) with summons to repent. And actually it causes him now to "pull in Resolution" (42): to rein in, more deliberately than ever before, his "Vaulting" (I.vii.27) ego.

But again that ego reasserts itself, though with far from its pristine vigor. His final mood in this scene is strikingly ambivalent: desperate weariness of spirit besets him along with a desperate yearning for martial action. He doubts "th' Equivocation of the Fiend / That lies like truth." But he refuses to see that the "Spirits that know / All mortall Consequences" (V.iii.4f) have been so overruled by the heavenly powers as to predict a "truth" which would be salutary for him if he would receive it as such. The weird advance of Birnam Wood, abetting the cause of the rightful heir to the throne—Malcolm, whom Macbeth has tried to scorn and persistently refrains from mentioning here —means that the tyrant should penitently resign his crown. But he will not do so. Yet he determines to emerge from his mighty "Castle" (2), "his main hope" (V.iv.10), and give battle to his thronging foes in the open, with the almost certain prospect, as he now believes, of defeat and death. Wearily hopeless yet arrogantly self-assertive his soul solicits, but at the same time fights against, death.

"Arme, Arme, and out!" (46) he shouts with hollow strenuousness; the words mimic his "Out, out, brief Candle!" above (23). Then his tone lowers:

> If this which he avouches does appeare,
> There is nor flying hence, nor tarrying here.

[96] Shakespeare conspicuously avoids it in the present scene hitherto and in the three preceding scenes.

"If. . . ." But his conscience tells him that the Messenger's strange story is essentially true: it is "sooth" (40).[97] In his mind's eye Macbeth is seeing "this which" is well avouched, "this" ominously moving "Birnam Wood" (34-46) which he will not now refer to explicitly. He does not need, and does not here propose, to verify this mystic phenomenon with his physical eyes. His soul recognizes it as one "more," and a mighty one, of those "sights" (IV.i.155) which, at the time of his lowest descent, he determined to exclude forever from his consciousness. It means that for him there can be no "tarrying here." And the "here" is not just his castle: it connotes the "Here" that is this bank and shoal of time (I.vii.5f), this "world" beneath "the Sun":

> I 'ginne to be a-weary of the Sun,
> And wish th' estate o' th' world were now undone.   50

That word "Sun," suddenly uttered by lips that have hitherto eschewed it (and shall not speak it again), is infinitely suggestive. In the foggy opening scene of the play we heard of a mysterious battle that would be "lost and won . . . ere the set of Sun."[98] And now, ere this day is over (V.vi.7), a final battle, sequel of that other but fought in clearer air, will be won and lost. It is ended already in Macbeth's inmost spirit. He has lost all those "Good things of Day" (III.ii.52) which, loved sincerely by his better nature, were necessary to him for his happiness. His first crime blackened the sun for him violently— "dark Night strangles the travailing Lamp" (II.iv.7)—and he never regained its light. But now he has realized that his career, designed to be "Golden" and lustrous (I.vii.33f), has been merely "a walking Shadow" (24). And so he is becoming ut-

---

[97] Cf. "sooth" as applied, at the outset, to another wondrous report (I.ii.36). But in the present instance the term is particularly effective; it connotes the sense of soothsaying, of prophecy. Macbeth's three "If's" (38,40,47), all capitalized in the Folio, become progressively fainter.

[98] In two other passages in the first Act the word "sun" appears in ominous contexts (I.ii.25, I.v.62). For the symbolic meaning of the sun in Shakespeare's total writings see G. Wilson Knight's *The Mutual Flame* (1955), pp. 59ff.

terly weary of the sun and of the "world" (50) for which the
sun provides light, life, "time" (21), and fair order.

And there is a touch of new humility in this world-weariness.
Formerly he defied the universal organism, "the frame of things
. . . Both the Worlds" (III.ii.16); he defied it violently in word
and deed. But he does not do so now. Merely he yearns that,
for him, the estate of the world "were"—could be what he
knows it cannot be—"undone." His present couplet summarizes
the theme of his despairing speeches above. His real yearning
here is that his own "way of life" (V.iii.22), "diseased" (V.iii.
40), unnatural, idiotic (27)—condemned by "the Sun," by the
world of reason and reality—could be "undone." He utters that
word with head more deeply bowed than ever before.

Thereupon, to be sure, he lifts his head and (closing the
scene) exclaims to his cowed soldiers:

> Ring the Alarum Bell, blow Winde, come wracke,
> At least wee'l die with Harnesse on our backe.

But the opening clause is a fateful repetition of Macduff's outcry in Macbeth's castle, "Ring the Alarum Bell" (II.iii.79),
after the secret murder of Duncan: another regicide, open and
justified, the killing of Macbeth, is imminent now. And the first
line as a whole has a cumbrous hastiness conveying the speaker's
present mood:[99] the "Alarum" in his soul is wearily heavy like
the last four words of that line. These words are a spectral echo
of his grandiose conjuration to the Witches in the Cauldron
scene. There with sinful zest he pictured the powers of evil
untying "the Windes," wrecking the ordered world of nature
and humankind, "till destruction sicken" (IV.i.52-60). But now
his own spirit has sickened; and the "Winde," sounding in imagination along with the fatal "Bell," proclaims his own "wracke"[100]

---

[99] Therefore the three commas of the Folio are expressive. They are replaced in modern editions by exclamation-points; and sometimes a dash is inserted after the (decapitalized) "bell."

[100] Like the preceding Thane of Cawdor, Macbeth has labored in the
"wracke" (I.iii.114) of his country (V.ii.28, V.iii.51). He "lives yet, / But

—the destruction about to "come" upon him from his enemies but, far more, the ruin already present within him. One deed is left to do: "wee'l die" in full armor, in the open field, fighting desperately to the very end (V.iii.32f). That, he well knows, is exactly what his "constrained" adherents (V.iv.10-14) when freed from the castle will not do. So his emphatic "wee" denotes his royal self, utterly lonely now, proud only of his bravery, and mortally weary of the royal "Sun."

k. *leavy Screens* (V.vi)

The wild clanging of the "Alarum Bell," within, yields to the rhythmic throb of an advancing *"Drumme"* and to the sound of many feet marching steadily. *"Enter Malcolm, Siward, Macduff, and their Army, with Boughes."* Malcolm says, "Now neere enough"—the soldiers halt and stand very still. For a moment, a deeply silent moment, we contemplate the "Birnam Wood" that has "come to Dunsinane" (V.v.44-46). And our sense of mystic consummation is sharpened by the fact that it is not in the least shared by those who have brought the event about. Malcolm, elsewhere very conscious of providential aid, evinces no jot of that awareness here. And in this scene no reference is made to "Birnam" and "Dunsinane," so bodefully prominent in the four preceding scenes.

Malcolm continues, with a mien (the opposite of Macbeth's, above) of modest and tactful, while supreme, command:

> Your leavy Skreenes throw downe,[101]
> And shew like those you are.—You, worthy Uncle,
> Shall with my Cousin, your right Noble Sonne,
> Leade our first Battell. Worthy *Macduff*, and wee,
> Shall take upon's what else remains to do,   5
> According to our order.

---

under heavie Judgement beares that Life / Which he deserves to lose" (I.iii.109-111).

[101] This line is combined in modern texts with the three preceding words, quoted above, to form one verse. My dash after "enough" replaces the Folio's colon.

Siward and his son, here warmly, and prudently, reminded by the prince of their kinship with him, shall lead into combat the main division of the army in recognition of Siward's famous soldiership. But Macduff is no less "Worthy" (4,2), though he and "wee" the kingly plural (as in Macbeth's last line, above), but here comprising the Scottish thanes, who are all Malcolm's "Cousins" (V.iv.1) in a clannish sense—shall, in the present case, play a subordinate though potentially effective role (5); on that point the speaker is both modestly vague and firmly confident. In short, the whole procedure shall be in accordance with "our order" (6), with the plan determined by the leaders (mainly the prince himself, we may surmise) in council.

As for *heaven's* plan or "order" anent the shattering effect upon Macbeth of the marching forest, the prince knows nothing of that. For him those weird boughs are merely a helpful camouflage (V.iv.3-7); and his candid soul is glad—together with old Siward, so intent upon plain and downright warfare (7f, V.iv.20)—to have done with it now and to have the soldiers show themselves "like those you are" (2). For us, however, the boughs are climactically suggestive here. Those green leafy ("leavy," a term new in this play and arresting) branches are emblems of the "many . . . youths" (V.ii.10) who, after bearing them aloft, now cheerfully cast them down—ready to lay their lives down, too, in young Malcolm's battle against a blighting tyranny, a diseased "yellow Leaf" (V.iii.23).[102] A poignant instance is Siward's "right Noble Son" (3), young Siward, who is to fall in single battle with the tyrant in the ensuing scene.

1. *the Grace of Grace* (V.vii)[103]

In this final scene the action of the play comes full circle. Here is shown, clearly, the ultimate result of the misty opening

---

[102] The word "leavy," used in *Much Ado About Nothing* (II.iii.75) and expressive of the summery air of that comedy, has a sudden, significant freshness in *Macbeth*, wherein images such as the "Rooky Wood" (III.ii.51) are normal.

[103] Most editors have followed Pope in dividing this scene into two at Mac-

battle (I.i. and ii). That combat, taking place unlike the present one entirely off stage and recounted by messengers in doubtful, violent terms, imaged the secret struggle proceeding in Macbeth's soul. His will was violently divided: he was fighting loyally for king and country but at the same time disloyally, though not yet fatally so, on behalf of himself; as discerned by the powers of evil that were with him invisibly. At the end of the first Act his evil ambition, stimulated by those powers, conquered him. And now, at the end of the last Act, he and they are defeated by opponents in the service of the powers of good. This battle, like that which opened the play, is symbolical. The spirit of Macbeth—more than his outward power, which has been shown in the previous scenes to be increasingly weak—is finally overcome.

Suggestively at the end of the preceding scene Malcolm's military forces disappear: off stage they march onward unseen while their "Trumpets speak" vigorously, blown with "all breath, / Those clamorous Harbingers of Blood and Death" (V.vi.9f). Thereupon *"Enter Macbeth,"*[104] alone, and strangely gesturing. His will is divided, as in the first Act, but now very differently. His brief first speech emphasizes the ambivalent mood of his last lines above: he at once desires, and defies, death. "They"— all the forces arrayed against him, Malcolm's army, his own deserting soldiers, equivocal prophecies, "time" itself (V.v.21)— "have tied me to a stake; I cannot flye"—here indeed there is no "flying hence" (V.v.48)—"But ⸗Beare-like I must fight the course." He whom the evil world encouraged to be "Lion-mettled, proud" (IV.i.90) must now fight bear-like, hemmed in on every side, baited ignominiously. With cynical desperation he recalls the prophecy that he must "feare" only a man "not born of Woman" (3f).

---

beth's second entrance (30); and some have made a third scene beginning with Malcolm's second entrance (64); see Kenneth Muir's edition. For line-numbering of the undivided scene see the Oxford Edition.

[104] Compare the rhyming of his name with "death" at the beginning (I.ii.64-67).

Instantly appears a "right Noble" youth (V.vi.3)—not "the Boy *Malcolm* . . . born of woman" whom Macbeth is expecting (V.iii.3-7) and has been trying to disdain, but one unknown to him, a brave stripling in the "first of Manhood" (V.ii.11). Young Siward approaches swiftly and, instead of announcing himself, demands the other's "name." Macbeth, motionless, surveying him with admiration, well aware that the too boldly eager youngster is no match for himself in single combat, would fain spare him. Doubtless this obscure opponent will be dismayed by the famous name which the great warrior presently utters with laconic impressiveness: "My name's *Macbeth*" (5-7). But now, for the first time, this Macbeth has to hear himself denounced to his face, utterly and terribly. His underlings have continued to address him even in his decline with such titles as "my good Lord" and "Gracious my Lord" (V.v.8,30). All that, his heart knew well, was mere "Mouth-honor" (V.iii.27); but, ever susceptible to outward signs of honor (I.vii.32-35), he could still hearken to it with some satisfaction. Here, however, a nameless youngling, completely within his power, evinces not the slightest sign of respect for his great name. Instead he stigmatizes it (6ff) as a hellish "name," "a Title" as "hatefull to mine eare" as any the "devil himself" could pronounce, a name designating an "abhorred Tyrant." And Macbeth, heretofore so profuse and powerful in rejoinders,[105] makes none now: tacitly he admits that his enslaving, diseased tyranny has been justly judged by the spirit of free and vital young manhood. Merely he urges again that his name, though evil, remains at least overpoweringly "Fearefull" (5,9). "Thou liest," cries the youth advancing his weapon—like the "Sword" of truth—forcing Macbeth to make use of his own; and he proves "the lie" by fighting dauntlessly until slain.

In spirit the contest has been won by Young Siward: he, "born of woman" (11), represents nature's invincible protest against the unnatural. "But Swords I smile at," Macbeth now boasts, in terms palpably forced and artificial, "Weapons laugh to

---

[105] Eminently in II.iii.114-124.

scorne." At the same time, however, he contemplates regretfully the dead figure at his feet, so youthful and comely, so lacking in the strength of a full-grown man—too clearly "of a Woman born" (13). Then he departs hastily; plunging into the thick of battle, as "*Alarums*" announce, while Young Siward's body is carried mournfully by his followers off the field.

Macduff appears, seeking the "face" of the "Tyrant" (14). His own face and his whole demeanor show him haunted by "My Wife and Children's Ghosts." With characteristic humaneness he has refrained, and will refrain, from killing any of the tyrant's underlings. At the beginning of the play Macbeth, seeking his chief opponent, Macdonwald, carved out his passage through swarms of "Kernes," his sword smoking "with bloody execution" (I.ii.13-20). But here Macduff "cannot strike at wretched Kernes." His "Sword," held high and pointing ahead towards his hidden wronger, gleams bloodless and "unbattered." It shall remain "undeeded," unrenowned—void of the slaughterous fame achieved by Macbeth—unless it finds its sole right mark. And now "the noise" ahead (14), rising to a "great clatter" (21), seems to bruit (we know it does) the presence of his main enemy. "Let me finde him, Fortune." Thus he begs in departing the aid of the mysterious demigod that often sways or seems to sway affairs in our turbulent world, under the supreme governance of the "Heaven," God, to whom he earlier prayed devoutly (IV.iii.227,231,235).

But now the continual "*Alarums*" suddenly cease. A minute of deep quietness comes when Old Siward, pathetically ignorant of his son's death, ushers in young Malcolm, with quiet dignity and deep respect. "This way, my Lord;[106] the Castle's gently rendered." Incidentally, as if by way of return for Malcolm's commendation of his "Noble Son" (V.vi.2-4), he praises the "Noble Thanes" (26), the prince's Scottish leaders. And he now acknowledges an event expected by them but doubted (in Scenes iv and vi) by his own realistic, martial mind: "The Tyrant's

---

[106] This title, not hitherto given to Malcolm by Siward, or by anyone else, is significant in its present context.

people on both sides do fight." This he has witnessed with his
own eyes. Malcolm, smiling, intimates that he himself, on his
part of the field, has had still better fortune: he has "met with
Foes" who fought on one side only, namely his own.[107] Politely
he refrains from saying plainly that many of Macbeth's Scotch-
men who would have fought against Siward and his forces, patri-
otically anxious to "scour these English hence" (V.iii.56), have
changed sides quickly on being confronted with their lawful
prince. As such he enters "the Castle" (29), the usurper's great
stronghold—its main gateway faces us, in dramatic imagination,
at the rear of the scene—to take possession of it in due form.
And now, with the battle in the field virtually won, "little is to
do" (28), as the practical Siward puts it. But the deed of greatest
importance "remains to do," allotted by heaven and fortune to
the "Worthy *Macduff*" (V.vi.4f).

As "*Alarum*" is renewed, Macbeth re-enters, entirely un-
wounded, staring strangely at the bloody weapon he holds before him, "mine owne sword" (31). His life is a poor "Player,"
a tale told by an "Idiot" (V.v.24,27); but he will not "play the
Roman Foole": he will not kill himself with his own and, seemingly, invincible sword. He has sought "Death" (V.iii.59) in
battle, at once yearningly and defiantly, assailing overwhelming
swarms of foes; but it has withheld itself from him—as it did at
the first when he defied it utterly, doubly redoubling "strokes
upon the Foe" (I.ii.38). So far, death has avoided him miracu-
lously. Therefore "whiles I see lives," he declares with grim
ennui, "the gashes / Do better upon them" (31f): he will slash
at "lives," at all the living beings he can "see," until death ends
his seeing, taking from him the tedious light of "the Sun"
(V.v.49). With weary "fury" (V.v.27, V.ii.14) he brandishes
his sword and begins to stride away.

But he halts and stands rigid when a voice behind him summons him. It is the voice of the one who would not come when
summoned by himself (III.iv.128-130); who had earlier knocked
loudly at the gate—that unforgettable "knocking" (V.i.73)—

[107] Malcolm's "beside" (29) alludes to Siward's "sides" (25).

after the murder of Duncan; who discovered and denounced that "sacrilegious" horror (II.iii.72); who took his stand along with Banquo in "the great Hand of God" to fight against hidden evil (II.iii.136-138)—but thereafter disappeared. Pursued he could not be found. But in spirit he has constantly pursued Macbeth, and has found him (22) now. The voice comes as from heaven assailing and judging him who has done the work of the devil and hell (7f): "Turne, Hell-hound, turne" (32).

Macbeth, not repudiating that "Title" (8), turns slowly to confront Macduff; starts and recoils (V.ii.23), covering his eyes —here is one living being whom he cannot bear to "see" (31); then speaks very huskily, sinking his bloody sword:

> Of all men else I have avoyded thee—
> But get thee backe, my soule is too much charged
> With blood of thine already.   35

The phrase "blood of thine" is significantly comprehensive. His "soul" is burdened, virtually, with the blood of Macduff himself, whom after an inward struggle he resolved to kill (IV.i. 82-86); actually, with the blood of this man's "Wife and Children" whose "Ghosts" (16) have haunted Macbeth, as they haunted his wife (V.i.47ff), consummating her heartbreak. His memory of that brutal slaughter of innocents is *the* thing within him which most condemns itself for being there (V.ii.24f). Accordingly he has "avoided thee," not anyone "else"; indeed he has avoided, as he strikingly does here, the very name "Macduff." Here we are made suddenly and dramatically to realize that hitherto in this last Act Macbeth, though he has named "Malcolm" (V.iii.3) and has often alluded scornfully to his adherents, has tried to banish from his thoughts the one who is the prince's leading adherent and his own great enemy.

Macbeth's chief enemy in the warfare at the beginning of the play was the king of Norway (I.ii.31ff), who had invaded Scotland with a great army. Taking advantage of a native rebellion, he seemed assured of success. But Macbeth was not dismayed. Though he had already endured a dreadful battle he encountered Norway's fresh assault with renewed and terrific energy. Fighting his way through the opposing forces he confronted the Norwegian monarch, engaged him arm against arm, and subdued him, the upshot being a glorious "Victory" (I.ii.58). And now he is perfectly certain of being able to conquer, in single combat, the leading foe confronting him here. The eventual "Victory," this time, belongs to the great host of his combined enemies; already it is "almost" (27) entirely won. Beforehand, however, he can have the great glory of overcoming him who, next to himself, is Scotland's chief warrior.

Instead, he does what he declared to Banquo's specter (and to the world invisible) he would never do even if confronted with the most powerful of mortal creatures (III.iv.99-106): he shrinks back trembling from the man before him. Though "lapped in proof," and armored as ever with complete physical courage, Macbeth is not now "Bellona's Bridegroom" (I.ii.54). He is a "Hell-hound"—a very human one however, who, while pursuing his own advantage evilly, has been pursued constantly, and now is overtaken wonderfully, by divine "Grace" (101). A moment ago he was ready, as at the first, "to bathe in reeking wounds, / Or memorize another Golgotha" (I.ii.39f).[108] But now he fears to inflict and to "see" any "gashes . . . upon" (31f) the man before him; he fears to draw from him a single drop of "blood" (35). He will not "memorize" (make famous) this his final battlefield by gloriously defeating his greatest single foe. Above, he had grace enough to be reluctant to destroy an unknown young nobleman who heaped opprobrium upon him; and now he is completely subdued, for the time being, by Grace.[109] Macduff's three-word challenge, so curt in comparison with Young Siward's reproaches, cuts him to the quick because it announces a spiritual presence that dismays him absolutely. In

[108] In the deposition scene of *Richard Second* the "field of Golgotha" (Calvary) appears in a context full of references to Christianity, including an allusion to the inspiration or grace of God (IV.i.133,144,83-175).

[109] Thus the combat with Macduff is dramatically prepared for by the lesser combat with Young Siward. That fact justifies my otherwise questionable interpretation, above, of Macbeth's attitude towards Young Siward.

the middle of the play Macbeth was dismayed by the presence of Banquo, at first in bodily (III.i), later in ghostly (III.iv) form. Now he is appalled, climactically, by a presence that is for him at once bodily and spectral. "There is none but he / Whose being I do feare," he declared of Banquo; that "being" rebuked his very "Genius" (III.i.54-57). But the present opponent rebukes his whole "way of life" (V.iii.22) most awfully. And so his continual, self-centered remorse is here converted, for the first time, into actual penitence: he wills to make amends by renouncing all desire for a final, self-glorying victory.[110]

But presently his penitence begins to weaken. Macduff responds sternly, "I have no words, / My voice is in my Sword" —justice requires acts rather than words—and attacks with all his might. Macbeth defends himself. But he is still resolved, all the more firmly because the other now terms him an unspeakably bloody "Villaine" (36f), not to draw blood from this opponent; who, however, despite his utmost efforts, is unable to draw blood from *him*. Therefore the combat comes to a standstill. And now Macbeth's penitence should cause him to yield. But he does not. And the humility which had entered his "soul" (34), above, departs in the course of his next speech (37-42). He begins quite soberly, "Thou losest labour," but his pride mounts more and more with each succeeding line:

> As easie mayst thou the intrenchant Ayre
> With thy keene Sword impresse, as make me bleed—

Ominously he feels himself as unwoundable "as the casing Ayre" (III.iv.23), that air (I.i.10, I.iii.81) which is the realm of the mighty but very vulnerable powers of evil. And the sound of "Ayre" is repeated suggestively by "beare" when he proceeds: "Let fall thy blade on vulnerable Crests, / I beare a charmed Life. . . ." Finally with head and proud "Crest" held high he recalls, now with full assurance, the prognostication he had repeated cynically in the opening of the scene (3f). Fatally trust-

---

[110] The modern opinion that he shows here his first sign of *real remorse* confuses remorse with penitence and ignores the real weight of remorse that has burdened his "soul" (34) all along.

ing the equivocating "Fiend" (V.v.43)—who seems to have predicted truthfully that even Macduff cannot wound him—he declares that his "Life . . . must not yeeld / To one of woman born."

Instantly the justice of heaven speaks to him through the mouth of his opponent: "Despaire thy Charme." "Despaire" echoes, with emphatic irony, Macbeth's "Ayre" and "beare": the "Charme" upon the "charmed Life" he bears is a thing of air, the air through which heaven hurled down the "devil himself" (8), the great angel whose pride wrought his fall:

> And let the Angell whom thou still hast served
> Tell thee, *Macduff* was from his Mother's womb
> Untimely ripped.   45

This abrupt disclosure—made in terms as violent as the images in the initial battle-story (I.ii.18ff)—recalls for Macbeth the "potent" *Second Apparition* of the Cauldron scene, the "*Bloody Childe*" (IV.i.75ff), thereafter unmentioned in the play until now: Macduff resummons it unawares, mystically and providentially. And more *humanly* than any other image in the play— notably the weird phenomena in nature after the first murder (II.iv.1-20)—it intimates that "Nature" (IV.i.59) is violently reacting against a tyrant who has assailed her violently and increasingly.[111] And also, with greater significance, the anomalous birth is associated here with the rebel "Angel," Satan, who is the author of all disorder. Once Macbeth, in a transient religious moment, averred that he had given his soul to "the common Enemy of Man" (III.i.69). But, with pride derived from Satan, he has always refused to see himself as a servitor of Satan. Now, however, he has to hear that the devil, always able to disguise himself in angelically alluring ways—e.g. the sweet bodements of the Third Apparition (IV.i.96)—is the one he has "still [constantly] served" (43).

Absolutely shattering is the effect upon Macbeth. He stands dumb for a moment, with head sunk low, his sword-arm quak-

[111] Now is the "time for such a word" (V.v.18) as Macduff's word "Untimely" (45).

ing as never before. Now he should condemn the devilish will within himself; but wrongly, though very humanly, he inveighs against the words that have unmanned him. He mutters:

> Accursed be that tongue that tells mee so;
> For it hath Cowed my better part of man—

He does not curse Macduff whom, still more than before, he shrinks from naming; nor will he here defy, as he earlier did, the supernatural "World" (III.ii.16) of which Macduff is the instrument. Merely he curses, with sullen, childish evasiveness, "that tongue that" has entirely daunted his very spirit, his "better part of man."[112] Thereupon and rightly, though perforce and at long last, he objurgates the "Juggling Fiends" whom he has encouraged (this fact he suppresses) to inspire him with false "hope" (51). He eyes his opponent, sinks his gaze again, and concludes bluntly: "I'll not fight with thee."[113] This line, with its emphatic final word, returns upon his initial declaration above —before he learned of Macduff's unnatural birth—"Of all men else I have avoided *thee*" (33). What he most deeply fears is, not the "thee" fulfilling the prophecy of a juggling fiend, but the "thee" who embodies, awfully, his own conscience. No "shape" other than "that" (III.iv.102), no other living being (31), could so daunt him; all else would be "too weak" for "brave Macbeth" (I.ii.15f). His present opponent is a "Strange Image," *made by Macbeth himself*, of "death" (I.iii.96f), the "death" (V.v.23) that during this last Act has more and more overcome his "soul" (34). So now he experiences an ultimate humiliation: he cannot and will not fight, further, with this "thee."

And that humiliation is touched with a humility which *could* now master him: his penitent state, emergent from long and terrible remorse, might be converted to real repentance. But divine grace, so often rejected, cannot in the end be easily accepted by him. And at once his new humility is put to a severe, decisive

---

[112] See the note on this phrase in Kenneth Muir's edition, page 166.
[113] These words should constitute, as not in the Folio, a separate short line.

test. Macduff, who has hitherto been intent upon slaying (15) his foe, exclaims unexpectedly (52-56): "Then yeeld thee, Coward, / And live to be the show and gaze o' th' time"—like a rare "Monster" in captivity, with a painted sign above him advertising "the Tyrant"! The prospect is certainly fantastic—as, in retrospect, is the career of this "Tyrant," like "a Tale / Told by an Idiot." The bizarre existence proffered to him now by a merciful "even-handed Justice" (I.vii.10) is perfectly relevant: it is exactly the sort of penance·he must accept and endure for real, entire repentance. In the close of the preceding Act Macduff exclaimed, with proleptic irony: "if he scape," escape "my Sword," "Heaven forgive him too!" (IV.iii.234f). There this noble thane—like the good Doctor who prayed in the next scene "God, God forgive us all" (V.i.83)—confessed his own need of forgiveness for the "demerits" (IV.iii.226) he shared with all mankind. And now, as fruit of his purgatorial sufferings, he is willing to sacrifice his very strong natural desire, favored by "Fortune" (22), to kill his bloody wronger or, at the least, to occasion his execution. So Macbeth is providentially offered the chance to suffer repentantly the flagrant degradation called for by his flagrant self-glorification.[114]

But that purgatory is rejected by the very thing which it is designed to subdue, Macbeth's great pride. Yet his demeanor, in his last speech of all, has much of the dignity of his best moments. Unlike the first Cawdor he does not, at the end of his life, "set forth a deep Repentance" (I.iv.7). On the other hand he does not in the least palliate his evil deeds; accordingly he refrains from replying in kind to the opprobrious words he has just listened to. Singling out Macduff's mildest term "yeeld," he replies in a low tone, while slowly raising his sunk head:

> I will not yeeld
> To kisse the ground before young *Malcolm's* feet,
> And to be baited[115] with the Rabble's curse.

[114] That sort of "tomorrow," resulting from all his "yesterdays," would *not* signify "nothing" (V.v.19ff).

[115] This word resumes his initial image (1f) of a bear tied to a stake and baited by dogs.

Deeply he feels, and knows that he deserves, that which he will not endure to see enacted: the utmost scorn of the whole realm, from the prince down to the lowest of the people. And "the Boy" whom earlier he disdained boastfully (V.iii.3) he now regards, with due respect, as the rightful and victorious new sovereign, "young Malcolm." That victory, he knows, has been brought about by high and righteous powers: he now alludes to their mysterious instruments, the moving forest and, above all, the person confronting him, whom he still will not name:

> Though Birnam wood be come to Dunsinane,[116]
> And thou opposed, being of no woman born,   60
> Yet I will try the last. Before my body,
> I throw my warlike Shield—

He addresses the "thou opposed," not violently as above (46), but in a tone of quiet awe: this personage "of no woman born"[117] figures forth a potent supernatural order. And though he will not yield to that order and to that personage he will not disrespect them. Merely and indefinitely he declares, with a novel touch of meekness, "Yet I will try the last." He will not assault this foe; yet he will shield "my body"[118] with all his force and skill. He will be at the last, and at the least, what he was so greatly at the first—"warlike."

So far his speech has evinced the composed dignity which can render human pride, despite its radical sinfulness, exceedingly attractive.[119] But in the end that mien is abruptly discarded: the speaker's tone, which has been steadily and naturally rising, becomes unnatural and blatant. Addressing his opponent *by name*, for the first time, he vaunts: "Lay on, *Macduff*, / And damned be him that first cries, hold, enough!" Three of those words are fatally ironic. In the Cauldron scene the First Apparition

---

[116] Shakespeare has artfully omitted, above, any indication that Macbeth has learned the *natural* cause of this phenomenon.

[117] This phrase varies emphatically from the three versions used above (3,11,42): the "no" is reserved by the dramatist for the present climax.

[118] His *bodily self*, naturally born of a woman, unlike Macduff's (60).

[119] Compare Spenser's Lucifera. See *The Faerie Queene*, I.iv.8, in its full context.

screamed out: "Beware *Macduff* . . . dismiss me. *Enough!*"
(IV.i.69-72). And in the close of that scene, when Macbeth had
heard the mysterious galloping that signalized the providential
escape of Macduff, he shouted that all who trusted "the weird
Sisters" should be *"damned"* (IV.i.136-142).

And now, so far from merely defending himself, he attacks
this *"Macduff"* with sudden, weird "fury" (V.ii.14) and drives
him—*"Exeunt Fighting"*—from the scene. Soon, however, they
re-enter *"Fighting"* with Macbeth in retreat, showing more and
more signs of exhaustion. His spirit, rather than his body, is
tired, as it has increasingly become throughout this Act and,
indeed, though not so obviously, throughout the four preceding
Acts. His proud strength, while renewing itself by fits and starts,
has constantly declined; while Macduff's humble power has constantly, though at first not apparently, progressed. So this final
combat is a summary image of the whole course of the *Tragedy
of Macbeth.*

Macduff, not present nor mentioned in the first Act, and devoid unlike Macbeth of martial fame, began a *spiritual* conquest
of the guilty hero when, still unseen, he knocked at the gate
after the regicide, and notably when he stigmatized that deed
as a most "sacrilegious" murder breaking open, and stealing the
"Life" of, the "Lord's anointed Temple" (II.iii.72-74). Soon
he retired from view with "God's benison" upon him (II.iv.40).
And, at the height of the new king's evil power, Macduff left
the realm, accompanied by the "Prayers" of good men (III.vi.-
49)—to reappear in a scene (IV.iii) illumined with continual intimations of divine grace. And now, though forced at first to
retreat by his foe's *diabolic* energy, he has a great reserve of
power derived from on high. Macbeth, contrariwise, is defeated
in spirit—"fallen into the Sear" (V.iii.23)—before he is quelled
in body: he is enfeebled by remorse which, not converted into
repentance, has become disastrous. His "soul" is so "much
charged" (34) with guilt that his final warlike efforts are futile.
He speaks no further word; he fights silently and desperately

—as in the play's opening battle;[120] and at the end of the story, as at the beginning, he is "brave *Macbeth*" (I.ii.16). But otherwise all his magnificent natural gifts, misused by the ambitious evil in him, signify precisely "nothing" (V.v.28).

Dramatically symbolic of that fact is the very ignominious mode of Macbeth's ending. Driven back steadily by Macduff he is "*slaine*" when about to disappear through a side exit; and his body, followed by the victor, is dragged out of sight by the hands of obscure persons barely glimpsed by us. Thereupon a "*Retreat*" is sounded; then a grand "*Flourish*." Malcolm with his entourage re-enters, centrally, from the surrendered (24) castle, while his victorious "*Soldiers*" come pouring onto the stage through other entrances, then line up at the rear with ceremonious mien.[121] Characteristically the prince's first concern, expressed with simple sincerity, is for "the Friends we misse .... *Macduff* is missing, and [to Siward] your Noble Sonne."[122] And now, with exquisite effect—with no overt allusion to Macbeth[123] but in vivid contrast with his exit in the preceding episode —the ending of Young Siward is commemorated.

His death is announced to his father by him who earlier brought distressful news to others (IV.ii.1ff, IV.iii.159ff), the commonplace but kind and tactful Ross. Through his careful speeches and the abrupt replies of Old Siward, grief-stricken but bravely mastering his grief, a deep pathos is established. But

---

[120] One of Shakespeare's purposes in having that battle fought entirely off stage is to keep Macbeth suggestively silent there: no word from him is quoted or alluded to by those who recount the story of the battle.

[121] Thus the play ends, as it began, in the open—not inside the castle as a good many have supposed—though of course without the initial fogginess: at the close of the play Malcolm's cause comes out, entirely and triumphantly, *into the open*. And apparently the last battle, lost and won so differently from the first, is, like that, concluded ere the set of sun (I.i.4f); cf. line 27 of the present scene in connection with V.vi.7.

[122] Contrast Macbeth's more rhetorical concern for "our deere Friend *Banquo*, whom we misse" (III.iv.90).

[123] The fact that he was the killer of Young Siward could have been proclaimed here if the dramatist had so desired. But that, while melodramatically striking, would have spoiled the whole tone of the present episode. Moreover the withholding of Macbeth's name here accentuates the effect of Macduff's re-entrance with the tyrant's head.

also the episode expresses conclusively the fact alluded to in several previous passages: unnatural tyranny is ever opposed by all that is fresh and vital, veritably natural, in humanity. And that opposition, we are now made to feel more than before, is sacrificial—as in the case of Macduff's little Son (IV.ii)—and, above all, religious. Young Siward was in his "first of Manhood" (V.ii.11): he "lived but till he was a man," until in "the unshrinking station where he fought . . . like a man he died" (69-72); but his *real* life is not ended. "God's Soldier be he . . . God be with him" (76,82). So the old father concludes, bowing his head for a silent moment, submitting to God and receiving His comfort. Then, using the word "comfort" in its religious sense (denoting strength and hope), he declares with lifted eyes, upon the entrance of the other missing nobleman: "Here comes newer comfort." That word "newer" is intensely meaningful: Siward, having humbly found divine comfort for the loss of his noble son, can find it also, unselfishly, in the fact that the "Noble" thane (26), Macduff, presumably fallen, is still living.[124] Macduff, with the eyes of Siward and all the others fixed upon him, advances rapidly to where Malcolm stands in the front center of the scene—young Malcolm in whose cause Young Siward died —and salutes him reverentially: "Haile, King, for so thou art!"

Then Macduff turns and gazes (all the company do likewise) at a weird *apparition*—a helmeted head borne aloft on the pike of a soldier who, entering after Macduff, has stationed himself in the extreme rear:

Behold where stands[125] [Macduff points with his sword]
Th' Usurper's cursed head—

Thus is fulfilled the thunderous prediction of the "power" that spoke through the lips of the First Apparition in the Cauldron

[124] Even if it is assumed (wrongly, I think) that Siward, having already caught sight of Macbeth's head, speaks here in a *grim* tone my interpretation of the main intent of his words is not invalidated. Incidentally his religious humility here is the more striking because of his predominantly martial attitude (75), sometimes stridently martial (V.iv.16ff, V.vi.7f).

[125] These three words, like the six quoted above, constitute a separate line in the Folio.

scene, *"an Armed Head"*—"thou unknowne power" (so addressed by Macbeth) who (so said the First Witch) "knowes thy thought" (IV.i.69). "Thou hast harped my fear aright," Macbeth declared; but he presently subdued his fear in a way that was dreadfully wicked. Accordingly he banished from his memory that First Apparition; unlike the Second and Third, whose significations he twisted to his own advantage with the aid of the evil spirits, it was never again mentioned by him. Nor has it ever been alluded to (unconsciously of course) by other persons—with one strange exception. Macduff bizarrely envisioned Macbeth, if he should yield, as "Painted upon [i.e. his picture at the top of] a pole" (55). And now the tyrant's armed (and uncrowned) head is suddenly displayed upon a pole, in vivid parody of his unyielding pride. He refused the warning that the invisible powers of good, overswaying the powers of evil, gave him through the First Apparition. And so heaven, working through Macduff, has brought about the present result. The head that armed itself against moral law and divine grace was, and is, the head of Macbeth. For a moment the whole company (on the stage and in the theater) gaze with awe at this definitive *apparition.*

But quickly Macduff reconcentrates attention upon the new and true and vital *head* of the realm; "the time is free," he continues:

> I see thee compassed with thy Kingdom's Pearle,   85
> That speake my salutation in their minds;
> Whose voices I desire aloud with mine:
> Haile, King of Scotland!

ALL   Haile, King of Scotland![126]

Malcolm, the legal heir to the throne, is, far more importantly, "King" by reason of his royal character. He is "free" from the

---

[126] The rhyme of "free" and "thee" (84f) is significant. And the threefold capitalized "Haile" (83,88f) recalls, with dramatic irony, the threefold "haile" that once greeted Macbeth (I.iii.48ff).

vices that "cursed" the "Usurper" (84); and he has evinced unawares all the "King-becoming Graces" which he is too modest, and too religiously humble, to claim for himself (IV.iii. 91ff). On his first appearance in the play he, so unlike Macbeth, was devoid of any distinction in battle; but he *was* distinguished by princely gratitude, simple and warm, to a sergeant, a "brave friend," who helped to save him from captivity (I.ii.3-7).[127] And now, in the close, his gratitude and "Bounty" (IV.iii.93) are finely manifested. His words, upon his attainment of supreme power, have no touch of self-glorification, nor of studied condescension. Instead, with simple dignity and kindliness he declares: "We shall not spend a large expense of time[128] / Before we reckon with your severall loves"—he glances from face to face— / "And make us even with you." At once he makes their rank more "even" with his own by conferring the earldom, for the first time in Scotland, upon "My Thanes and Kinsmen" (cf. V.iv.1). And much more shall "be planted newly with the time"—shall take part in the fresh and natural growth prefigured by the Third Apparition, "a Childe Crowned, with a Tree in his hand." Exiled "Friends" shall be called "home," while Macbeth's "cruell" instruments, throughout the realm, shall be produced and (he implies) justly dealt with.[129]

And now, suddenly and briefly, with a gesture towards the severed head displayed at the rear, he alludes to

> . . . this dead Butcher, and his Fiend-like Queene;
> Who, as 'tis thought, by selfe and violent hands
> Tooke off her life. . . .   100

[127] This passage is so worded as to imply, what Malcolm refrains from saying, that he himself fought bravely in an advanced and dangerous position, and that he has already, off stage, commended to his father the "good and hardy Soldier" who crucially came to his assistance.

[128] His tone is one of modest and friendly-smiling understatement: he proceeds to give his thanes an immediate reward. Incidentally we should note the significant iteration in this play of the word "time" (84,94,102, cf. V.v.18,21, and earlier passages).

[129] Humanely he does *not* say that they shall be *cruelly* punished.

Such is the epitaph pronounced upon the preceding king and queen by the new monarch. It is the more dreadful because, uttered casually by a gracious prince, with no note of *personal* animus against the two who had wronged him so extremely, it expresses that which is "thought" (99) by all the "minds" (86) here present. It signifies the sort of fame which Macbeth, who loved fame, has eventually won: an infamy far surpassing that of the "merciless" rebel whose "Head," at the outset, was fixed upon the royal battlements (I.ii.9,23). In the close of that scene the victorious hero was acclaimed, by the king, as "Noble Macbeth"; in the close of the last scene of all he is passingly referred to, by the new king, as "this dead Butcher."[130] And the brutal violence denoted by those words is accented by the quick suggestion that it was shared by the woman who was his "Queene": both of them had "violent hands." For us that phrase recalls her declaration to her husband: "My Hands are of your colour" (II.ii.64). But the term "Fiend-like," we know, applies far less to her career than to his. The strength she derived from the evil spirits at the outset (I.v.41ff) was soon exhausted; but he increasingly served the purposes of the "Fiends" (48).

But this inhuman tyrant was formerly regarded by good men as upright and lovable (IV.iii.13): he was distinguished for human-kindness. His devoted wife knew he was so full of it (I.v.18ff) as to be in constant dread of doing wrong to others. What she did not know was that his human pride, surmounting his human-kindness, and becoming* more and more devilish, must eventually drive him to despair—unless overcome by *superhuman* grace. In Malcolm, as in his meek and gracious father (I.vii.17, III.i.66, IV.iii.109), that grace appears greatly, without his awareness: the very humility that enables him to have it prevents him from knowing that he has it *distinctively*. He per-

[130] In the opening battle scene the name "Macbeth" is uttered four times with carefully climactic effect (I.ii.16,34,65,67). In the present scene it is mentioned twice (7,18) during two introductory episodes; otherwise he is anonymously referred to in opprobrious terms, climaxing in the present degrading epithet.

ceives it in others: in Macduff's mien of "Grace" (IV.iii.22-24); in the conduct of the English king so "full of Grace" (IV.iii. 159); in all, indeed, who are "Instruments" of the heavenly "Powers" (IV.iii.238f). He knows that those powers are equally kind and severe. Grace rejected is awful in its judgment upon a tyrant inspired by a "slaughterous" (V.v.14) lust for earthly honors: hence Malcolm's final pronouncement (quoted above) upon Macbeth. Grace accepted can make the "dearest" earthly thing appear "a carelesse Trifle": hence his very different epitaph upon another but repentant traitor, Macbeth's immediate predecessor (I.iv.2-11). Those two utterances of this prince, the one at the outset and the other at the end of the tragic action, represent the two poles upon which the world divinely turns: lovely mercy and austere justice.

Thus the play's closing monologue, spoken in a steadfast, gracious tone by the head of an ordered realm, is the antithesis of the wild opening trialogue (I.i) representing the realm of ambitious, chaotic evil. It is also antithetic to the monologues wherein Macbeth in the course of this final Act exhibits his world-weariness. Those speeches, marked by a magnificence of style and personality which Malcolm lacks, signalize the tragedy of great human qualities gone to waste through evil pride. Christian self-esteem would have rendered Macbeth what deity and nature designed him to be, and what Macduff is now, the noble chief supporter of "King" (88) and country. As usurper he lost increasingly that which Malcolm has increasingly won: "Golden Opinions from all sorts of people" (I.vii.33), "Honor, Love, Obedience, Troops of Friends" (V.iii.25). Malcolm's native and *natural* humanity, far more limited than Macbeth's, has been more and more nourished by that "Milke" (I.v.18) of supernatural grace which is "the sweet Milke of Concord," of "peace" and "unity" on "earth" (IV.iii.98-100). His final speech, as a whole, evinces "modest Wisdom" (IV.iii.119) and constant human-kindness *crowned by Grace*; it concludes:

... This, and what needfull else   100
That calls upon us, by the Grace of Grace,[181]
We will performe in measure, time, and place:
So thankes to all at once, and to each one,
Whom we invite to see us Crowned at Scone.[132]

[181] The phrase "by the Grace of Grace" modifies "will perform" as well as "calls"; and its casualness denotes, climactically, the unobtrusiveness of Malcolm's piety and "love of Grace" (*Hamlet*, III.iv.144). Elsewhere Shakespeare speaks in fuller terms of immanent and effective grace of spirit derived from the transcendent grace of God (see *All's Well That Ends Well* II.i.139-179, especially line 163). Here he alludes with utmost concision to "the Grace of [derived from] Grace." And the ensuing lines evince Malcolm's royal "Graces" (conferred by Grace) of "Temperance," "Perseverance," and "Patience" (IV.iii.91-94) together with gratitude, courtesy, and firm dignity, this last illustrating right self-esteem as contrasted with wrong pride.

[132] Contrast the "unnatural" and doubtful atmosphere in which Macbeth departed, *unseen*, to be "invested" with the sovereignty in the sacred parish, "Scone" (II.iv.10, 30-32).

THE INITIAL CONTRAST IN *LEAR*

ADDITIONAL ESSAY

The Initial Contrast in *Lear*

IT IS WELL KNOWN that in Shakespeare's greatest plays the opening episodes are very significant: here he foreshadows the whole
trend of his story. Therefore a critic who misinterprets the introductory passages of the play gets off on the wrong foot. And
that, I think, has been commonly done by critics of *The Tragedy
of King Lear* because, obsessed by certain modern notions, they
have missed the Elizabethan and Renaissance viewpoint of the
author. This does not mean that in order to interpret rightly
the beginning of *Lear* we must go *back* to the Renaissance standpoint: we need to go *forward* to it. In other words we need to
re-employ that entirely *dramatic* view of persons and events
which, though extraordinarily prominent in Renaissance literature, supremely in Shakespeare, is not for an age but for all
time. Below is an attempt, imperfect enough, to disinter the
introductory portion of this play from the nondramatic concepts imposed upon it by modern criticism and to interpret it
in a Renaissance—that is, in a dramatic—manner.

A main feature of dramatic art is vivid contrast; and a striking contrast is provided by reason and passion. When the reasonable creature man becomes beside himself with sudden, violent
passion his conduct is extremely dramatic. Renaissance play-
wrights worked that fact for all it is worth—and more; often
the passion is not adequately motivated. In Beaumont and
Fletcher a protagonist may give way abruptly to a passion that,
instead of putting him merely *beside himself*, transforms him
into an entirely different person. But at their best, Elizabethan
dramatists achieved sufficient probability in matters of this kind.
It is interesting to watch Shakespeare striving to do so in the
initial climax of the first scene of *Titus Andronicus* (supposing
that melodrama to be his), wherein Titus with sudden fury kills

{ 235 }

his disobedient son Mutius (l. 290). A dozen years later the dramatist could manage more successfully a similar situation in the chief crisis of the first scene of *Lear*: we are shocked, but not confounded, when the old king, suddenly enraged, curses and casts off his disobedient daughter Cordelia (ll. 110ff.). In both cases, however, the author drives at the tragic change produced by uncontrolled passion in a *more or less* reasonable, and therefore representative, human being: we are shown the intensely dramatic contrast between his present and his previous state of mind.

In order to achieve that tragic contrast Shakespeare endeavored to make Lear, before his outbreak against Cordelia, as reasonable and normal as possible. Certainly that task was difficult because of the conditions imposed upon the dramatist by the strange old story he was handling; moreover, in this crowded drama the Introduction—so to term lines 1 to 109—had to be extraordinarily brief and condensed. Hence the main intent of the Introduction, though no doubt apparent to the Elizabethan audience, is not unmistakably clear to the average modern reader; and he has been hindered rather than helped by the critics. They have made the mistake of reading back into the initial episodes the subsequent folly of Lear. They have ruined the great contrast described above by regarding him as, from the very first, unreasonable and abnormal. This view renders him unbelievably different not only from Shakespeare's other tragic heroes but also from what he himself is increasingly shown to be from the fourth scene onward, a very representative human being. That he is essentially such from the very start is shown by the dramatist in the Introduction.

Proponents of the contrary view are numberless. Mention of its two chief promoters, Coleridge and A. C. Bradley, will suffice. Coleridge declared that Lear's conduct at the first is "improbable"; and that his trial of his three daughters' love for him "is but a trick . . . a silly trick."[1] Bradley, fundamentally agree-

---

[1] Thomas M. Raysor, *Coleridge's Shakespearean Criticism* (London, 1930), I, 55, 59.

ing with Coleridge though more elaborate, speaks of Lear's "complete blindness to the hypocrisy" of Goneril and Regan; declares that his "original plan," the threefold division of the kingdom, is "foolish and rash"; and even goes so far as to assert that the very first lines of the play "tell us that Lear's mind is beginning to fail with age."[2] Very different, however, is the actual effect of the opening speeches:[3]

KENT.   I thought the King had more affected the Duke of
         Albany, than *Cornwall*.

GLOSTER. It did alwayes seeme so to us. But now in the division
         of the Kingdome, it appeares not which of the Dukes
         he values most, for qualities are so weighed, that
         curiosity in neither, can make choice of either's moiety.

In Shakespeare's other tragedies, notably *Hamlet*, *Othello*, and *Macbeth*, the opening lines are exciting and ominous. But *Lear*, the most tempestuous of all, opens very quietly—in order to make the threefold division of the kingdom seem as natural as possible. For the double purpose of economy and suspense the dramatist does not yet inform us that Cordelia's "third" is to be the most "opulent" (l. 88). But suspense is far from the mood of Kent and Gloster here. Their reaction to the equality of the other two shares is surprise of the mildest sort, notably so in the case of the bold and critical Earl of Kent. His casual tone is continued in his next speech, "Is this not your Son, my Lord?" And during the rest of the dialogue his mood is equable, kindly, and tolerant while Gloster chatters with gross humor about the bastardy of Edmund. In short, the opening episode (ll. 1-34) of this stormy play is, as a whole, calm in tone and increasingly *humorous*. It establishes the mood in which the dramatist wishes us to watch what immediately ensues.

And the play's first lines, far from telling us that "Lear's mind is beginning to fail with age," suggest exactly the oppo-

[2] *Shakespearean Tragedy* (London, 1911), pp. 250, 281.
[3] Quotations are from the First Folio (1623). The original spelling and punctuation are retained when they seem at all significant for sound and sense.

site. In the past—with right intuition, as future events will demonstrate—he has had more fondness for the Duke of Albany than for the Duke of Cornwall; but he has refrained from showing obvious and impolitic favoritism: note Kent's "I *thought*" and Gloster's "It did always *seeme* so." And now, having weighed very carefully a difficult problem, he has finally decided that the shares of Goneril's husband, Albany, and Regan's husband, Cornwall shall be so equal in value that neither couple shall be tempted to envy the other's "moiety." Moreover, to counteract any previous sign that he may have given of a special affection for Albany, he presently and publicly addresses the two dukes in the following politic manner, gently featuring Cornwall though he is the *second* daughter's spouse (ll. 42-46):

> . . . Our son of Cornwall
> And you our no lesse loving Sonne of Albany,[4]
> We have this houre a constant will to publish
> Our daughters' severall Dowers, that future strife
> May be prevented now. . . .

In that passage the dramatist recalls for us and confirms the point of the play's two opening speeches. Lear had pondered long the question of his two older daughters' dowers before reaching the "constant" determination that, despite his personal preference for Albany, he must make the two dowers entirely equal to forestall "future strife." In that respect the king's warm heart is controlled by his statesmanly head.

Nor is there any suggestion of senile folly in his original plan considered as a whole. His tone from the first (ll. 35ff.) is both masterful and sane:

> Give me the Map there. Know, that we have divided
> In three our Kingdome. And 'tis our fast intent
> To shake all Cares and Businesse from our Age,

---

[4] The reader may decide whether the difference between "son" and "Sonne" is meaningful.

> Conferring them on younger strengths, while we
> Unburthened crawle toward death . . . .

Obviously that last line does not refer to his immediate future:[5]
he is still, and will continue to be during the first half of the
play, powerful in body and mind. But at his "Age," emphasized
by the capital letter and the metrical pause, he must think of
his approaching end; and he speaks with graphic urgency of
that final "crawle" in order to justify in his hearers' minds the
crucial decision he has just announced. Like a number of aging
rulers in history he has prudently resolved to retire while still
in full possession of his faculties. And his plan for the "younger
strengths" is natural enough in view of the difficulties of the
situation. He has no son; and, whether or not the principle of
primogeniture applies to his oldest daughter, he has determined
(wisely, as the event will show) not to entrust the supreme rule
to Goneril and her husband. He will entrust it, in defiance of
convention, to his youngest daughter Cordelia—and her husband-
to-be, the monarch of France.

That last point, to be sure, is not made unmistakably clear
by Shakespeare: dramatic economy or patriotism, or both, kept
him from having Lear make plain his intention that the French
king should be co-ruler of Britain. But certainly Lear, together
with Cordelia, prefers France to Burgundy at the start; later,
despite his wrathful impatience, he evinces a deep regard for
the "great King" (l. 211) who, in the last part of the scene,
is shown to be a truly great gentleman, fit mate for Cordelia.
In any case, it is perfectly clear that she, aided by a foreign
and powerful prince as husband, herself strong and true in
character, is to have, in her father's wise design, the overlord-
ship of the kingdom. The "bounds" (l. 64) of her special domain are left suggestively vague. Evidently, since the word
"Albany" indicates the northern part of the island and "Corn-

[5] Which *may* be the reason for the omission of this line in the Quarto
version of the play, published in 1608, reprinted in 1619, containing some
three hundred lines absent from the Folio.

wall" the southwest, she is to have the traditionally most important region, the center and southeast. And as Goneril's and Regan's shares are so very extensive—"plenteous" (l. 66) and "ample" (l. 82) stretches of an ideally vast landscape, far transcending the actual Britain—Cordelia's "more opulent" domain (l. 88) must be very great indeed. Moreover, her father's mantle will descend upon her. Prudently he iterates his intention of entirely divesting himself of "Rule" (ll. 40, 50): he wishes full responsibility to be thrown from the first upon his successors, above all Cordelia. But her regime will derive great prestige from his residence with her. He is to "set [his] rest / On her kind nursery" (ll. 125f.)—stake his all upon her who will cherish him and foster the peace and welfare of his beloved kingdom.[6]

Lear's original plan, then, was carefully pondered and rational. But certainly it was unusual; and therefore he determined that its inauguration should be marked by an impressive public *ceremony*. This word is the key to the whole affair. In the close of the opening dialogue between Kent and Gloster the latter, quickly dropping his light tone, says very formally: "The King is comming" (l. 34). A "Sennet" is heard, a set of trumpet notes announcing the approach of a grand procession. Then *"Enter one bearing a Coronet,"*[7] doubtless upon a gorgeous cushion, held high; then King Lear, followed by the other principals and a number of attendants. And Lear's long opening speech, quoted in part above, is highly ceremonial. But in the second half of it (ll. 46ff.) his formal tone, while firmly sustained, is increasingly and gently lightened:[8]

> . . . The Princes, *France* and *Burgundy*,
> Great Rivals in our youngest daughter's love,

[6] The word "nursery" alludes to gardening; "set my rest" refers to the stakes in a card game. Lear is thinking of his land's future together with his own: both were to have the "kind" ministration of Cordelia.

[7] From the stage direction in the Quarto.

[8] Obviously wrong is the actor who speaks the following passage in a heavy and senile manner.

Long in our Court have made their amorous sojourne,
And heere are to be answered. Tell me, my daughters,—
Since now we will divest us both of Rule,   50
Interest of Territory, Cares of State,—
Which of you shall we say doth love us most,
That we our largest bountie may extend
Where Nature doth with merit challenge. Goneril,
Our eldest borne, speake first. .   55

Lear's lightened tone, indicated particularly by the words "amorous sojourne" and "shall we say," suggests that Goneril's speech
is not to be taken too seriously. And indeed hers and Regan's
oratory is a dramatically heightened version of the formal
speech-making that takes place (in democratic as in monarchic
times) when a ruling statesman announces his retirement. That
is why the spectators in the theater, unless misled by critics
and/or actors, are not repelled by the present ceremony. Goneril
and Regan remind us of the politicians who, disliking the re-
tiring ruler in their hearts, rise to the present occasion with glib
eloquence. But whereas those politicians may to some extent
mean what they say, the dramatist makes the two daughters
say what they cannot possibly mean—and what all rational hearers, including Lear, must obviously disbelieve—namely that
their love for their father is unique, absolute, and perfect.
He says no word in commendation of their speeches. Only half
listening to them he keeps his eyes fixed on the map (l. 37) of
"our faire Kingdome" (l. 82) which he so fully loves. And the
true magnificence of his praise of that land (ll. 65f.),

With shadowie Forrests and with Champains riched,
With plenteous Rivers, and wide-skirted Meades . . . .

is thrown into high relief by his two daughters' glittering
rhetoric; which shall presently be superseded, Lear expects, by
a simple and truthful declaration by Cordelia of her love for
him. Thus his extraordinary decision to assign the central government to the "youngest" (l. 47) of his heirs shall be publicly

justified: all will see that his "largest bountie" is the just due of her true heart and great "merit" (ll. 53f.). Lear's own hands will place the "*Coronet*" on her head. Then "the Lords of France and Burgundy" shall come on, ushered by the Earl of Gloster (l. 35); and Lear with Cordelia's assent will choose the good French king for her husband: such is the plan. But the real climax of the scene is to be the very ceremonious coronetting of Cordelia, symbolizing Lear's transfer of all his "power" (l. 132) to her. He, retaining the crown and title of "King" (l. 138) during the remainder of his life, will reside with her and invest her government with the aura of his great authority.

The whole affair, particularly the declarations on the part of the three daughters, has been carefully "weighed" by Lear beforehand, with the full awareness of his intimate counsellors, Kent and Gloster; and the fact that they were mildly surprised by one feature of the scheme (ll. 1-7) suggests that they knew and approved all the rest of it. Kent's calm and cheerful mood, so fully displayed (ll. 1-31) in the initial episode, persists when he listens silently to Lear's long opening speech culminating in the command to his three daughters: Kent's mien in hearing that command is as casual as the king's tone in uttering it. He gives no sign of uneasiness here. Nor does the equally silent Cordelia. But she, unlike all the others present, on the stage and in the theater, is deeply disturbed by the ensuing speech of Goneril, so insincerely and ingeniously worded (ll. 56-62). Aside she whispers intensely: "What shall *Cordelia* speake? Love, and be silent." That curt, tumultuous pentameter line is in striking contrast with Goneril's smooth finale—"Beyond all manner of so much I love you"—and also with Lear's ensuing stately passage, "Of all these bounds even from this Line, to this. . . ." And her intense agitation, as indicated by her gravid aside (ll. 78-80) after Regan's speech, constantly increases; unobserved by the rest of the company, notably Kent, who keeps watching with looks of deep devotion the old king intent upon the map of his beloved realm. Hence not only Lear but the good Kent and all the others are astounded when Cordelia refuses to play her part in the present great ceremony.

The king, setting his map aside, addresses her with stately but fine tenderness, smiling happily: "Now, our Joy,"

> Although our last and least: to whose young love
> The Vines of France, and Milke of Burgundie,
> Strive to be interest. What can you say, to draw
> A third more opulent than your Sisters? speake.

CORDELIA. Nothing my Lord.

LEAR. Nothing? 90

CORDELIA. Nothing.

LEAR. Nothing will come of nothing, speake againe.

CORDELIA. Unhappie that I am, I cannot heave
My heart into my mouth: I love your Majesty
According to my bond, no more nor lesse. 95

LEAR. How, how, Cordelia? Mend your speech a little,
Lest you may marre your Fortunes.

The words "a little," prominent at the line's end, stress the obvious fact that she was not required to make an elaborate, emotional speech, to "heave / My heart into my mouth" as she puts it with sullen bitterness. She was expected to utter her love briefly, simply, and sincerely, in happy contrast with her sisters. But instead of that right kind of plainness she has used the wrong kind: she has spoken, as Lear perceives and as every reasonable person must perceive, with "pride which she calls plainnesse" (l. 131). The deep tenderness of her love for her father, equalling his for her, has been overcome for the time being by blind, unconscious, angry pride. And this vice is here marked, as it generally is, with unsound self-pity: she regards herself as "Unhappie" (93) and as "poore *Cordelia*" (78) even while richly gratified by her own bluntness. Humorlessly wrathful at her sisters' oratory, she has resolved not to utter a single word that might seem similar to it. Goneril referred to the king as "Father" (60); Regan addressed him as "your deere Highnesse" (78). So Cordelia will call him "my Lord" (89) and

"your Majesty" (94). And she continues to avoid the words
"dear" and "father" when, adjured by him to mend her speech
a little, she amends it in the following wrong fashion:

> Good my Lord,
> You have begot me, bred me, loved me.
> I returne those duties backe as are right fit,
> Obey you, Love you, and most Honour you.   100
> Why have my Sisters Husbands, if they say
> They love you all? Haply, when I shall wed,
> That Lord, whose hand must take my plight,
>   shall carry
> Halfe my love with him, halfe my Care and Dutie.
> Sure I shall never marry like my Sisters—⁹   105

LEAR.   But goes thy heart with this?
CORDELIA. Ay, my good Lord.
LEAR.   So young, and so untender?
CORDELIA. So young, my Lord, and true.

Ironically, after avowing extreme brevity, she has now uttered
a speech somewhat longer than those of her sisters and, though
truthful unlike theirs in diction, equally untrue in *tone*. If in
a tone of penitent, simple tenderness she had said merely, "My
Father," instead of "Good my Lord," "I . . . Obey you, Love
you, and most Honour you," all would have been well. She
would have indeed obeyed him by showing, on this crucial
occasion, that she loves him as he loves her with inmost "heart"
(l. 106), thus justifying publicly the great public trust he has
designed for her.

But Shakespeare with finest art makes us sympathize with
Cordelia. He knows that we know that a young woman about to
be married is preoccupied with that event. Its imminence in the
present case, twice warmly emphasized above by Lear (ll. 46-
49, 85-87), is now alluded to by Cordelia with a maidenly

---

⁹ The dash is mine. Instead, the Quarto has a comma and adds the phrase
"to love my father all," thus putting into Cordelia's mouth the word "father"
so studiously avoided by her.

reserve—"Haply, when I shall wed" (l. 102)—that betrays how much her heart and mind are engrossed with it. And beneath the harsh sophistry of her iterated word "Halfe" (l. 104) there is a truehearted resolve to give her husband the same loving care and duty that she has always had, and will continue to have, for her father. Her coming husband is vividly present in her imagination: he is as real as the present "Husbands" (l. 101)—she points to them—of her untruthful sisters (both of whom, eventually, will be untrue to them). And her impending marriage ceremony makes the present political ceremony seem to her repellently unreal and false. We must sympathize fully with her state of mind.

Nevertheless her fault, though later the penitent Lear will term it "most small" (I.iv.288), is great and crucial. Her chill words regarding her filial "bond" (l. 95) are not only cruel to her father but publicly misleading. Her sisters, *so far as we yet know*, acknowledge that bond as much as she does: despite their coldness of heart they may, at present, intend to do their minimum "duties" to him who "begot" them, "bred" them, "loved" them (l. 98f.). Cordelia's *present duty* is to make fully clear to the assembled court and, by implication, to the whole "Kingdome" (l. 82) that her ties to her father far surpass the mere filial bond; that she loves him with her whole "heart" (l. 106) and with a tenderness (l. 108), a fine sensitiveness, enabling her to enter fully into his plans; thus justifying her good "Fortunes" (l. 97) and providing the right climax for a ceremony designed to give high prestige to the very unusual sort of regime about to be instituted. But the whole affair is spoiled by her recalcitrant mood. Her climactic speech, admirable for courage and strength of will, is fundamentally wrong in its self-assertive pride: "So young, my Lord, and true." Extremely untrue is her tone.

Such is this play's Introduction. And it renders Lear's ensuing outbreak a great *dramatic surprise*, i.e., sudden and astonishing yet carefully prepared by the dramatist beforehand. It is astonishing because of his deportment hitherto, his statesmanlike deliberation and self-control, the more remarkable because of his obviously autocratic and imperious temperament. This he manages to restrain, extraordinarily, during the dialogue with Cordelia quoted above; the subtle art of which exceeds anything given or suggested by Shakespeare's sources at this juncture. Cordelia's curt "Nothing" might well have made the old king furious; but his actual response is far from that: his comments (ll. 90-97) are sharp and warningful but, considering the circumstances, remarkably patient. And his ultimate exclamation, "So young, and so untender?" (l. 108), recalls his opening words regarding her "young love" (l. 85ff.): the "Vines" and "Milke" image renders exquisitely the clinging tenderness of his affection for her. But at the same time there is a constant suggestion that Lear is exactly the kind of person who, exactly on the present occasion, *could* be very angry if crossed. Astounding, however, is the *extent* of his wrath: he is not merely very angry; he is utterly beside himself, overcome by violent and "barbarous" (l. 118) rage. And the ground of that extreme mood, though prepared for under the surface by the Introduction, becomes *patently* clear only in the whole course of his terrific speech (ll. 110-122).

It begins with a quick uptake of Cordelia's final word "true": "Let it be so, thy truth then be thy dower . . ."[10] This tells us that his present mood is a violently magnified echo of hers—like a sudden crash of thunder following a near but moderate peal. *Her* pride spoke in harsh plainness (l. 131); *his* speaks in a dreadful magniloquence. Earlier, he had pictured the majestic reaches of his kingdom, enriched with forests and plains, great rivers and wide meadows (ll. 64ff.). Now his imagination rises from that vast landscape to the still vaster and mightier skies above it: the "sacred radiance of the Sunne," the "mysteries of Hecate and the night . . ." "all the operation of the Orbes, / From whom we do exist and cease to be. . . ." In the climax his thought ranges to far, benighted realms where cruel barbarians

---

[10] The comma after "so," in Quarto and Folio, generally replaced by a semicolon in modern editions, indicates rapidity of utterance.

devour their own offspring. And it is patent that throughout he is furiously, and progressively, hardening his "heart" against her who has, for the time being, hardened her "heart" (l. 106) against him: in the close she is cast out entirely, so he declares, from his "bosome" (l. 120). In public she has refused to show a wholehearted love for him, refraining even from addressing him as "Father"; so now in the finale, wholeheartedly (he fancies) discarding his love for her, he publicly stigmatizes her as "thou my sometime Daughter."[11] But that final word "Daughter," uttered with a choking passionateness that reduces the speaker to silence for a moment, betrays the hidden depth of his love for Cordelia; for to be wroth with one we love (as in Coleridge's famous verse) doth work like madness in the brain. And we realize completely now that Lear, like Othello in his attitude toward Desdemona in the second half of the play, is trying, vainly, to kill his great love by means of great hate: the mightier the love, the more furious the mood of hate.

Doubtless that factitious mood would have yielded to his great love now—as it does later (I.iv.79ff.)—if Cordelia, pierced by the phrase "thou my sometime Daughter," had mended her speech a little, had put all her heart into a few simple, *contrite* words of affection for her father. But, instead, the following happens:

KENT. Good my Liege—
LEAR. Peace Kent.
    Come not between the Dragon and his wrath,
    I loved her most, and thought to set my rest   125
    On her kind nursery.—Hence and avoid my sight.—[12]
    So be my grave my peace, as here I give
    Her Father's heart from her . . . .

[11] This phrase stands out in contrast with his opening address to her, "Now, our Joy" (84) . . . . The term "Daughter" is the more emphatic in that Shakespeare has kept Lear from applying it to Cordelia since his first reference to her in this scene: "our youngest daughter's love" (47).

[12] The two dashes, like the one after "Liege" above, are mine. The Folio has a colon after "sight."

There the dramatist reiterates the fact that Lear's singular rage is occasioned by his singular love. And the piercing words, "I loved . . . kind nursery," spoken in a low intense tone, are surely designed to make an ultimate appeal to Cordelia. But she remains silent, her mien as recalcitrant as ever; and her father, in his loving hate, can no longer bear the "sight" (l. 126) of her near to him. She moves away—obeying him (l. 100), with dramatic irony, in this one respect—while he consummates his separation from her in words the more dreadful because of their monosyllabic simplicity: "So be my grave my peace," a peace *not* harbingered by "her kind nursery." That brief invocation exceeds in awfulness the melodramatic oath of his preceding speech (ll. 111ff.); and replete with tragic meaning is the phrase, hitherto unused, "Her Father's heart."

Certainly that heart is now hardened, wickedly and foolishly; but the folly is not due to senile infirmity. Lear's mind, throughout the first scene, is remarkably active and powerful. His first division of the kingdom was carefully politic; and the new plan, announced in the remainder of his present long speech, is—so far as we now know—a shrewd second best. Presently Kent will term it "hideous rashnesse" (l. 153); and such it will prove to be, in retrospect, when Goneril and Regan take over the rule of the kingdom; as they prepare to do in their private colloquy, carefully feeling each other out, at the close of this scene (ll. 286-312). But that is not in accordance with Lear's design. In the whole course of the scene there is no indication that the "mad . . . old man," in Kent's brash terms, "bowes" to their "flattery" (ll. 148-50). And now, disregarding them entirely, he assigns the supreme rule to their husbands, Cornwall and Albany (129-41). Giving them Cordelia's third of the kingdom he invests them "joyntly" with his power. But he reserves for his own command "an hundred Knights," a considerable army, to be supported by his sons-in-law, with whom he will reside by monthly course; retaining the "name and all the addition," all the titular honors and prestige, of a "King." By thus forestalling rivalries, jealousy and strife, he will establish the peace and order of the realm "now" (ll. 45f.). And his plan, though it has doubtful aspects, is very far from weakly irrational. It can be successful if Albany and Cornwall shall prove to be loyal, firm, and temperate. And such they appear to be when, using their new authority as joint heirs, they effectually restrain his violent gesture threatening the life of the violent Kent: together they exclaim, "Deare Sir, forbeare" (l. 165). And that speech, their sole utterance in scene i, must be regarded as indicating their demeanor throughout the scene: they are not flatterers like their wives, nor emotionalists like all the others. Lear's final trust in them, prepared for in the Introduction (ll. 1-7, 42-46), is, so far as we now know, quite justifiable—unlike his final and utter repudiation of Cordelia.

Gradually, in the course of his present long oration (ll. 123-41), he masters his vociferous rage against her by hardening his heart toward her. And that loud fury, thereafter rearoused by Kent (ll. 141ff.), is far less tragic, though more theatrical, than his present heart-hardening; which is the more dreadful from the very fact that his new plan for the kingdom seems reasonable. He employs hard, brainy logic. Cordelia has refused to take part in a great public ceremony inaugurating a new regime with her at its center. So now he will thrust her as far as possible from that center, and from the center of his heart. He will bury, as in his "grave," all his love of her, turning his "Father's heart" entirely to "Cornwall and Albany." All the great prestige he had designed for her shall be conferred upon them—not upon Goneril and Regan—with great ceremony. Rising from his throne he lifts from its cushion the Coronet that was to have been placed upon Cordelia's head. Bending it into equal halves[13] —which his sons-in-law, now addressed by him as "Beloved Sonnes" (l. 140), shall break in two—he commands them in a hard, clear tone: "This Coronet part betweene you."

In short, Shakespeare in the outset of this drama tries to

[13] This action, a guess on my part, seems appropriate. Consciously or not Shakespeare makes the bending and breaking of the Coronet symbolic of what happens later to Lear and to his kingdom.

make Lear, like his other main tragic heroes, as humanly representative as possible. Like Hamlet, Othello, and Macbeth he is very extraordinary, and dramatically very interesting, in his own individual way; but he is no more abnormal than they are. He is extreme, but also extremely typical. So far from being a silly and pathetic, instead of tragic, oldster, he is, the more strikingly because of his advanced age, entirely virile in body, heart, and mind; and he is essentially noble. He has our sympathy, not in the main because he is old, but, as I have tried to show, because he is a great person greatly provoked. Cordelia's fault is precisely the sort that is hardest for him to bear under the present circumstances. But her fault is immeasurably outdistanced, with supreme tragic irony, by the selfsame fault in himself. Proud obstinacy becomes in his case, as not in hers, the occasion of cruel, subhuman wrath, a wrath altogether deadly because, instead of exhausting itself in stormy outbreak, it assumes a rationalistic form—his careful plan whereby the two dukes shall govern under himself as titular king. He sinfully justifies and fixes his anger against Cordelia by converting it into a policy, a policy that is apparently almost, if not entirely, as statesmanlike as the threefold division of the kingdom originally planned. Thus his anger becomes hellish, recalling the heat and *the cold* of Dante's Inferno, and representative of the human heart and the human *reason* at their tragic worst. The contrast between Lear at the beginning of this scene and Lear after his outbreak of fury exemplifies what may happen to Everyman when he lets himself be governed by the "Dragon," i.e., the Devil,[14] of pride and "wrath" (l. 124).

[14] The word "Dragon," especially when capitalized, suggests Satan. See *The Faerie Queene* I.iv.10 and I.xi, *passim*.

INDEX